the sexual life of
adult women is a
'dark continent'
for psychology.
Sigmund Freud

[Women] can be taught
that their territory is black:
because you are Africa,
you are black.
Your continent is dark.
Hélène Cixous

[Woman is]
the privileged object
through which [man]
subdues Nature . . . .
[She] is the fixed image of
his animal destiny.
Simone de Beauvoir

men call that barbarisme,
which is not common to them . . . .
we have no other
ayme of truth and reason,
then the . . . opinions and
customes of the countrie we live-in.
Michel de Montaigne

The Shakespearean Wild

Geography, Genus, and Gender

Jeanne Addison Roberts

University of Nebraska Press
Lincoln and London

Library of Congress
Cataloging-in-
Publication Data
Roberts, Jeanne Addison.
The Shakespearean wild:
geography, genus, and
gender / Jeanne Addison
Roberts. p.   cm.
Includes bibliographical
references (p.) and index.
ISBN 0-8032-3899-1
(cloth: alk. paper)
1. Shakespeare, William,
1564–1616 –
Knowledge – Natural
history. 2. Wilderness
areas in literature.
3. Nature in literature.
4. Animals in literature.
5. Sex in literature.
I. Title. PR3939.R58
1991 822.3'3 – dc20
90-13037 CIP

Acknowledgements for
the use of previously
published material
appear on pages ix - x.

70484

For Markley

Contents

Illustrations

Acknowledgments

I am profoundly grateful to the staff and trustees of the Folger Shakespeare Library. They have been unfailingly supportive and helpful in many ways over many years. Particular thanks go to Betsy Walsh and the Reading Room staff; Nati Krivatsy, reference librarian; and Julie Ainsworth of Photography. A Folger Short-term Fellowship enabled me to bring my work to completion. I am grateful also to David Bevington, S. Schoenbaum, and Cyrus Hoy, who were supportive and encouraging in the early stages of this work. Susan Snyder and Russ MacDonald made valuable criticisms and suggestions at a later stage. My colleagues at the American University, especially Edward Kessler, Judith Lee, and Jonathan Loesberg have been most helpful in reading and improving the manuscript. The university granted me leave without pay to finish my manuscript, and the Mellon Fund of the College of Arts and Sciences made the illustrations possible.

Generations of students have provided stimulation, support, and challenge. Special thanks go to Peggy O'Brien of the Folger Shakespeare Library and the staff and participants of three Teaching Shakespeare summer institutes who afforded me a receptive and demanding critical forum. Mary Tonkinson of the Folger provided invaluable editorial assistance.

As always, my deepest gratitude is to Markley.

Portions of Chapter 2 were previously published as "Horses and Hermaphrodites: Metamorphoses in *The Taming of the Shrew*," *Shakespeare Quarterly* 34 (Summer 1983): 159–71, and are used by permission of the Folger

Shakespeare Library; and as "Animals as Agents of Revelation: The Horizon-talizing of the Chain of Being in Shakespeare's Comedies," in *Shakespearean Comedy*, edited by Maurice Charney, a special issue of the *New York Literary Forum* 5–6 (1980): 79–96, and are used by permission of the Department of Romance Languages, Hunter College of the City University of New York.

Portions of Chapter 3 have been previously published as "Strategies of Delay in Shakespeare's Comedies: What the Much Ado Is Really About," *Renaissance Papers* 1987, pp. 95–102, edited by Dale B. J. Randall and Joseph A. Porter, published by the Southeastern Renaissance Conference, 1987, and are used by permission of the Southeastern Renaissance Conference; and as "Crises of Male Self-Definition," in *Shakespeare, Fletcher, and "The Two Noble Kinsmen,"* edited by Charles Frey, and are used by permission of the University of Missouri Press, copyright © 1989 by the Curators of the University of Missouri. "Shades of the Triple Hecate in Shakespeare," modified in Chapter 3, appears in *Proceedings of the PMR Conference* 12–13 (1987–88): 47–66, and is used by permission of the Augustinian Historical Institute at Villanova University, which hosted the Patristic, Medieval, and Renaissance Conference for which the paper was originally commissioned.

All references to Shakespeare's works are from *The Riverside Shakespeare*, ed. G. Blakemore Evans et al. (Boston: Houghton Mifflin, 1974).

Introduction

A story told about Thales (and sometimes about Socrates) reports that he declared himself grateful to Fortune for three blessings: that he "was born a human being and not one of the brutes ... a man and not a woman ... a Greek and not a barbarian." (The very order is illuminating—women are above animals but below barbarians.) Page duBois, in discussing fifth-century B.C. Greek society, sees this statement as reflecting a paradigm of early Greek definition of culture. She concludes, "The other—alien, female, bestial—is excluded ... from culture and set at the boundaries of the city to define it as a circle of equals." Although she does not use the term, her picture evokes an image of the peripheral groups as inhabiting a Wild.[1] (I have capitalized the words *Culture* and *Wild* to emphasize the special sense in which I am using them.) Culture thus becomes identified with the central "equals," Greek male humans. DuBois further suggests that this model was threatened by the ambiguous position of women (excluded yet necessary), eroded by the Peloponnesian war, and supplanted by the Platonic/Aristotelian model of the "Great Chain of Being" (4–6). The picture imagined earlier, however, is a forerunner of some current anthropological models of societies and remains extremely useful in analyzing subsequent Western culture.

Shakespeare's England differs from fifth-century Greece in having a female ruler, in its somewhat more fluid boundaries between male and female, its rigidification of the human/animal hierarchy, and its multiplication of the varieties of potentially invasive "barbarians." Still, the Cultural center remained male, and the rulers (in spite of the obvious exceptions), recorders, and interpreters of that Culture were and have continued to be overwhelmingly male. Forces outside that ethnic human male Cultural core were and have continued to be thought of as parts of the Wild.[2]

The Wild seems to be envisioned by Shakespeare as inhabited by strange and untamed creatures, fascinating and frightening, offering the lure of the hunt with the goal of capturing or killing the Wild's imagined denizens, but at the same time as providing a reservoir of necessary resources for the maintenance of Culture. Slaves, wives, and beasts of burden are to be drawn from the Wild. Shylock, Othello, women, and domesticated animals are incorporated into Shakespeare's Culture, but they never quite shed their foreignness or become totally trustworthy. Shylock is never more than marginal. Othello retains the taint of the "Old black ram"; the "woman's part" elicits both lust and revulsion; the "harmless" cat is tolerated as "necessary" but the dog is scorned as fawning and hypocritical; the monkey becomes the symbol of lust and the instrument of Jessica's betrayal of her semiacculturated father. Even when domesticated inhabitants are admitted provisionally into the bounds of Culture, their space becomes ghettoized, and the male seems to fear being engulfed by the requisite cohabitation. In his central Cultural position he preserves a fantasy of freedom in an idyllic male Wild which excludes intruders, except possibly as prey, and celebrates the pleasures of warfare as sustained and glorified by the complementary delights of male camaraderie and male rivalry. The male Wild offers escape from the complexities and confines of Culture. Sometimes it superimposes itself over a vision of the perils of the female Wild, erasing its unknown threats and ambiguities. Although Shakespeare reflects the traditional Culture/Wild distinctions, he also often proves gratifyingly capable of subverting and transcending them in ways I hope to demonstrate.

There have been several recent efforts to define and diagram the relation of male Culture to female Wild. I have used duBois, Sherry Ortner, and Edwin Ardener; but since none of their diagrams is wholly satisfactory, I have designed my own, more complex, model, which I will use in this work.

Page duBois suggests that Thales's imagination of the subject of *polis* Culture might be diagrammed as a circle of equals (Greek male humans) surrounded by "others" or the Wild (animal, barbarian, female) set at the boundaries as defining entities. But as duBois points out, this picture involves some ambiguities because females must at some point become, however briefly, part of the *polis* (4–6). The same problem complicates Sherry Ortner's provocative argument (1973) that woman is to man as nature is to culture, an argument which, like duBois's, seems to imply separate spheres for male and female. These spheres might be diagrammed, simply but not wholly satisfactorily, as two discrete circles.[3]

Ortner later modified her argument to suggest that women are seen as *closer* to nature than men. She describes something like a diagram of the relationship: "We may envision culture … as a small clearing within the forest of the larger natural system. From this point of view, that which is intermediate between culture and nature is located on the continuous periphery of culture's clearing; and though it may thus appear to stand both above and below (and beside) culture, it is simply outside and around it" (1974:85).

In reaction to Ortner, Edwin Ardener developed a modified diagram for society which shows overlapping rather than separate spheres for male and female ("Problem Revisited" 23).

Ardener explains that ABCD is an unbounded field, metaphorically the Wild, in which "circle *x, plus* the unshaded overlap of circle *y*, is the model of society where the male model is dominant." For men, the shaded portion of circle *y* is mysterious, identified with the Wild, whereas for women the crescent portion of circle *x* is a sort of ambiguous male Wild whose contents (modified) have become familiar through literature and legend. Ardener comments on the "fortuitous homology" between the purely ideational concept of Wild as a field against which "society" is defined and "that part of the actual territorial world which is not socially organized—the 'wild.' " He adds, "It is a mere confusion that [the 'wild'] may … also be walkable into, and be found to contain sounding cataracts and unusual beasts" (23–24, 30). But such fortuitous homologies provide the very stuff of literature. Indeed, since the ideational is merely reflected in literary works as a construct of a literary imagination, the "walkable into" natural settings of drama are already metaphorical. I will suggest that ideational and metaphorical Wilds are inextricably linked and that in

Shakespeare the one frequently serves as a metaphorical exploration of the other. Wild forest, Wild animals, and Wild men and women provide insights into the structure of male Culture, which is defined and threatened by them.

Ardener's diagram is helpful in suggesting a model for the relationship between dominant and muted, male and female cultures, and in resolving the ambiguities of duBois's and Ortner's models by showing women both inside and outside Culture. And Ortner's geographical image is suggestive of my own approach. But neither picture is wholly satisfactory. They omit the animal and barbarian elements so important in Thales's self-definition, and they understate the complexity of Culture/Nature relationships.

DuBois posits that Thales's world picture was superseded by the concept of the Great Chain of Being, a model with which virtually all students of the Renaissance have been indoctrinated as basic to their study. This design, which, as A. O. Lovejoy convinced us, was accepted "through the Middle Ages and down to the late eighteenth century," was based on a principle of unilinear gradation incorporating a chain "composed of ... an infinite number of links ranging in hierarchical order from the meagerest kind of existents ... to the highest possible kind of creature" (59). This diagrammatic picture is useful in its clear hierarchical structure and its inclusion of animals and barbarians, and admittedly the concept of the Chain is often helpful in Shakespeare. It seems to lie behind Luciana's moral injunctions to her sister in *The Comedy of Errors* (2.1.15–25), Kate's advice to women in *The Taming of the Shrew* (5.2.136–79), and, if ambiguously, behind Ulysses' famous speech on order in *Troilus and Cressida* (1.3.78–137). E. M. W. Tillyard made it one of the keystones of his influential, though currently unfashionable, *Elizabethan World Picture.*

Both the Chain and the World Picture are quintessentially male constructs, rooted in Aristotle, codifier of patriarchal theory, and committed to a Christian teleology, which often seems foreign to the more cyclically oriented female. Carol Gilligan has suggested that because of their early conditioning, men see the world in terms of ladders and naturally assume hierarchies, whereas women, shaped by different conditioning, are more likely to see (and be seen) in terms of nets or webs (62). Female readers, if they can be freed from immasculation, that is, the internalization of male values, may see patterns not readily apparent to the usual male.[4]

The patterns perceived by Lovejoy and Tillyard are indubitably there in Shakespeare's works; but because he was a creative artist and not a philosopher, a poet of intense "negative capability," and, as we now see him, a man of profound ambivalences, there is much else there as well. Critics inevitably choose what they need. New Historicists and Cultural Materialists are right to reject the simplistic dependence on earlier paradigms. For feminists, too, those paradigms are of primarily negative value, illuminating by omission or by oblique reference the marginal, the partially repressed, the hidden premises, and the terrors of the texts. In their assumptions that Nature and order are coterminous, such systems seem to have tamed the Wild. But the untamed Wild is also there in Shakespeare's works, and I am concerned to discover and explicate it.

My own suggested model of the play worlds, an attempt to combine the male Cultural center with the Wilds of female, animal, barbarian, and even the semivisible male Wild modifies duBois with Ardener and incorporates some element of the hierarchy implied in the male view.

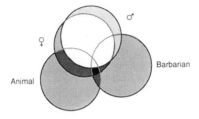

This model is intended to represent a male perspective and to be suggestive rather than precise. Its unshaded area is male-defined Culture. In its shaded portions it shows areas defined as Wild by a dominant white male Culture, indicating considerable overlap between male, female, and animal, and male, female, and barbarian. Female, animal, and barbarian all participate marginally in male Culture. The barbarian world partakes of both male and female Wilds in addition to its own; the animal world overlaps with the female Wild and also adds its own. The lightly shaded male Wild, impinging on but never coinciding with the female Wild, contains, as we have seen, imagery of male fantasies outside of the model of Culture but relatively accessible in male literature—images of warfare, male bonding, and the hunt.

Using this stylized diagram merely as a suggestive model, I will examine the frontiers of Culture in Shakespeare's works as they impinge on the three others identified by Thales: the female Wild, often associated with the malign and benign forces of the green world; the animal Wild, which offers, by contrast with Culture, the reassurance of special human status and, through its similarity to Culture, the threat of loss of that status; and the barbarian Wild populated by marginal figures such as the Moor and the Jew as well as various hybrids. In each world are figures that threaten the clarity of Cultural definition but also provide visions of possible new modes of being. Because barbarian or outsider characters like Othello, Shylock, and Cleopatra have been treated insightfully and extensively in other works (especially those of Leslie Fiedler, Marilyn French, and Janet Adelman),[5] I have devoted little space to them here, focusing rather on the metaphorical language and stage imagery that reveal glimpses of worlds behind the overt stage world. Finally, I consider certain male and female characters as revealing projections of suppressed fears and fantasies which haunt the Cultural constructs of the male psyche. The males I have chosen to discuss represent, often almost schematically, such figures as lover, husband/cuckold, and father, negotiating between Culture and the various Wilds—particularly the female. The female figures are recurring archetypes—maid, wife, widow, or more mythically virgin, whore, and crone—which seem to personify both positive and negative poles of male stereotypes of women. I have limited my discussion to Shakespeare's comedies, tragedies, romances, and "Venus and Adonis" and have treated them very selectively. The effort to look with new eyes has frequently led me to focus on plays about which there is relatively little criticism and to pay proportionately less attention to much analyzed works.

The Wild in Shakespeare is associated with Amazons, Scythians, cannibals, and undomesticated animals. Unexplored continents provide mental images of untamed Wilds. Perhaps the most inclusive and evocative single image of the Shakespearean Wild is Africa, the dark continent, locus in the Renaissance mind of plenitude and undisciplined riot, of mystery and menace, the exotic and the erotic. It is the home of lions, tigers, elephants, apes and monkeys, and crocodiles. It fuels the passions of Othello and Cleopatra. Cesare Ripa's illustration (Fig. 1) is richly suggestive, with its black Venus portrayed against a natural landscape, a figure with provocatively bared leg, with elephant tusks on her head and a lion and three serpents at her feet, offering in one hand wheat sheaves and in the other a scorpion.[6] In Shakespeare, the imagined Africa is linked with all varieties of the Wild—barbarian, female, and animal. It produces the villainous Aaron the Moor of *Titus Andronicus*, the childlike Prince of Morocco, seduced by gold and happily banished by Portia in *The Merchant of Venice*, the noble but ultimately savage Othello, and above all the fatally fascinating Cleopatra. Africa is the original home of the foul witch Sycorax of *The Tempest*

1. *Africa*. Cesare Ripa, *Iconologia*. Rome, 1603, p. 337. By permission of the Folger Shakespeare Library.

and the site of the exile of Alonzo's daughter Claribel. Ethiope is a term of opprobrium, usually associated with women, as in *Love's Labor's Lost* (4.3.116), *As You Like It* (4.3.35), *Two Gentlemen of Verona* (2.6.26), and *Much Ado About Nothing* (5.4.38), and as in *A Midsummer Night's Dream*, when Lysander scorns Hermia for her dark complexion (3.2.257). It becomes part of a figure of exotic beauty, however, as Romeo envisions Juliet hanging "upon the cheek of night / As a rich jewel in an Ethiope's ear" (1.5.45–46). Africa is a rich repository of "golden joys" (*Henry IV, Part II*, 5.3.100), but it is clearly beyond the borders of male European Culture, and the points at which it impinges are points of potential conflict and danger, as in the opposition of Caesar's masculine Rome to Cleopatra's feminine Egypt.

America, with its more freshly evolved Renaissance traditions, similarly offers visions of a Wild female eroticism and plenitude combined with the fearful specter of cannibalism, danger, and death. Cesare Ripa suggests these qualities (Fig. 2) with his voluptuous seminude woman, depicted with a bow and arrow and the severed head of an enemy and a crocodile behind her feet. Ripa's representation of Nature (Fig. 3) is similarly ambivalent. Nature is depicted as a nude woman with swollen breasts flowing with milk, signifying nurture and abundance, but on her hand sits a vulture, suggesting the imminence of devouring death and reminding one of the cyclical pattern of Nature, which destroys as well as sustains corruptible bodies. As late as 1758–60 Johann Georg Hertel in his new edition of Ripa's *Iconologia* printed an illustration of "Earth" (Fig. 4) based on Ripa's 1603 description, which shows Earth's participation with Nature and fertility in her proximity to forest and waterfall. But in the background the Earth opens to swallow those who rebelled against Moses.

Such ambivalences are at home in drama. Its dialectical nature makes it a particularly useful forum for the exploration of such Cultural assumptions, uncertainties, and dilemmas as those set up by the Culture/Nature opposition; and Shakespeare constantly uses drama as such a forum. The most obvious vehicle of the dialectic is, of course, dialogue, with its potential for playing out the counterpoint of opposing ideas; but dramatic settings, characters, and metaphoric language offer subtler forms of multiple vision, serving, like dialogue, to counterpose conflicting values and to confirm or challenge traditional patterns. The dialectic between the fluid "picturing" of language and the embodied imagery of the stage is an important energizing force in drama, enabling it to adapt itself to generation after generation. Stage pictures pin

2. *America. Cesare Ripa, Iconologia*. Padua, 1611, p. 360. By permission of the Folger Shakespeare Library.

3. *Natura*. Cesare Ripa, *Iconologia*. Padua, 1611, p. 374. By permission of the Folger Shakespeare Library.

4. *Earth. Cesare Ripa: Baroque and Rococo Imagery.* Ed. and trans. Edward A. Maser.
New York: Dover, 1971. (Repr. of Johann Georg Hertel, *Historiae et Allegoria* . . . .
Augsburg, [1758–60].)

down meaning, but verbal images, in their ability to excite multiple and disparate visions in different readers and auditors, maintain a power to generate new meanings. The interplay between the two kinds of imagery creates an unstable equilibrium between being and becoming which is unique to drama. Such power can be enlisted in the search for new dimensions of the human.

It is, I suspect, apparent from the above that my primary interest is in Shakespeare and women and in how the construction of Culture and Wild shapes our perceptions of females. There is, indeed, an underlying question: how can women learn to read the sacred literary texts by male authors without being either seduced into total acceptance of their world or so alienated as to reject their world altogether? This question has concerned feminist Shakespeareans intensely for the last fifteen years. Various approaches have been attempted with varying degrees of success. And serious questions impede our progress.

The first question, which may initially seem simple-minded, is, Can we define *women* in ways that do not reduce them to predictable and restrictive Cultural traditions? The very term *female perspective* is suspect, as is the idea that women read as a group. Various important modern critics, beginning most notably with Simone de Beauvoir, have argued vigorously and persuasively against such essentialist theories of femininity.[7] Later critics have posited that binary oppositions such as male/female always serve the purposes of hierarchy and that, by accepting patriarchal definitions of women as "other," women become instruments of patriarchal power. Michel Foucault has contended that the obsessive modern discourse on sexual roles and differences is a relatively recent development dating from the seventeenth century and that we need to learn to free ourselves of such "disciplining" distinctions to establish or reestablish a heterogeneous liberation that will permit the arrival of that "day, perhaps, in a different economy of bodies and pleasures [when] people will no longer quite understand how the ruses of sexuality, and the power that sustains its organization, were able to subject us to that austere monarchy of sex" (*Sexuality* 159).

I am sympathetic to this antiessentialist position, and I can imagine progress toward achieving its goals. I have nonetheless chosen in this work to adopt the views of Nancy Chodorow and Dorothy Dinnerstein that Western patriarchal society—itself a Cultural construct, but a long-standing one—and especially the patriarchal family have fostered certain predictable patterns of male and female identity. My definition of female is thus based on the admittedly simplistic but ubiquitous distinction of genders according to reproductive function and on the assumption that this distinction was as powerful in Shakespeare's day as in our own. The study of male writers may always entail such dichotomies. I also posit the even more controversial premise that we can begin to analyze these patterns, regularly depicted in traditional literature from a male point of view, from a female perspective which observes from a position primarily outside the cultural center. Because of centuries of conditioning, this is, of course, extremely difficult, perhaps impossible; but the hope is that the resistance to male stereotypes and a gradually increasing awareness of female potentialities, combined with the self-conscious development of alternative values, may serve to open new vistas.

In attempting to develop a female perspective on Shakespearean drama, we must address a second important question: were there any women on the Shakespearean stage? Some modern critics have paid particular attention to the impact of boy actors in "female" roles. Lisa Jardine concludes of boys playing "women" such as Julia, Portia, and Rosalind that "these figures are sexually exciting *qua* transvestied [sic] boys, and that the plays encourage the [presumably male] audience to think of them as such." She adds that they "reveal nothing of 'real' womanly feelings" (29, 33). Stephen Orgel has similarly emphasized the erotic appeal to the men in the audience of boy actors in female roles ("Nobody's Perfect").

In line with Foucault's premises, Stephen Greenblatt has approached the question of boy actors from a somewhat different angle. Basing his hypothesis on Renaissance theories that women are unfinished men and that thus "there are not two radically different sexual structures but only one—outward and visible in the man, inverted and hidden in the woman," Greenblatt develops the idea that "Shakespearean women are ... the representation of Shakespearean men, the projected mirror images of masculine self-differentiation." He goes on to elaborate: "Men love women precisely *as representations*, a love the original performances of these plays literalized in the person of the boy actor. . . . We have a theater that reveals, in the presence of the man's (or boy's) body beneath the woman's clothes, a different sexual reality. The open secret of identity—that within differentiated individuals is a single structure, identifiably male—is presented literally in the all-male cast" (77, 92, 93).

Jardine, Orgel, and Greenblatt all suggest, then, that the primary identity of Shakespearean "women" is male and that their appeal is as males to males, although Greenblatt acknowledges "the fictive existence of two genders and the [importance of] friction between them." I do not deny the possibility, even the probability of transvestite eroticism on Shakespeare's stage, but surely the artist's imagination of females—witches, wives, and crones as well as romantic heroines—has some further dimensions, a basic element of otherness stronger perhaps than any sense of similarity. I argue that Shakespeare's women are neither male nor female but may be understood as projections of male fantasies of the Wild female other. Animals and barbarians are similarly constructed in ways that serve the needs of patriarchal Culture. Attempting to see these figures from a perspective that acknowledges this premise can be illuminating to both male and female audiences.

In a curious way Greenblatt's analysis of a form of Renaissance essentialism that denies distinct genders conforms to the long tradition of Shakespeare criticism before the last decade. Neoclassical, romantic, and Victorian critics regularly celebrated Shakespeare's astonishing representations of "universal human" values, and it has only very gradually become apparent that those "universal" values were axiomatically male values. Only very recently in feminist literary criticism have women begun to extricate themselves from the spell of that vision.

Feminist literary criticism has flourished most notably and perhaps most easily in dealing with works by women, especially those of the nineteenth and twentieth centuries, when an emerging feminist consciousness often began to free itself from "immasculation," that internalization of patriarchal values that marks much women's writing of earlier periods.[8] Modern feminist critics working in the Renaissance, also concerned with writing by women, have opened up new windows on the period by rediscovering previously forgotten works by women and by writing about the lives, education, influence, and perceptions of women.[9] But all students of the Renaissance return repeatedly and inevitably to the work of the white male writers who have constituted the canon enshrined in the Western Cultural heritage and in our educational bastions.

The work of Shakespeare in particular is the perennial mystery that feminist Renaissance scholars have circled and recircled in the attempt to find insights useful to the feminist enterprise. They have tried to analyze the degree of his affiliation to patriarchy, his attitude toward women and his uses of them as characters, his psychological conditioning, and his relationship as a male to his historic moment. Probably all feminist critics, but indubitably all of a certain age, are hampered in their efforts by the immasculation ensured by readings of Shakespeare shaped by generations of male critics, male teachers, and patriarchal values. Obviously, critical generations change, as the history of Shakespeare criticism abundantly attests, but historically the changes have offered few occasions for women to formulate unmediated critical responses or at least to achieve the freshly imagined engagement that feminist critics are currently attempting. We are in the process of trying to reimagine Shakespeare even as we work at the larger enterprises of rewriting the Renaissance, reshaping family life, and restructuring political and economic realities. I should like to emphasize that reimagining Shakespeare does not necessarily mean rejecting him. On the contrary, he remains for many of us our most valuable and varied resource.

Reimagining Shakespeare has taken different directions. There have been attempts with varying success to claim Shakespeare as a proto-feminist,[10] to highlight and critique the formation in the plays of male identity,[11] to focus narrowly and specifically on women characters,[12] and to analyze the relation of gender to genre.[13] Most feminist studies retain some sense of the value of Shakespeare as a consummate artist, but a few seem to conclude that feminists must jettison him altogether.[14]

In this book my interests are closest perhaps to those of the critics who have studied the patterns of male identity. I approach the works of Shakespeare by taking as given the assumption that they are products of male imagination, centered in a male-defined conception of Culture, and that they record overtly and subliminally confrontations with the surrounding Nature or Wild, conceived as the world of females, animals, and barbarians. My study includes consideration of the lures and primordial memories of the Wild, as well as of its terrors and threats to Cultural boundaries. Although this is not primarily a historical study, I have used illustrations available to Shakespeare's period with the belief that they not only illuminate Shakespeare but also force a recognition of assumptions and connotations that are still operative.

My purpose, then, is to explore some of the areas of the Wild as they are represented by Shakespeare and in particular to examine them as projections of male vision. *Male vision* is, of course, like *female vision*, a term fraught with problems. That the central Cultural vision of Shakespeare's works is that of a white (as opposed to barbarian) male human (as opposed to animal) of Renaissance England is, on one level, self-evident, but questions immediately arise from the premise. Can males be lumped together any more than females? Is

Shakespeare a typical white male? To what extent does he represent Renaissance England? Rather than attempt to answer these probably unanswerable questions, I am consciously opting for a simplistic generalization that depends on a belief that there has been a historical continuity of male values dating from classical times and still dominant in our culture. My hope is to help in the process of exposing, appraising, and changing responses to Shakespeare based on those values—responses that have prevailed for so long that they have come to seem universal.

The human essentialism that celebrates universal values has been a powerful force in past Shakespeare criticism. It enabled Darwinians to deal comparatively easily with received notions of the Great Chain of Being[15] and has helped even non-English audiences at least vaguely cognizant of Shakespeare's ethnocentrism and chronological and geographical locus to demonstrate remarkable facility in accepting and exploiting the poet's depictions of foreigners, outsiders, and barbarians. In spite of its historical eminence and traditional usefulness, however, I believe that women readers and audiences of Shakespeare must now try to extricate themselves from traditional patriarchal modes and develop their own values in responding to the plays. I recognize that my argument substitutes a kind of male/female essentialism for human essentialism, but it seems a justifiable risk.

Although the patriarchal system has shaped Western Culture for millennia, feminists, most recently Gerda Lerner in her landmark work *The Creation of Patriarchy*, have persuasively argued that it is a historic construct, not rooted in some mysterious "human nature," and is neither necessarily universal nor unalterable.[16] Indeed, it is the goal of the feminist enterprise to rethink this history, to imagine a world in which women are central, and ultimately to alter the patriarchal system.

This system has traditionally, even in disparate circumstances, shaped male and female development in different ways. Modern feminist theorists such as Nancy Chodorow and Dorothy Dinnerstein, modifying Freud, have argued that basic male/female differences are generated in Western societies by the universal practice of early child nurture by women—mothers and others—and the more distant authority of fathers and other male presences.[17] Infants' experience of union with a benign and seemingly powerful female is followed by divergent experiences for males and females in relating to this primary attachment— experiences that cultivate in the male an independent spirit and residual contempt for and fear of the female, whereas for females a less violent separation encourages powers of relationship, tainted nonetheless by contempt for females and a conviction of their own inferiority. Although it is doubtless possible to imagine exceptions to these patterns, and although later development obviously complicates and modifies early experiences, these theories seem to me to provide a credible explanation for observed phenomena. The theories illuminate the effects if not the origins of patriarchy and help to show why the Western patriarchal tradition has tended to identify Culture as male. Historically conditioned as it is, the tradition dominates all of Western written history. My intention in this work is to listen to the most powerful English voice in this tradition with a new ear—to chart some of the characteristics of his visions of Culture and hear clues to the characteristics of the suppressed Wild, both what it contains and what it is imagined to contain.

The following pages, then, reveal a search for clues in Shakespeare to the imagination of human Culture: the use of landscape, animal forms, hybrids, and human figures—male and female—reflections of the Wild that define the Cultured by their difference. What I hope will emerge is some small progress toward a new understanding of how male psychological development conditions worldviews, how traditional intellectual concepts may change, and how psychological dimensions, personified in stage characters, may play out recurring male visions of gender. In Shakespeare these visions are sometimes evoked and abandoned, frequently in process of evolution, occasionally progressive throughout the works, often expressive of the unique play worlds of the works in which they appear. I am concerned to acknowledge and delineate male-centeredness but also to discover how the plays may variously engage both male and female audiences.

Chapter 1 deals with Natural landscapes. *Titus Andronicus* and *Venus and Adonis*, both early works, play out the association of the female with the forest, revealing a barely repressed fear of and revulsion to the mysterious "other" and emphasizing the importance of male Culture and male rivalry over erotic attraction. Later plays, beginning with *As You Like It*, show increasing demystification of the forest Wild and increasing certainty of the primacy of male Culture, while continuing to focus more on male preoccupations than on relations with the female. In this chapter I focus strongly on early works, in which the forest Wild seems central and actively operant, and skim lightly over later plays that banish or suppress the Wild landscape. I believe that this shift in geographical emphasis is the result of a shift in the central concern of the works. Whereas the early plays deal with the mating of young lovers—the male's foray into the mysterious female forest—the later plays focus on the problems generated by having incorporated Wild creatures uneasily into Culture. Once the male is enmeshed with the precariously "domesticated" Wild, emphasis shifts toward fears of unbridled lust, infidelity, infertility, entrapment, intractable virginity, incest, and, above all, the menace of women who are not primarily sex objects but cronelike reminders of death (witches, Lady Macbeth, Goneril and Regan, Volumnia, Cymbeline's Queen, Paulina, and Sycorax). The Wild landscape of the later plays is not the fertile forest but the sterile heath, the isolated island, the foreign outpost, the treacherous sea, or the rocky "desert" place. Some of the struggles of these plays are treated in later chapters.

Modern scholars have demonstrated the progressive constriction of female roles in society in the sixteenth and seventeenth centuries, paralleling this development with the rise of Puritanism, the decline of Catholic hegemony, and the growing domination of Nature. Some have also linked these developments with an accelerated revulsion from and fear of women, manifested most flagrantly in widespread witch burnings.[18] Shakespeare's evolution in depicting male control of Nature and women seems to parallel what was actually happening in seventeenth-century society. In this regard he is a man of his time, but the disappearance of the Wild forest seems to signal in Shakespeare the suppression rather than the defeat of the formidable forces of the Wild.

Chapter 2 explores Shakespeare's use of animals in ways both conventional and innovative. Although women are not central in this chapter, their pervasive association with animals makes them constantly relevant. I deal here particularly with plays that feature a heavy concentration of animal figures, references, and images. I show how the conventional animals of *The Taming of the Shrew* are used unexpectedly to express character transformations and to provide an original and ingenious early variation on the expected pattern of strict hierarchy. I also show how animal markers such as snakes and lions occur at transitional points of plays and seem to facilitate evolving visions, sometimes bridging boundaries of Culture and Wild. The chapter traces the abandonment of the comic alazon, defined by Northrop Frye as "someone who pretends or tries to be something more than he is" (*Anatomy* 39). This figure is personified in such man/animal hybrids as Bottom and the Falstaff of *The Merry Wives of Windsor*, but the alazon vanishes when he begins to seem too threatening to be funny. The chapter also examines both the erotic and the violent suggestiveness of the love hunt.

The erosion of man/animal, male/female, and male/barbarian boundaries through hybrid metaphors in such plays as *Troilus and Cressida* and *Timon of Athens* prepares for the terrifying collapse of man/animal boundaries that leads to the descent into madness in *King Lear* and to the horizontalizing of the vertical Chain of Being in *King Lear* and the later plays. Considerable evidence in other Renaissance works points to a parallel weakening of the chain image in other writers so that again Shakespeare's evolution seems to echo what was happening in Renaissance thought, although it runs counter to the trend toward male domination of female Nature outlined in Chapter 1.[19] Animals and barbarians encroach on male Culture even as it moves to confine the female. In this chapter I deal particularly with plays that feature a heavy concentration of animal figures, references, and images.

Finally, in Chapter 3 I take up depictions of the problems of males in confronting the female Wild, not primarily epitomized by landscape or entangled with animals but embodied by female figures themselves. These problems are expressed in schematic representations of both males and females. Embodiments of the conflicting aspects of the maturing male as he attempts to preserve Culture while he encompasses the necessary female Wild are presented in especially interesting ways in *The Comedy of Errors*, *Much Ado About Nothing* and *Two Noble Kinsmen*. *The Comedy of Errors* shows the effort to harmonize male lover with husband. In *Much Ado* Benedick labors to integrate his scattered "five wits" and to overcome the fear of cuckoldry which seems to loom so large in male Culture, while Palamon, Arcite, and Theseus of *Two Noble Kinsmen* play out in graphic detail components of male struggle for mastery of the female. The Wild that is tamed in that play is in the male imagination of the mysterious and threatening region of male-female unions.

In the last section of this chapter, I focus on the imagined female, both as Shakespeare's characters reveal her and as the plays preserve traces of the archaic memory of the Triple Hecate. The clichés of virgin, whore, and crone as male images of the female are pervasive throughout Shakespeare, but three plays interest me particularly as early and late studies. The early *Comedy of Errors* depicts these clichés with curious flatness and almost archetypical clarity. The ending brings them together in a very uneasy union. *All's Well That Ends Well* recapitulates the struggle—again with a less than wholly satisfactory conclusion. The late romance *The Winter's Tale* addresses the problems yet again in a final scene strikingly similar to that of *The Comedy of Errors*; but in this play the reconciliation of aspects of the female is miraculous and, at least momentarily, persuasive. A *Midsummer Night's Dream* and *Macbeth* are especially useful in revealing aspects of the shadowy "memories" of Hecate.

Examining characters and plays in this way helps to point up recurring male anxieties and projections of male experience, which are crystallized by Shakespeare in an endless variety of ways. The chapter hypothesizes neither progress nor regress but reveals rather the pervasive instability of Cultural equilibria. I have drawn from works throughout the canon with little regard for chronological rationale because I see no consistent "progress." The works discussed are those that seem to me to illustrate most vividly the problems caused by the female Wild, now a ghettoized part of Culture, as its inhabitants assume the ambiguous roles of wife/whore and mother/crone.

In this book I have ranged widely over Shakespeare's works, but I have made no attempt at an inclusive chronological study or a thorough review of the criticism of various plays, although I have greatly profited over the years from such criticism. I have felt free to choose plays that seem especially relevant and to ignore others that may be relevant but have already been much discussed. I deal in detail with some plays and only cursorily with others. In a work of such broad scope thorough and detailed examination of each play is impossible. I hope and expect that readers will make extensions of my analyses as well as objections to them.

A female reader may find Shakespeare's dramatic forays from the center of male-defined Culture into the mysterious realms of female, animal, and barbarian others brilliant and illuminating or shocking and confusing. In any case, attempting to examine his world from a female perspective should enlighten both sexes. Such a perspective is obviously partial and reductive, and Shakespeare's progresses and changes are, of course, less simple and schematic than I have made them seem. His voice modulates from revulsion at female sexuality to celebration of female power, from delight in human animality to horror at bestial perversions, from derision of the Ethiope to insistence on the humanity of the Jew. His status as a creative artist identifies him as one who, like the madman and the lover, imagines worlds beyond common experience. Because his voice is so powerful and so varied, it demands and repays repeated reexamination. The process ought to help us all as we try to reimagine the human, to understand some of the impediments to this process, to redefine boundaries, to negotiate, like Hamlet, between the "paragon of animals" and the "quintessence of dust," and most particularly as we struggle to bring women to a more central position in our definition of Culture.

As we attempt this reimagination, we realize that we have very little idea of how or whether females might construct Wild/Culture paradigms. Trying to establish a female view of Culture and Wild is extremely difficult because only recently have women writers undertaken to record their own special experiences; and even now the immasculating forces of literary images and values and habits make the achievement of fresh visions based on female perceptions very slow work. Still, the best sources of insight would seem to be modern writing by women.

Natural settings are important to these women writers, and, interestingly, Africa continues to be a significant symbolic landscape. But instead of connoting the sensuousness of Cleopatra and the savagery of Aaron the Moor, fertility and fatality, license and mystery, for modern women writers, Africa is often a landscape of freedom and fresh opportunity. Doris Lessing and Beryl Markham, for example, seem to have owed their ability to think of female possibilities in unstereotyped terms at least in part to their African upbringing. Isak Dinesen found independence in that foreign space, partly through the loss of a lover, and Dian Fossey records how she learned to be more at home with gorillas than with men. Women's green worlds, though central, are not typically sites of rapprochement with the male inhabitants of Culture. They evoke neither the fear of engulfment nor the specter of male/female violence. They are, rather, neutral territory that permits and encourages self-discovery. Like Shakespeare in *Venus and Adonis*, women identify landscapes with the female body, but their purpose is to explore and comprehend rather than exploit or escape.

The Wild as viewed by women is inhabited by many animals. Sometimes, like witches' familiars, they are extensions of power, not of the diabolical power invoked in *Macbeth* through the use of dissected toads, newts, bats, dogs, and lizards, but the power of living guides to new vistas. Women's Wild experiences may include green world lovers, but such lovers are rarely integrated with their women into Culture as they are in Shakespeare. In women's novels the alliance between women and animals often extends to foreigners and social inferiors as creatures outside the dominant Culture.

Characters in women's fiction also present a striking contrast to those in Shakespeare. Predictably, in women's works that focus on female experience, male figures are often shadowy and stereotyped. But one is struck by the vividness and variety of the females. Female writers no longer chronicle feminine trinities. For protagonists struggling, successfully or unsuccessfully, to discover themselves and pursue their destinies, virginity or lack of it is meaningless— female heroes are rarely, and usually only briefly, virginal. The status of wives is so volatile as to be unclassifiable. The experiences of older women, although still underrepresented, are sometimes explored in great detail. These figures, no longer defined simply as maternal, or asexual, or harbingers of death, become crones of great dignity and complexity. Female/female relationships, as we might expect, take on great importance and are explored in detail.

But perhaps the most striking feature of modern women's writing is its resistance to closure. Marriage may still be the culmination of popular romances, but in more serious works it almost never is. Unlike Shakespeare's dramas, the works rarely end neatly. Marriage and death are not the only female options. Because death, when it occurs, seems a part of a Natural cycle larger than individual experience, the crone, even in her most terrible aspect, can be tolerated with equanimity.

In women's works the Wild is celebrated as a Natural home, the site of self-discovery and fresh perceptions of identity and value. Culture is usually not so much abandoned as enriched by women who have profited by their Wild experiences. Mary Daly provides an example of how female redefinitions of Wild words and images may be liberating and inspiring. Using Cultural vocabulary, Daly redefines its terms. She sees Sirens as guides to the Realms of Deep Memory, Haggards as Wild-eyed "women reluctant to yield to wooing," and Harpies as those who harp on Haggard themes. Amazons are A-mazing creatures who can lead us out of Cultural mazes. Daly rescues Gorgons, Hags, Harridans, Battle-axes, Furies, and Fates from centuries of opprobrium. Revolting Hags become for her social heroes who bring hope of change. Daly's goal, she says, is to Wildize our consciousness. We might attempt something similar in reading Shakespeare. The resistant reader is often the most responsive reader.

Rethinking terms that have long shaped our visions of ourselves and our worlds is an exhilarating but difficult enterprise. It does not mean that we should stop reading Shakespeare, who remains the towering literary figure of our Culture, but it probably does mean that we should stop reading him in isolation as the voice of special revelation. We must view his works with a critical eye, emphasizing both his glories and his limitations, annotating his vision with other records of human experience.

Chapter One

he Wild Landscape

WOMEN AND NATURE

The Shakespearean Wild, whatever is not encompassed by the central male vision of Culture, frequently manifests itself metaphorically in terms of Natural landscape—typically introduced through journeys out of the court and city or through incursions of external forces into the court and city. Such landscapes may be associated with any or all of the three varieties of other under considera- tion—women, animals, and barbarians—but in this chapter I am concerned with their associations with women, the most unsettling segment of the mysterious Wild.

In recent criticism, discussions of this Natural world have been dom- inated by analyses of Shakespeare's "green world," a term that became a catch phrase in the vocabulary of modern Shakespeareans as a result of the powerful influence of Northrop Frye, who in *Anatomy of Criticism* opposed the "green world of romance" to the "normal world" as major locales of Shakespearean comedy. Frye speaks of the forest as part of a benign green world expressive of the "ritual theme of the triumph of life and love over the waste land" and "the victory of summer over winter." He categorizes the green landscape as a territory analogous to the "dream world of desire." (The desire is, of course, male, and Frye points out that a recurring green world theme focuses on the "ritual assault on a central female figure.") Viewing the forest in comedy and romance as a harmonious part of the green world, he notes that the place of conversion in *Two Gentlemen of Verona* is "the embryonic form of the fairy world of *A Midsummer Night's Dream*, the Forest of Arden in *As You Like It*, Windsor Forest in *The Merry Wives of Windsor*, and the pastoral world of the mythical sea-coasted Bohemia in *The Winter's Tale*." In elaborating what he calls "phase two of romance," the phase of the innocent youth of the hero, he visualizes a pastoral setting characterized by a "pleasant wooded landscape, full of glades, shaded valleys, murmuring brooks, the moon, and other images closely linked with the female or maternal aspect of sexual imagery" (182–83, 199–200).

By defining his green world in association with dramatic genre, specifically with comedies and romances with happy endings, Frye predetermined that this world would be for him and his followers benign, harmonious, and restorative, bringing "innocent youths" together with receptive and comforting females. Looking at much the same evidence with a more jaundiced eye, Jan Kott, another strong and influential commentator, moved critics and directors to a darker view of the Shakespearean Wild. In *Shakespeare Our Contemporary*, Kott vividly delineates a "Bitter Arcadia" as the setting of *As You Like It* and imagines the forest of *A Midsummer Night's Dream* as one inhabited by "devils and lamias, in which witches and sorceresses can easily find everything required for their practices" (335–42, 225–26).

Contradictory as these two visions of the Wild are, they share one striking characteristic. Both men describe their mythical Shakespearean green worlds in female terms. As he himself suggests, Frye's pastoral landscape with its glades and shaded valleys sounds stereotypically feminine, evoking specific aspects of female anatomy and resonant of the nurturing presence of the "good mother." Kott's lamias, witches, and sorceresses reflect the darker side of fantasies about women, the vision of the seducer and the "wicked stepmother." The convergence, in two such different visions, of assertions of the femininity of the green world provides some basis for further speculation about the underlying significances of this world in the works of Shakespeare.

Although both Frye and Kott base their descriptions of the Shakespearean green world on comedy and romance, other notable forms of Wild can be found in other genres. Metaphorical patterns do not necessarily conform to generic boundaries. I shall suggest that Shakespeare's use of the forest topos cuts across genres and that an analysis of a narrative poem and a tragedy may cast light on shadowy significances more obscurely present in comedy and romance. In each case my hypothesis is that for Shakespeare the Wild is the locale for the male's necessary, seductive, and terrifying confrontation with the female, his braving of the perils of maternal regression and destructive erotic abandon in order to annex a woman into his Cultural context.

The Wild world in Shakespeare's early works is frequently a forest—mysterious, magical, and ambiguous. Elaborated or suggested forests occur in at least seven of Shakespeare's early works: *Venus and Adonis*, *Two Gentlemen of Verona*, *Titus Andronicus*, *Love's Labor's Lost*, *A Midsummer Night's Dream*, *The Merry Wives of Windsor*, and *As You Like It*. Later forests tend to become tamer: the Forest of Arden may not be a forest at all,[1] and the mountain fastness of *Cymbeline* and Prospero's magically controlled island are male preserves virtually untouched by memories of the female Wild. The forests of *Timon of Athens* and *Two Noble Kinsmen* are almost parodic, whereas other Wild zones veer from the fertile and potentially generative sites of the forests to the sterile and barren worlds of *Macbeth* and *King Lear*. Shakespeare's gradual denaturing of the Wild and his increasing suppression and control of the green world recapitulate what I have suggested is the typical sequence of male experience—first, separation from the dangerously seductive maternal Wild and consolidation of his position in male Culture, and then the venture into the foreign territory once again to acquire a mate. The final step is the return to Culture and the taming and suppressing of the Wild, now precariously and marginally incorporated. The process is never wholly completed. This tamed Wild always harbors the possibility of rebellion (like Bianca's in *The Taming of the Shrew*), betrayal, real (like Gertrude's, Goneril's, and Regan's) or suspected (Mrs. Ford's, Hermione's, and Desdemona's), and death—actual, feigned, or supposed (Ophelia's, Lady Macbeth's, Hero's, Hermione's, Thais's). The landscapes that contain these hazards are no longer fertile forests but sterile heaths, oceans, rocky and desert places, and isolated islands. My primary focus in this chapter is on the earlier works. Some of the later plays are taken up in more detail in Chapters 2 and 3.

The equation of women and Nature is so ancient and so ubiquitous as hardly to need documentation. From Aristotle on, philosophers have seen women as formless matter upon which men must imprint shape, even as Nature was the raw material from which human Culture was to be constructed. Francis Bacon defined primordial Nature as matter "entirely despoiled, shapeless, and indifferent to Form," concluding that matter is "a common harlot" with forms as suitors (4:320). Women were seen as closer than men to animals in the Great Chain of Being, barely rational and dominated by passion and appetite. They were the vessels that carried male fertility to fruition. Seen as passive and receptive, women were repeatedly linked by tradition and specifically by Shakespeare with the earth; the affinity of wombs and tombs became a cliché. Like Nature, the female was fixed and given, if chaotic and shapeless, whereas the male, like Culture, belonged to the intellectual world of becoming. Woman's fertility, her cyclical anatomical processes, and her subordinate position in most societies confirmed her closeness to Nature and reinforced the view that she was to be controlled by male Culture. Using the mythical Prometheus as a model, Renaissance scholars saw the role of man as completing, improving, and refining Nature.[2] This view is admirably adumbrated in the famous passage in *The Winter's Tale* (4.4.80–95) in which, after Perdita, identifying with Nature, rejects the streak'd gillyvors as "Nature's bastards," Polixenes reproves her, praising the art (presumably male) that mends and changes Nature.

Although Nature and the female are clearly linked in Shakespeare, it would be folly to try to set up a system of exact equivalence between man and Culture and woman and Nature. Sherry Ortner has argued, however, that such an equivalence does seem to prevail in many cultures; and it is worthwhile to examine ways in which the Wild provides in Shakespeare the setting for the male's confrontation with the female—a confrontation sometimes violent, as in *Titus Andronicus*, sometimes unfruitful, as in *Venus and Adonis*, and sometimes resulting in the successful establishment of a new generation, as in the forest comedies. If we posit the concept of a central Cultural citadel defined by and for males, we must also acknowledge a surrounding feminine landscape that is both essential and threatening.

Recent theories of male development, based on Freud, greatly modified by Nancy Chodorow and popularized by Carol Gilligan help to illuminate the dilemma symbolically suggested by geography. To negotiate the Oedipal crisis successfully the young man must separate himself from his attachment to his mother and identify with the more distant world of his father. This process is facilitated by a growing, socially induced sense of the inferiority of the female species and the superiority of his own; and it is abetted by an increasing consciousness that the powerful mother will deny and punish as well as nurture and protect. Having successfully completed his identification with the male world, however, the young man must, for the sake of property and progeny, learn to relate in a new way to the female world. Seduced by the memory of his Natural childhood idyll but convinced now of the superiority of the male world of Culture, he is confronted with the twin perils of being paralyzed, devoured, or engulfed by maternal powers on one hand or castrated or destroyed by male rivals on the other. Illustrations in Renaissance books attest to the currency of male fantasies of being dismembered and/or devoured by inhabitants of the Wild—female, barbarian, and animal. Editions of Ovid, often illustrated, were, of course, widely circulated and probably known to Shakespeare. The illustrations in the 1591 Antwerp edition graphically depict the dismemberment of Pentheus (Fig. 5) and Orpheus by women. Accounts of the Arctic voyages of William Barents in 1594, 1595, and 1596 were apparently so well known that most scholars agree that the line about the "icicle on a Dutchman's beard" in *Twelfth Night* (3.2.27–28) glances at Barents. Girard Le Ver's French edition of the travels includes a picture (Fig. 6) that might well serve as an illustration for *The Winter's Tale* of how the "bear din'd on the gentleman" (3.3.106) (see also Fig. 15). And the earliest known woodcut, dating from 1505, of New World Indians (Fig. 7) shows a family scene of cannibals, one of whom is dining on the arm of a European guest, the rest of whose mangled corpse hangs from a nearby tree. We know that such reports of cannibalism—not wholly baseless—persisted in the European imagination for generations. Interestingly, three of the scenes—Orpheus, Barents, and the Indians—are set in the marginal land at water's edge where Culture has confronted the Wild. In spite of the risks, real and imagined, however, for progeny, food, and property the male must venture into the Wild.

Western literature richly documents the varieties of male experience in embarking on this adventure. Green worlds harbor the primary versions of the female—virgins, whores (devils and lamias), and crones (good mothers, bad mothers, witches). It is no surprise that Diana's woods are also the playground of Venus and Ceres. The conventional view of the pastoral is suggestive but misleading. Walter R. Davis in *A Map of Arcadia* describes a traditional vision of the pastoral journey. He sees the hero (always a male) as a sojourner passing through a pastoral world, which Davis maps as three concentric circles, one defining an outer "real" world, urban, complex, and sophisticated, which surrounds a second circle representing a classical literary tradition. Both these circles surround a "supernatural" center, usually a shrine or cave, ruled over in almost every case by a female—Venus, Calliope, Diana, a nymph or other semidivine figure. On this site the hero experiences "rebirth" (34–38). The pattern could hardly be clearer—the hero must brave the perils of the Wild to get his woman and must negotiate the mysteries of female anatomy—the shrine, the cave—to achieve the promise of fertility.

But Davis's map is inaccurate. The diagram suggested in my introduction offers a more realistic representation of the male journey. As the diagram shows, the female is not at the center of the hero's world but in a strange, enticing, and threatening Wild territory overlapping but not identical with his own. And he is indeed a sojourner there who will leave it as soon as his mission is accomplished. His Culture includes both experience of the "real" world and knowledge of classical antiquity—his tradition—but the mysterious unknown region is the female/foreign/animal Wild. The male must venture into this territory; he may even find its terrors exciting; but he will eagerly return to his familiar world.

THE FRIGHTENING FOREST

Shakespeare's early works reveal the possibilities and the anxieties of the male journey with astonishing clarity, again and again recapitulating experiences of the male as he braves the female Wild. Sometimes, as in *Venus and Adonis*, *Titus Andronicus*, and *A Midsummer Night's Dream*, Shakespeare's renditions are filled with vivid and explicit evocations of the attractions and fatal entrapments of a numinous forest world. In other cases, such as *Two Gentlemen of Verona*, the feminine presence is virtually eradicated. *Love's Labor's Lost*, *A Midsummer Night's Dream*, *The Merry Wives of Windsor*, and *As You Like It* occupy intriguing middle grounds. Viewed in the most simplistic and reductionist terms, the 1592 poem *Venus and Adonis* lays out many of the central themes of green world drama. Adonis inhabits a determinedly male Wild where the hunter resists sexual possibilities and concentrates on his animal prey. But male and female Wilds briefly intersect. Venus offers a feminized Wild with an erotic prize. She herself sets up the analogy between her body and the landscape, offering to be a park where her "deer" can feed, grazing on her lips and enjoying "pleasant fountains," "Sweet bottom grass," "high delightful plain," and "Round rising hillocks" (lines 232–37). But nurturing and maternal as this sounds, Venus also serves as sexual love object, arousing some faint interest in Adonis, most notably as she lies passive and unthreatening in a swoon. At the same time, she embodies the frightening figure of the "terrible mother," devouring rather than satisfying. She unmans Adonis by plucking him from his horse; she feeds "glutton-like"

5. *Pentheus*. Ovid, *Metamorphoses*. Antwerp, 1591, p. 97. Illustration by Pieter van der Borcht. By permission of the Folger Shakespeare Library.

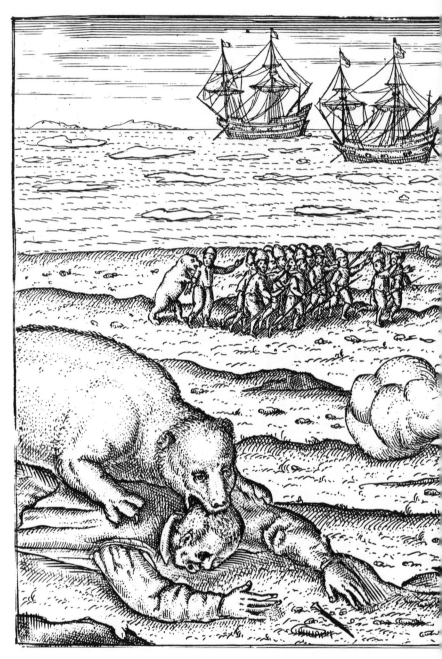

6. *Arctic Expedition of William Barents*. Girard Le Ver, *Vraye Description des Trois Voyages*. Amsterdam, 1600, fol. C3v. By permission of the Folger Shakespeare Library.

7. Woodcut of New World Indians, probably South American. Printed by Johann Froschauer. Augsburg, 1505. Spencer Collection. Astor, Lenox and Tilden Foundations, New York Public Library.

on her "yielding prey" and yet "never filleth." Her lips are conquerors; she forages with "blindfold fury." Her face reeks and smokes, and her blood boils with careless lust. She kisses him

Even as an empty eagle, sharp by fast,
Tires with her beak on feathers, flesh, and bone,
Shaking her wings, devouring all in haste,
Till either gorge be stuff'd, or prey be gone;
(lines 55–58)

The theme of male rivalry surfaces more subtly, but the very first lines set up the antithesis between the "purple-color'd face" of the royal-paternal sun rising from his amorous bed and that of the "Rose-cheek'd" son, Adonis, piously abjuring love. There is surely an implication, reinforced later in the poem, of the dutiful son renouncing the libidinal territory of his father. He retreats to the safe male Wild of the hunter of animals, continuing to resist sexuality, even though Venus encourages him to "Be bold to play" because "our sport is not in sight." When the forest shadows forsake them and Titan, the paternal god of the sun/son, enviously discovers them, observing them with burning eye and wishing himself in Adonis's place, the young man suddenly cries, "The sun doth burn my face, I must remove" (186). Even after the descending sun has set, he continues to resist, fearing the moonless but feminine "black-fac'd night, desire's foul nurse," as much as the paternal sun (773). Venus points up the son/sun rivalry when she warns the morning sun,

There lives a son that suck'd an earthly mother,
May lend thee light, as thou dost lend to other.
(lines 863–64)

Later she reminisces hyberbolically that the sun lurked like a thief to rob Adonis "of his fair," forcing him to go bonneted for protection from its light. And Venus's final apostrophe to the dead Adonis, now diminished into a purple flower, depicts the son/father rivalry most baldly. Although the father she refers to is literally Adonis, the language clearly evokes the Oedipal triangle and depicts the return of the son to safe, regressive bliss:

Here was thy father's bed, here in my breast;
Thou art the next of blood, and 'tis thy right.

Lo in this hollow cradle take thy rest,
My throbbing heart shall rock thee day and night.
(lines 1183–86)

Even Adonis's death in the encounter with the boar and the retreat of Venus to Paphos suggest the victory of male principles over female. As a hunter of animals, Adonis has chosen the known perils of the male Wild over the perilous pleasures of the female forest. One might even argue that the boar is the specter of a vengeful father that has forced his son back to infantile regression to the mother, a kind of death. Male rivalry is stronger than heterosexual eroticism.[3]

By exploring the anxieties of father/son rivalry in *Venus and Adonis* Shakespeare may have succeeded in allaying his own, at least temporarily—although such rivalry surfaces again in *Hamlet* without the powerful female ambiance of the forest milieu. The problems of the male in dealing with the female continue to exfoliate in forest settings. Perhaps the starkest exposition of the forest topos as site for the power struggle between masculine Culture and the recalcitrant Wild—both feminine and barbarian—occurs in *Titus Andronicus*. The opening scene in Rome—locus classicus of patriarchy in Shakespeare—emphasizes almost to absurdity the importance of male rivalry and male domination. Saturninus's first speech invokes *pat*ricians, *pat*rons, arms, country*men*, right of succession, swords, first born *son*, and *father*'s honors. Rivalry between Saturninus and Bassianus for political power modulates into a struggle over possession of Lavinia, and Titus kills one of the four remaining of his five and twenty sons rather than relinquish control over his daughter's destiny. The eldest son of Tamora, defeated matriarch, is sacrificed, but, in a temporary and ominous reversal, she gains fresh power, duplicitously acceding to a new role as "handmaid," "nurse," and "mother" (1.1.331–32) when Saturninus chooses her as a substitute bride. The nightmare of the dominion of the wicked stepmother is about to be played out.

Tamora has effected a superficial peace, persuading her new husband to seem to reconcile with his brother and the Andronici. (Saturninus's desire for Lavinia is quickly transmogrified into rivalry with his brother over what he identifies as her "rape" [1.1.404].) But almost immediately it emerges that, though Tamora may control Saturninus, *her* ruler is Aaron—she is faster bound to him, he boasts, than Prometheus to the Caucasus (2.1.17). His lust for her, however, is overshadowed by his lust for power—again male rivalry. Through Tamora

Aaron will dominate Saturninus and the Roman Empire. Tamora's sons, Demetrius and Chiron, fall out, not so much because of "love" for Lavinia, as through the passionate intensity of sibling rivalry and the ambition of "horning" Bassianus as Aaron has horned Saturninus. As for Lavinia, a "certain snatch or so" will serve their turns (2.1.88–95).

The struggle is between men, but the necessary pawns are women, and the arena of the power struggle is the forest. Titus views the forest with an auspicious eye, noting that "the [morn] is bright and grey; The fields are fragrant and the woods are green" (2.2.1–2). Having been troubled in his sleep, he finds the day inspiring "new comfort" and the promise of fulfilled harmony graced by the "emperor and his lovely bride" (2.2.1–10). Relations between the sexes are superficially tranquil; but the "musical discord" of the "uncoupled" hounds which wakes the lovers of *A Midsummer Night's Dream* to new harmony here signals the waking of lovers to the grim truth of "Roman hunting." The doubleness of the metaphorical hunt, inevitably linked to the forest, is repeatedly insisted on throughout Shakespeare's works, regularly suggesting both the pursuit of animals and sexual pursuit. Tamora puts it nicely: the two themes echo each other "As if a double hunt were heard at once" (2.3.19). And Demetrius combines the two meanings as he gloats with Chiron in anticipation of plucking "a dainty doe to ground" (2.2.26).

Tamora is a creature of the Wild—both female and foreign.[4] She comes to the forest, a devotee of Venus, expecting to enjoy the unlawful embraces of her lover, also a creature of Wild Nature, foreign in color as well as breeding. To her the forest sounds are "gleeful": the "chequer'd shadow" provides secrecy (shelter from the paternal sun); and her vision of the venereal modulates into the maternal: the sounds of horns, hounds, and birds will be a nurse's lullaby (2.3.10–29). Aaron, however, rejects Venus in favor of Saturn. For him the "snake rolled in the cheerful sun" becomes an adder (female) unrolled "to do some fatal execution." His is a male-dominated forest focused on "Blood and revenge"— doom for Bassianus and vengeance on Titus by means of Lavinia. Consummation is eclipsed by conquest; amorous passion is revealed to be "Spotted, detested, and abominable." Bassianus equates Tamora satirically not with a generative Venus but with a destructive Diana. Her earlier vision of the pleasant, receptive, female forest darkens into a description of "A *barren* detested vale," where "nothing *breeds*" (2.3.93–96, italics added). The soothing sounds of the maternal nurse change to the "fearful and confused cries" of fiends, snakes, toads, and urchins. The welcoming cave Tamora has remembered as the shelter of Dido and Aeneas is transformed in ghastly parody into the "abhorred pit," and the womb of the mother earth has altered, as it so often does in Elizabethan literature, into a tomb where Bassianus will shortly lie. Male rivalry breeds the plot against Bassianus and Lavinia, spurs the two sons to murder, and enhances their jointly executed rape. Tamora now rejects any implication that there might be pity in her "woman's face" or "womanhood" beyond concern for her sons in her role.

The transformation of the forest from a place of harmonious, if adulterous, union of the male with the female to the nightmare realm of revenge and rivalry is further demonstrated as Aaron leads Quintus and Martius to the "loathsome pit." All the worst male fears of the Wild are now realized. Revulsion against the female is spelled out with almost embarrassing clarity in the description of the "subtle hole ... / Whose mouth is cover'd with rude-growing briers, / Upon whose leaves are drops of new-shed blood," the "unhallow'd and blood-stained hole," the "detested, dark, blood-drinking pit," the "fell devouring receptacle, / As hateful as Cocytus' misty mouth." The "precious ring" on the "bloody finger" of the dead man lightens the hole like a taper in a tomb, shining only on the "dead man's earthy cheeks" and the "ragged entrails" of the pit. It is compared to the moon that shone on Pyramus "When he by night lay bathed in maiden blood" (2.3.192–236). The equation of female sexuality with death could hardly be clearer. One young male who has ventured into the Wild zone has been swallowed up through the agency of the seductive/destructive mother, and four more will be engulfed and destroyed before the play's grisly end. The sterile gold exhumed from the nettles at the base of the elder tree, "which overshades the mouth of that same pit," only confirms the image of female betrayal and abortive birth, an image which culminates in the despised black baby who seems to survive the end of the play. Male/male violence and by extension male violence against female "possessions" is unleashed in the Wild setting, and the emergence from the forest of the maimed and bloody remnant of Lavinia seems the only fitting conclusion to the series of grim triumphs of male violence over the potentially benign forest walks. Tamora's oxymoronic description of her sons' departure to "deflower the trull" exposes a male problem in his conquest of the Wild—he wants both virgin and whore and cannot reconcile the two.

The rape of Lavinia enacts overtly two important aspects of male fantasies.

By violating Lavinia, Tamora's sons have avenged themselves and their mother on Lavinia's father—the embodiment of patriarchal power with its threat to sons. The Wild disorder of the forest temporarily prevails over Roman Culture. The sons satisfy their bloodthirsty mother (who later literally "swallows them like the earth" [5.2.191]) by diverting their own appetites to the "dainty doe" conveniently provided them. They create in the mutilated Lavinia a gruesome icon of the "perfect" sex object—silent and powerless. But because Lavinia still proves capable of betrayal of the rapists with her writing in the sand and of her father by her very presence, she must die. The accomplished lust is sterile; Chiron and Demetrius's despised black half-brother is the only progeny. The rest of the play continues to objectify male fears—castration anxiety in the repeated images of amputated hands and the specter of Tamora as the nightmarish devouring female. The final bloody banquet brilliantly combines the acting out of maternal engulfment with revenge on both the ambiguous denizens of the female Wild—the seductive/destructive mother and the wife/whore/daughter/bride. Aaron's death by burial waist high in the earth and slow starvation provides an eloquent coda, a final vision of the nightmare of female entrapment and deprivation.

THE FOREST COMEDIES

These two early works expose aspects of the green world that are suppressed or disguised in much of Shakespeare's later work. The fear of female power and the revulsion from female sexuality displayed overtly in these two early works resurface in subtler forms in the more complex structures of subsequent dramas. In the forest comedies the males venture more successfully into the female Wild, but even here the deflection of interest from male engagement with the female to the struggle between males is a regularly recurring pattern.

Love's Labor's Lost starts with a specific enactment of the short-lived effort at a male bonding that will secure the citadel against female incursions and the necessary concessions to the world of the future. But almost immediately Costard is taken with Jacquenetta, who comes to personify the potential of the future through her pregnancy, presumably courtesy of Don Armado. The aristocratic women, confined at first to the castle park, a controlled hunting ground, will in time necessarily be incorporated into the castle proper. But meanwhile the Princess of France shows herself to be a formidable hunter, and the men are humiliated by the superior skills of the women in easily penetrating their disguises. Although the men finally concede their need of women, incorporation of the female is never sucessfully completed; it is rather suspended by the departure of the women. Only Jacquenetta guarantees a future, and one doubts that she is fully tamed.

Shakespeare's forest comedies, *Two Gentlemen of Verona*, *The Merry Wives of Windsor*, and *As You Like It*, highlight the young male's invasion of the female world in search of a spouse, but male rivalries continue to be a strong parallel theme. They take the form of oppositions between father and lover, lover and lover, and husband and lover. Again these conflicts are precipitated by the dilemmas of male efforts to deal with the female, and again they are resolved in the forest setting. The dilemma of the father is that he wants to retain possession of his daughter as an important property; but the value of the property lies in his ability to dispose of it—an essential step in his own immortality.[5] Egeus points up the irony in *A Midsummer Night's Dream*, declaring of Hermia,

As she is mine, I may dispose of her:
Which shall be either to this gentlemen,
Or to her death, according to our law
Immediately provided in that case.

(1.1.42)

He is determined to have his way even if it means losing his property, his daughter, and his hopes for the future in her fertility. Similar cases of fathers' determination to control the destiny of their daughters precipitate the action of *Two Gentlemen of Verona* and *The Merry Wives of Windsor*. In the former the Duke of Milan is set on pairing off Silvia with the lumpish Thurio, and in the latter Master Page relentlessly pursues his resolution to acquire the foolish Slender for a son-in-law. In each case the concern of the father is not for his daughter but for his own control and choice, and in each case the conflict leads from the Cultural center of the orderly patriarchal town or court to the risks of the disorderly but fertile forest.

As we have seen earlier, although the goal of the male's journey to the Wild is to secure the female, the process is fraught with potential conflicts—with other males, fathers and rivals—and indeed the focus often strays from the erotic to the competitive. The rivalry between male "lovers," one of the strongest themes of Shakespearean drama, is particularly evident in *Two Gentlemen of*

Verona. Although Shakespeare's "new comedy" purports to center around love for a lady, it more often appears to be either a masculine property dispute or a device to avoid a commitment to love—a method of clinging to the known perils of male Culture in preference to risking a new commitment in the Wild. Lovers are often more intent on challenging their rivals than pursuing their ladies. Proteus seems smitten more by Valentine's admiration for Silvia than by genuine affection—he has barely seen her. The rejected Thurio follows Silvia into the forest saying,

> I'll after, more to be reveng'd on Eglamour
> Than for the love of reckless Silvia.
>
> (5.2.51–52)

There is only one scene in all of *Two Gentlemen* in which male and female lovers are alone (2.2.1–15), and it lasts for only fifteen lines. There is much talk of love but very little demonstration of it.

Shakespeare's changing of the name of the Celia of his source to Silvia is of particular interest because it substitutes the confusion of the forest for the serenity of the sky. Jonathan Goldberg in *Voice Terminal Echo* links the new name to the *silva* literary tradition connecting leaves of the forest to leaves of books. He suggests that her name emphasizes the secondhand quality of the "literary." He concludes that all Shakespearean characters are thus "the generation of Silvia" (ch. 4). If this is true of the men, it is doubly so of the women, who are echoes of figments of the male imagination. Female characters are thus removed by a second generation from the "real." Silvia does seem to be a source of poetic inspiration in the play, but at the price of her own near obliteration. Geoffrey Hartman, speaking of the tale of Philomela, summarizes the poetic process— "A girl dies, song is born" (163). Goldberg, too, refers to the "Ovidian etiology of song in rape and mutilation." Art seems in this model to be grimly mimicking the "deflowering" or "dying" necessary to human procreation, and the implication seems to be that females must be sacrificed to achieve art.[6] They are also sacrificed to achieve other forms of male self-actualization. Threatened like Lavinia with rape, Silvia is saved only to become an object of barter for the male protagonists. She nearly vanishes at the play's end.

Other connotations also cluster about the name Silvia and the idea of the sylvan. Silvia is an alternate name for Rhea or Cybele—the earth goddess with power both to bless and to curse—and the Latin word evokes both the mystery and the plenitude of a place of massed vegetation, a benign Wild. In this sense Silvia suggests the good mother, source of nurturance and fertility. Descriptions of the actual forest of Shakespeare's England suggest similar female attributes, both mysteries and pleasures. But they also take for granted the dominance of the male. John Manwood, in his treatise on the laws of the forest, lingers repetitively on the forest's secrecy, fruitfulness, and recreational pleasure, describing it as a "territorie of wooddy grounds and fruitful pastures" stored with "couverts for the secret abode of the wild beasts." But although Manwood's dedication acknowledges the "great and provident" care of the Queen, his actual description of the forest overwhelmingly stresses that it is for "the princely delight and pleasure" of the King—offering a variant form of the droit de seigneur. It is inviting and inspiring, but it is also female—to be enjoyed and controlled.[7]

In the forest of *Two Gentlemen of Verona* Silvia and Julia are freed from some patriarchal strictures. But the forest is represented only minimally, and the freedom of the female Wild is severely limited. In some ways, the play is a comedic rewriting of *Titus Andronicus*. The frightening mother/step-mother/whore has been banished from the forest, and the two women who are permitted there are, like Lavinia, rendered speechless and powerless. The threat of rape, first by the outlaws and then by Proteus, silences Silvia—her last words follow Proteus's lines: "I'll woo you like a soldier, at arm's end, / And love you 'gainst the nature of love—force ye" (5.4.57–59). Julia, whose male disguise leaves her impotent (unlike Rosalind, who is empowered by hers), regains her lover only after becoming completely inert in her swoon. (There is, of course, a similar turning point in *As You Like It* when Rosalind's fainting finally reveals her true weakness and availability.) In spite of the male's surface idealization of women, Silvia and Julia are virtually invisible to the men of the play.

Indeed, though the men seem to have infiltrated the Wild, they are too thoroughly imprisoned in their own preconceptions to experience its liberating effects. For them the forest is a male Wild, differentiated from the city by its outlaw population. They cannot experience the forest as female except as territory for conquest. They seem arrested in prepubertal play. Indeed, we can account for the strangely flat and perfunctory quality of the forest of *Two Gentlemen of Verona* if we recognize the failure of the men to become truly engaged with the female world. There are so many references to the blindness of love and of lovers in this play that it seems clear that part of Shakespeare's purpose was to satirize such superficial and indiscriminate infatuation. Speed tells Valentine, "If you love her, you cannot see her" (2.1.68). Valentine says that Julia holds Proteus's eyes "lock'd in her crystal looks," leading Silvia to conclude that Proteus must then be blind. She rejects Valentine's claim that love has twenty pair of eyes, and Thurio reiterates love's eyelessness (2.4.89–96). Proteus falls in "love" with Silvia almost before he sees her and expects to be blinded when fully acquainted (2.4.211–12). Thurio's song to Silvia speaks of love's blindness (4.2.46–47), and Julia bemoans the power of the "blinded god" (4.4.196). Even when surrounded by the Wild, the men cannot see it.

Seeing eyes are a complementary and constantly recurring theme. The eyes of mistresses are much celebrated, not as parts of other living beings but as Lacanian mirrors, like those of a mother, which reflect flattering images of narcissistic male viewers. Thurio's song portrays blind love using and incorporating Silvia's eyes—again the female is sacrificed to art in the male imagination. Proteus remarks to Thurio that black men become pearls in ladies' eyes (5.1.12). He begs Silvia for "one fair look" and vows on the very verge of violence toward her that he would perform any dangerous action for "one calm look from Silvia" (5.4.41–42). When we first see Silvia, she reflects Valentine's greeting and multiplies it—he wishes her "a thousand good morrows" and she returns "two thousand" (2.1.96–101). We find that she has inspired him to the astonishing narcissistic act of writing a love letter to himself without knowing it and, as he later declares, to leave his "enthralled eyes" watching his own heart (2.4.134–35). His Silvia is an echo of male fantasy rather than a true spirit of the Wild forest, and because he cannot see her as a person, he is ready to sacrifice her to his friend.

If the men see themselves in their mistress's eyes, the women are created as erotic objects by male gaze. When the men are present the women exist chiefly as reflected images. Indeed, we see them in any detail only when males are absent. Otherwise they tend to be idols (2.4.144, 4.2.128) and shadows—shadows of males rather than females. Proteus contents himself with the idea of making love to a picture (4.2.120–25). Julia sees herself as reduced to a shadow in the absence of Proteus's love (4.2.128, 4.4.197–98) and declares that having thrown away mask and mirror in her sorrow, she no longer has rosy cheeks or fair skin. The masked Silvia is "invisible" to Friar Lawrence in the forest, and the disguised Julia is "invisible" to Proteus. Throughout the play women are associated with transparency—with "crystal looks," jewels, glass, tears, water, ice, streams, ocean. They are hardly present to the males, and the woods they inhabit reflect their sterility.

While Valentine and Proteus remain immune to the vitality and potential Wildness of the women even in the wood, Speed and Launce see the women in earthier but no less stereotypical terms. Revulsion from the feminine lurks just below the surface of their humor. The Petrarchan idealization of women, based on illusion, is balanced throughout the play by the "realism" of Speed and Launce, and although the juxtaposition is unquestionably funny, some of the humor comes from the degradation of the female. Speed deflates his master's high-flying rhetoric by informing him that the follies of love shine through him "like the water in a urinal" (2.1.39–40) and permit the easy diagnosis of his malady as mere illness. He goes on to suggest that Silvia is painted and deform'd (2.1.56–76). The Natural power of the female is denied and her Wildness is reduced to the animalistic. Launce designates his shoe with the "worser sole," that "with the hole in it," as his mother (2.3.16–17). His extraordinary account of his effort to give his dog to Silvia on behalf of his master surrounds her with images of violation and pollution. He tells how the dog steals a capon's leg from her plate, releases a stench under her table, and finally heaves up his leg and makes water against her farthingale (4.4.7–43). This may be humor for the groundlings, but the laughter grows from complicity in the degradation of woman (perhaps hinting at the much feared incontinence of women[8]) as well as from perception of the incongruity between noble lady and ignoble dog. The female, earlier subject of hyperbolic praise, now inspires derision and disgust.

Shakespeare's decision to depart from Jorge de Montemayor's *Diana*, the source of *Two Gentlemen of Verona*, by splitting in two the single male protagonist of that work (revealingly named Felix), who embodies the happy male fantasy of flitting like a bee from flower to flower without encumbrance, obscures the clarity of that vision, and reminds us that at least a certain modicum of fidelity is necessary to assure legitimate progeny. Indeed, the split enables us to experience concurrently both fickleness and fidelity. And as in *Titus Andronicus*, the memory of the source lingers in the play. Montemayor's heroine is Filesmena (a lost court play of 1585, *The History of Felix and Philiomena* may have been a more immediate source), and like Lavinia she echoes Ovid's Philomela, ravished, mutilated, and deserted in the forest by Tereus and transformed into a nightingale. The virtuous Valentine in Shakespeare moans that, except with Silvia in the night, the nightingale has no music (3.1.78–79), and in his forest cell (the only remnant of the pastoral cave—now colonized by the male) his distresses reverberate to the nightingale's complaining notes (5.4.5–6). At almost the same moment, his "counterfeit," his alter ego, Proteus, is attempting, like Tereus, to ravish the maiden in the forest, in this case Silvia.

Two Gentlemen of Verona thus transforms and conceals the material of *Titus Andronicus*, turning it to "comedy" by the male's success in resolving his conflicts without actual violence and appropriating the female in such a way as to allow for a more promising future. Silvia is silenced and Proteus is able to accept the inert Julia. The female rings are properly bestowed. Women are found to be interchangeable and exchangeable, and with that business accomplished, the men are able to leave the de-Natured female Wild behind and return to the business of ordering male Culture.

If the Wild of *Two Gentlemen of Verona* is minimally delineated, that of *A Midsummer Night's Dream* occupies most of the play. In *A Midsummer Night's Dream* Hermia and Lysander set forth from Athens to escape patriarchal tyranny by seeking out his wealthy aunt beyond the forest. But the forest, magnified and mystified, becomes the focus of the play. Titania, the Faerie Queen, is a powerful and appealing force—almost equal to Oberon. Puck associates himself with "the triple Hecat's team" (5.1.384), eliciting the powers of Luna, Diana, and Prosperina; and both the pregnant votaress of Titania, who has given birth to the changeling boy (2.1.123–37), and the chaste vestal, "imperial vot'ress" of Diana (2.1.157–64), are luminous presences even in their absence. The step-mother/witch/crone has disappeared from the Athenian forest and overwhelming pressure toward the fertility and consummation appropriate to Midsummer's Eve is blocked only by confusion of objects of passion, by the ineffectually resistant patriarchal decrees of Egeus and Theseus, and finally by the propriety of the city-bred Hermia herself who insists that her lover "lie farther off." Oberon promotes consummation for mortals and even temporarily unleashes the extramarital lusts of his wife. Ambiguous as it is, the Athenian forest displays and tolerates female eroticism. Hermia, Helena, Hippolyta, and Titania, though hardly subtly characterized, show varied and clearly defined aspects of the female. There are virgins in abundance—Hippolyta, the vanquished Amazon; Hermia, the confident, assertive woman in pursuit of a mate; Helena, the self-loather, unable to believe she is loved. Titania is a unique figure—a wife strong-willed and sensuously alive and probably adulterous but not condemned as a whore. The development from *Two Gentlemen of Verona* is extraordinary. The male lovers, sharply differentiated in the earlier play, have now becomed indistinguishable, while the females have proliferated and taken on individuality in direct proportion to the blossoming of the forest.

And yet certain patterns repeat themselves. Like Proteus, the males are easily distracted. Quickly and easily the "magic" of Oberon and Puck diverts Lysander from interest in consummating his love in a matriarchal setting to the passionate pursuit of his rival Demetrius to solve a problem between men. In the forest, Demetrius, like a pale shadow of the rapist of the same name in *Titus Andronicus*, imagines the possibility of raping even his rejected lover. The idea is implicit as he warns her not

> To trust the opportunity of night,
> And the ill counsel of a desert place,
> With the rich worth of your virginity.
> (2.1.217–19)

His threat becomes more explicit as he elaborates, "do not believe / But I shall do thee mischief in the wood" (2.1.236–37). The forest is the proper sphere of the feminine moon, and our first glimpse of this setting features servants of the Faerie Queen. But the ambiguous nature of the fairies and the disorder of the natural world point up an unstable equilibrium.

In the forest the female power embodied in Titania holds out, at least temporarily, against the demands of her husband; but the frightening prospect of female rebellion and the naked revelation of female lust are safely curbed in Oberon's final victory. Serving to veil unpleasant realities, "magic" is a metaphor for male power. Titania's display of lust, a game licensed by male magic, is at first enchanting both to her and to her audience, but it becomes a nightmarish memory after the restorative second application of magic juice. Oberon sees the fresh and fragrant flowers Titania has used for a coronet for Bottom's "hairy temples" as weeping at "their own disgrace." He taunts her "at his pleasure," and under the magic spell she begs his patience and quickly yields up the changeling boy. The male has achieved his "progeny" without bothering to beget it (4.1.51–63). The threat to patriarchy—suppressed in the city—is quelled even in the more permissive world of the forest. Primordial memories of the Faerie Queene as Great Mother or Triple Hecate and of Midsummer's Eve as the occasion for Bacchanalian fertility rites are evoked and suppressed. The forest trope allows the idea of matriarchy to surface but ends by denying it.[9]

The power of the idea of matriarchy, repeatedly subdued, persists, however, resurfacing in particularly striking form in *The Merry Wives of Windsor*, where the forest becomes the scene of female triumph over the male Wild personified by Falstaff. This play became associated early with a possibly apocryphal command from Queen Elizabeth, and it has been notably unpopular with male critics.[10] It is the only one of the forest comedies to celebrate female freedom in ways that promise its survival beyond the limits of the play. For once the forest offers and delivers feminine triumphs—although not without some compromise. As with *Two Gentlemen* and *A Midsummer Night's Dream*, the forest is the site of male-female confrontation; but unlike those two plays *The Merry Wives* somewhat dissipates the intensity of the conflict through the audience's knowledge that the spectacle at center stage is not a real struggle but that the conclusion is predetermined. The merry wives are not pursuing illicit erotic encounters in the forest but are colluding with their spouses to "punish unchaste desire." The real schism between Ford and his wife has been healed before the scene in Windsor Forest, and even the intensity of the tug-of-war in the subplot between the Pages over their daughter has been vitiated by our knowledge that Anne and Fenton have arranged to circumvent the intentions of both parents.

But many of the disturbing issues of *A Midsummer Night's Dream* persist in recognizable form. It is almost as if Shakespeare has chosen to repeat the themes in a demystified version. The powerful memory of the once potent Faerie Queene is again dimly present, and the possibility of the union of the "goddess" with her "horned god" paramour is surely latent behind the forest scene.[11] But the "goddess" has been fragmented into a servant and two faithful wives and the "horned god" reduced to a figure of fun.

Male rivalry abounds—between the three suitors aspiring to Anne Page's hand, between Ford and his wife's supposed lover, between Falstaff and his ex-followers Nym and Pistol, between Dr. Caius and Sir Hugh, and between the Host and Caius and Hugh. Like Oberon and Titania, Master and Mistress Page are rivals in asserting their power to dispose the destiny of the young—this time the female offspring of both—but in this case the daughter wins over both parents. And like Hermia, Anne succeeds in winning the man of her choice by establishing her marriage as a fait accompli. Ford's jealousy is frightening and as disruptive of the social order as Oberon's is of the Natural order. Both angry husbands conjure up semibestial suitors for their wives.

Although the comic genre foreordains the outcome, the spectacle enacted in the final scene of *The Merry Wives* plays out genuine problems. The female Wild is not wholly neutralized. The wives' rendezvous in Windsor Park embodies the overt display of female sexuality, controlled though it is by our knowledge of its innocence. Falstaff signals the entrance into a marginal world with his powerful soliloquy. It is midnight, and he imagines a mythical setting that, like Bottom's dream, dissolves boundaries between gods and humans, men and beasts, and promises to merge male and female. In his erotic zest he enjoys a recollection of the male rape fantasy as he evokes the example of Jupiter and Europa, and he reveals a momentary masochistic pleasure at the idea of being torn apart like a "brib'd buck" by the two amorous women. The Faerie Queen reappears in this play as Mistress Quickly, in what might have been parodic form, and yet she does not behave farcically but as a woman in power. If anyone is parodic, it is Evans and Pistol, masquerading as satyr and hobgoblin and serving as surrogates for the absent Faerie King. The sterility and corruption that follow the estrangement of male and female—sketched at length in *A Midsummer Night's Dream*—is played out in *The Merry Wives* only in the discovery by Caius and Slender that each has married a boy. All the pleasures, fears, and pains of a male view of male-female encounters are present in the forest scene, but it is a milder and more ambiguous landscape than that of earlier works. The outcome seems to some critics disturbingly problematic because the invasive figure of male libido is symbolically castrated. The male Wild is tamed; Falstaff is curbed; but still Master Ford, at the play's end, enjoys the certainty that he will that night lie with Mistress Ford. Familial fertility is rescued from the rival male.

No one woman is in complete control in this play, however. Mistress Ford and Mistress Page are ignorant of the Ford-Falstaff plot. Mistress Quickly underestimates Fenton. Anne, a powerful symbolic figure, is minimally developed. The plan for the final elopement seems to be hers—Fenton quotes her letter—but her audacious act is eclipsed at the end by the stage managing on the part of her new spouse. And yet women dominate in every aspect of the plot. Small wonder that the inspiration has been attributed to Elizabeth and that male critics have found the play so disquieting. The vision of female dominance may have been disquieting even to its author. He has hedged it with secure domesticity and neutralized it with homely prosaic language.

As You Like It similarly offers a tantalizing mirage of female domination, which it at the same time circumscribes and ultimately dissolves. Although the sudden onset of Rosalind's passion for Orlando coincides with the banishment of the women from the court, and the Forest of Arden to which they flee is the scene of male-female rapprochement, it is almost as much a male bastion as the forest of *Two Gentlemen of Verona*.[12] It is referred to as a wild wood and a desert place, but it has nothing of the magical midnight mystery of *A Midsummer Night's Dream* or *The Merry Wives*. Some feminine aura is evoked by Rosalind's statement to Orlando that she and Celia dwell "in the skirts of the forest, like a fringe upon a petticoat" (3.2.335–36) and by Jaques de Bois's reference to "the skirts of this wild wood" (5.4.158).[13] The forest seems to have the power to defuse the violent aggression of both Oliver and Duke Frederick and to provide pastoral nurturance for the various exiles. And yet Rosalind, the central female presence, derives her power from her male disguise, and much of her humor is actually antifeminine (see Park, 106–9). Celia radiates common sense without the opportunity to use it and capitulates to love with almost indecent haste, whereas Audrey and Phebe are primarily figures of fun.

The Duke's cave holds neither the terrors of the pit in *Titus Andronicus* nor the potency of the bower of the Faerie Queen in *A Midsummer Night's Dream*. Rivalries between pairs of brothers precipitate the action and resurface weakly in Touchstone's appropriation of Audrey after dismissing her sylvan suitor, but they are much less central than in the earlier plays. The city/country opposition is developed in some detail but in conventional ways that blunt the impression of any mysterious Wild. The urban invaders, both male and female, actually plunder and usurp the forest. Duke Senior and Jaques bemoan the plight of the slaughtered deer while enjoying the benefits of the hunt. And other forest denizens, the snake and the lion (both identified as female), are frightened away or killed. Rosalind and Celia colonize the shepherd's cottage coveted by Silvius, and Celia and Oliver will presumably continue to use it as their abode even after Silvius achieves Phebe. Touchstone seduces Audrey away from her country prospects, and Jaques assumes the right to the empty cave at the end of the play, in flight from the "couples … coming to the ark" (5.4.36). The forest thus de-Natured never recovers its full potency in subsequent Shakespearean drama. The quest of the young male to incorporate the female has been successfully completed and the forest tamed. In later plays, with the exception of the problematic *Two Noble Kinsmen*, forests are no longer the sites for premarital encounters, though they may still be associated with female powers.

THE BARREN DREAM

After reading *King Lear* and preparing to reread it, John Keats expressed the hope that when he had gone through the "old oak forest," he might not "wander in a barren dream." This feared sequence suggests Shakespeare's movement in his plays from the fertile forests of the comedies to the sterile landscapes of the tragedies. After *As You Like It* the fertile forest disappears from the Shakespearean canon, and characters begin to wander in barren dreams. This is explained in part by generic changes in the form of the plays and in part by the focus on more mature characters, less concerned with young love. In the later plays the associations of women with Nature become neutral or negative, and the struggle to contain female power seems increasingly urgent. A brief survey narrowly focused on Nature/female connections in *Macbeth*, *King Lear*, and *Timon of Athens* will illustrate this changed use of landscape. I also hope to show that in *Cymbeline*, *The Tempest*, and *Two Noble Kinsmen*, Nature has been successfully subdued and the female threat effectively suppressed.

The sterile heath of *Macbeth* is associated only with witches, female tricksters, betrayers, and, ultimately, harbingers of death and destruction. Macbeth's equation of the sickness of his wife with the sickness of the land is manifest as he moves in his conversation with the doctor from Lady Macbeth's "mind diseas'd" to his wish that the Doctor could "cast / The water of [his] land, find her disease, / And purge it to a sound and pristine health" (5.3.40, 50–52). The news of Lady Macbeth's death is followed immediately by the news that Birnam Wood, which Macbeth has viewed as rooted and eternally reliable, has metamorphosed and now betrays him by beginning to move toward Dunsinane. Female betrayal and abandonment merge with female encroachment. It seems wryly fitting that Macduff's final victory should solve the problem of necessary female connection by resurrecting the ancient fantasy of a man not born of woman. The relentlessly misogynistic visions of this play lead us to imagine for the moment that the only real salvation from female horrors lies in excluding female functions altogether.[14] Its revelation of the consequences is, of course, devastating, and the barren landscape seems appropriate to the barren world.

The theme of female betrayal grows to obsessive proportions in *King Lear*. The numinous and mysterious forest has virtually disappeared. The potentially benevolent mother is already entombed in earth. Whereas in the earlier plays the forest offered the promise of fertility as well as frightening sexual confrontation, the barren landscape of *King Lear* is haunted by the specter of the sterility conjured up by Lear against his daughter. Edgar finds sanctuary briefly in the hollow of a tree and deposits his father in a tree's shadow near the final battle; but such trees are merely fleeting and ineffectual memories of former fertility. Edmund does briefly invoke Nature as his goddess, but at the end of the same speech he turns to male gods as defenders of bastards. The pit of *Titus Andronicus*'s forest, recollected in less menacing and increasingly demystified form in *A Midsummer Night's Dream*, *The Merry Wives of Windsor*, and *As You Like It*, is starkly reimagined as a female hell: "There is the sulphurous pit, burning, scalding, / Stench, consumption. Fie, fie, fie! Pah, Pah!" (4.6.127–29). The revulsion against the female in *Titus* is now intensified into nausea and loathing, relieved only by Lear's reunion in an open camp with Cordelia, now a motherly nurse. And part of what makes the tragedy so painful is that no way is found to ensure the survival of the benign mother/daughter image after the destruction of the malign witch figures of the other two sisters. The perpetuation of sterility is guaranteed, and the landscape reflects this.

Timon's journey into the forest is a puzzling parody of the green world comedy, a retreat from the patriarchal city, but a retreat that will offer no hope of either fertility or harmonious return. Timon is in search of separation rather than union, and the forest is truly a desert place. The numinous female forest cave reappears totally transformed in *Timon of Athens*. As in *Titus*, the pit beneath the tree is associated with sterile gold and the violation of Mother Earth. The hope for fertility and a Nature/Culture rapprochement that will ensure a future seems no longer an issue. The females Timon confronts are whores, and he charges the maternal earth to "Ensear [her] fertile and conceptious womb" and "no more bring out ingrateful man" (4.3.187–88). He rejects both city and forest and fantasizes return to a womb that will reverse procreation and end life as it began. Timon's "mansion," now a desolate and lifeless cave, is built on "the beached verge of the salt flood," and eternal isolation is his only solace. Like *King Lear* and *Macbeth*, the play leaves neither surviving females nor visible offspring. It is Shakespeare's most relentlessly male play.

THE WILDERNESS COLONIZED

If the barren landscapes of the tragedies suggest a continuing struggle with female threats, the green worlds of the romances and *Two Noble Kinsmen* reflect female Nature under control. Potential Wilds are rarely frightening, and all are subdued to Culture. *Cymbeline* again features a cave in a Wild, if not forest, setting, but again it is a male bastion, where the disguised Imogene serves as a kind of "angel in the house." Referred to as "fairy" and "angel" as well as "boy," she wishes she could change her sex to be one of the men (3.6.86), although they cherish her in the benign "motherly" roles of housewife and cook. It is perfectly fitting that when the young men think she is dead, they should lay her beside their deceased "mother" Euriphile. The male-female confrontation in this almost neutralized green world has been reduced to a minimum. The plot revolves around male rivalry, sparked by Cymbeline's rejection of Post-humus, fueled by Posthumus's jealousy of Iachimo, and concluded by a war of domination. Cloten's vain quest to be Posthumus ends in "castration," decapita-tion by an angry male, and Imogene and Posthumus come together only briefly in Act 5.

What may be a residual form of green world in *The Tempest* seems more like a perfected male fantasy than a genuine Wild. The island modulates from the combination of "barren place and fertile" (1.2.338) perceived by Caliban, to the uninhabitable desert described by Adrian, to Gonzalo's lush and lusty grass (2.1.35, 53), and finally to the "filthy-mantled pool" that leaves Stephano and Trinculo smelling "all horse piss" (4.1.182, 199); but all the variations are subject to Prospero. Miranda, the lone female presence, is firmly under the magic control of the patriarch even when she disobeys him. Her mother, dead, we must imagine, from the time of her birth, exists only briefly in Prospero's memory (1.2.56). The cave, quite de-Natured, is the site of a decorous, if possibly duplicitous, game of chess (Miranda says that Ferdinand plays her false [5.1.172]). The ghost of Sycorax, the African witch, hovers over Caliban; and the king of Naples's daughter Claribel has been the object of successful male exchange with the African king of Tunis; but both women are physically absent from the scene.[15] Nature is effectively de-Natured of its feminine essence.

The association of female sexuality with the forest world resurfaces strikingly, however, in *Two Noble Kinsmen*, primarily in scenes that, though they may not be by Shakespeare, seem to fit coherently into the play, which is at least partly his. The jailer's daughter, who expresses her lust for Palamon freely and openly in the forest, is defined as mad, then imprisoned, and finally "re-educated" into accepting her father's choice of a husband.[16] Meanwhile, male rivalry over Emilia, a notably unresponsive sex object, dominates the play.

Shakespeare's green worlds seem, then, to progress, starting with the early scenes in *Venus and Adonis* and *Titus Andronicus* of premarital and extramarital sexual encounters fraught with fear of and revulsion from the female, moving through the sexual rapprochements, ambiguous as they may be, of the forest comedies, *Two Gentlemen of Verona, A Midsummer Night's Dream, The Merry Wives of Windsor*, and *As You Like It*, into the sterile landscapes of *King Lear, Macbeth*, and *Timon of Athens*, where the feminine presence is finally banished altogether. The female reappears in the paler green worlds of *Cymbeline, The Tempest*, and *Two Noble Kinsmen*, but in each case, most clearly in *The Tempest*, the world is safely dominated by pervasive male authority.

The patterns I have tried to trace in these works of Shakespeare may reflect a common, though surely not inevitable, sequence of male experience: resistance, union, suspicion, rejection, domination. They may also reveal regularly recurring aspects of male images of women: mother, daughter, virgin, whore, and hag. Shakespeare's progressively male domination of his own Wild worlds reflects and foreshadows what was actually happening, according to some analysts, in his society. In Shakespeare, as in the larger theater of the world, the suppression of the metaphorical Wild seems to have coincided with the progressive control and manipulation of Nature and with the constriction of the scope of female activity in seventeenth-century Europe.[17] One of the emblems in Johann de Bry's *Procenium vitae humanae* (Fig. 8) epitomizes a male fantasy of controlled Nature—a virgin-bearing tree in a garden with eager men below waiting to harvest the domesticated virgins.

As exploration and colonization increasingly subdued "virgin" lands, and the development of mechanized means of mining and farming encouraged the invasion of "mother" earth, and as doctors learned to anatomize the human body, the beginning of industrialization and the rise of Puritanism seem to have fostered both the domination of Nature and a contraction of the sphere of women. The "progress" of society at large seems to have recapitulated the "progress" of the individual artist. Uncovering and analyzing such changes may help us to see more clearly the influences that have shaped our thinking and perhaps to discover ways of reversing or modifying these forces.

FELICES IVVENES, QVIBVS HÆC EST ARBOR IN HORTIS.

8. *Virgin-bearing Tree.* Johann Theodor de Bry, *Proscenium Vitae Humanae*. Frankfurt, 1627. By permission of the Folger Shakespeare Library.

Chapter Two

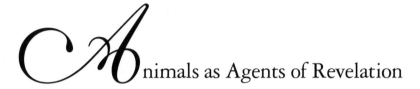

nimals as Agents of Revelation

VALUE REVERSALS

There is an affinity between Shakespeare's green worlds and the animal world, but the two operate in almost opposite ways. As the green world is conquered, the animal realm is liberated. Many of Shakespeare's animals are "natural" inhabitants of forests, wildernesses, or mythical landscapes—the lion, the tiger, the serpent, the deer, the wolf, the fox, the crocodile, the elephant, the basilisk, the phoenix, and countless other birds and insects. Many are domestic—the ass, the horse, the lamb, the ox, the dog, the cat—or at least urban—the rat, the mouse, the spider. All have in common, however, that like females they are peripheral to the central core of male/human definition. I have spoken earlier of the Greek model for this definition—the imagination of the male/human defined as what is not female, not animal, and not barbarian. Shakespearean animals often function to reinforce but sometimes to blur that central definition.

Metaphorical figures of animals provide ways of thinking, both of passing on conventional wisdom and of facilitating the emergence, gradual or sudden, of new ideas. Animals are peculiarly suited for these roles, serving humans as mirrors which, even as they reflect shapes of haunting familiarity, have traditionally reassured people of their own distinctive uniqueness. Figurative language that uses animals may stress the familiar or the strange or blend the two.

Many animal epithets, ejaculations, and beastifications are so central to Western traditions that they pass through the consciousness of audience and probably author only as stereotyped allusions to popular wisdom. The great abundance of dog and ass comparisons are funny precisely because they fit into readily recognizable categories, eliciting stock responses which include only the faintest evocation of any authentic animal figure. To the Elizabethans they were already clichés, prefabricated and dependable terms of derogation.

Audrey Yoder, one of the most useful of Shakespearean image-catalogers, reports that there are more than four thousand allusions to animals in Shakespeare's plays. She concludes that, with rare exceptions, Shakespeare used animals to express the fundamental human "essence of sensuality, stupidity, or cruelty" (62). Wolfgang Clemen similarly demonstrates that all of the animal language in *Richard III*, most of it used to characterize Richard, is derogatory (51). Given the Elizabethans' reputedly strong belief in the Great Chain of Being, this pattern is not surprising. And if Culture centers on the male human, the imagistic crossover into the animal Wild is both perilous and degrading. The majority of Shakespeare's uses follow such standard patterns. Thus, in *The Merchant of Venice* when Gratiano wants to express the violence of his hatred for Shylock, he does it in terms of animals, entertaining for a moment the heretical possibility that Pythagoras's metempsychosis might be the only explanation for Shylock's behavior:

O, be thou damn'd, inexecrable dog!
And for thy life let justice be accus'd.
Thou almost mak'st me waver in my faith
To hold opinion with Pythagoras,
That souls of animals infuse themselves
Into the trunks of men. Thy currish spirit
Govern'd a wolf, who hang'd for human slaughter,
Even from the gallows did his fell soul fleet,
And whilst thou layest in thy unhallowed dam,
Infus'd itself in thee; for thy desires
Are wolvish, bloody, starv'd, and ravenous.

(4.1.128–38)

In cursing Shylock, Gratiano considers espousing the philosophical position Ovid seems to embrace at the end of his *Metamorphoses*—an acceptance of Pythagoras's doctrine of metempsychosis.[1] The doctrine led Ovid to advocate a benign vegetarianism, which would prevent a man from being faced with the regrettable possibility of eating his brother (1977, 2:371–77). Gratiano, on the other hand, resorts to metempsychosis to express the most extreme revulsion and wonders whether the souls of men and animals could indeed be inter-changeable because this is the only explanation he can offer for the bestiality of the Jew. *The Merchant of Venice* presents the idea of mingling of species, the interpenetration of Culture by the animal Wild, as shocking; Christian doctrine viewed it as heretical. Even the union of human and animal forms in costume was forbidden by the medieval church; and in spite of abundant evidence of the popularity of animal representations on the Elizabethan stage, as late as 1615 one I.H. inveighs in *This World's Folly* against players "barbarously diverting *Nature* and defacing God's owne image, by metamorphising humane shape into bestiall forme."[2]

And yet most Elizabethans clearly found fascination and humor in metamorphic variations on the human form, the deliberate violation of Culture by the playful importation of the Wild. In his early plays, Shakespeare's intermingling of human and animal figures reflects the ambiguity of his age, but his language shows considerably stronger affinity with the pleasures of dallying with metamorphoses than with the piety embodied in the anti-Semitic fervor of the Venetian. Shakespeare's variations on animal themes often have surprising effect. Richard III's sinister power is enhanced by the vividness of animalistic vituperations against him—as he merges with venom toads, lizards, bottled spiders, boars, hellhounds, and cockatrices, he moves into the realm of the Wild and becomes a contaminated outsider greatly to be feared by guardians of Culture. His is not simply a double step down on the Chain of Being, from male below female to animal, but an invasion of a Wild which blurs the margins of culture. His Wild, however, overlaps animal and male Wilds and is energized by lust not for women but for power. Animals seem to occupy a more honorable place than women.

A similar ironic elevation of animals can occur in comedy. Shakespeare's favorite beastification of low comic characters as asses, language usually put in their own mouths, achieves almost the level of Encomium Asinorum as it rises exuberantly and affectionately from Dromio of Syracuse to Bottom to its glorious crescendo in Dogberry. Rosalind lightheartedly claims to have been an Irish rat in Pythagoras's time (*As You Like It* 3.2.176–78), and the pretended Sir Topas toys with the unfortunate Malvolio in *Twelfth Night* in a similarly flippant mood:

CLO. What is the opinion of Pythagoras concerning wild-fowl?

MAL. That the soul of our grandam might happily inhabit a bird.

CLO. What think'st thou of his opinion?

MAL. I think nobly of the soul, and no way approve his opinion.

CLO. Fare thee well. Remain thou still in darkness. Thou shalt hold th' opinion of Pythagoras ere I will allow of thy wits, and fear to kill a woodcock lest thou dispossess the soul of thy grandam.

(4.2.50–60)

The encounter is funny because the supposedly mad Malvolio gives the "right" answer and the supposedly sane Sir Topas rejects it. The effectiveness of these figures springs from their flirtation with boundaries that, because they are firmly fixed, can be playfully transgressed with pleasure and safety. The voicing of a view, even in jest, however, makes it thinkable, and repetition reinforces the vision. Shakespeare's own work shows a movement in the direction of Sir Topas's pretended position, though the earlier examples of animal use tend to side with Malvolio. The violations of the boundary between Culture and the animal Wild, whether violent or playful, smooth the way for further interchange.

Typically the animalistic humor of the earlier plays starts from well-established conventions that honor the accepted lines between Culture and the animal Wild, conventions which, because they are axiomatic, can be humorously transgressed. But even in such cases, Shakespeare displays a dazzling ability to surprise and delight. *The Taming of the Shrew* is a good example. In this play the convention of human superiority and the use of animals for derogation operate with predictable denigratory effect, but Shakespeare has paradoxically used them in such a way as to highlight the positive potentiality of metamorphosis.

It is a truth universally acknowledged that Shakespeare was well-versed in Ovid and that Ovidian literature shaped and permeated his writing. Ovid's influence is clearly manifest in the playwright's early works, especially in *Venus and Adonis* and *Titus Andronicus*. *The Taming of the Shrew* advertises its Ovidian connection with two Latin lines from Penelope's letter to Odysseus in *Heroides*, quoted in Cambio's first Latin lesson with Bianca (2.1.28–29), and in the reference to *The Art to Love* (the *Ars Amatoris*) in the second Latin lesson (4.2.7). In addition there are allusions in the play to the outcast Ovid and to Adonis and Cytherea, Daphne and Apollo, Io, Leda's daughter, Europa, Dido, Hercules, and the Cumaean sybil, all of whom Shakespeare could have learned about in the *Metamorphoses*. Even two dogs have Ovidian names: Echo and Troilus. And most suggestive for my purposes, there is, at the crucial moment of the play, a submerged but significant reminder of the myth of Salmacis and Hermaphroditus, to which I will return later. Finally, it is apparent that the whole play, like another of its sources, Gascoigne's *Supposes*, is concerned with the possibilities for change in human beings.

Metamorphoses ought to be useful in comedy—a form committed by its nature to the belief that people can change. Muriel Bradbrook has illustrated the use of such changes in early Elizabethan dramas such as *The Old Wives' Tale, Love's Metamorphoses*, and *The Maid's Metamorphosis*. She suggests, however, that the influence of such Ovidian changes rapidly faded and that Shakespeare never employed the device, being deeply concerned in his comedies with the subtler forms of change involved in growing up (88). I think Bradbrook is essentially right. Although I find hints of Ovidian metamorphoses in the transformations of Bottom and Falstaff, which I will discuss later in this chapter, these hints pose a basic threat to comedy because their changes are apparently for the worse. Ovid's metamorphoses are, in fact, not true changes but terminal revelations of stasis. People cross the boundary between Culture and Wild and turn into animals, trees, or stones because they are trapped by character or circumstance and cannot change as humans.[3] They are exiled from Culture and permanently marooned in the Wild. The changes of characters in Shakespearean comedy are more likely to be positive. They are signaled by mini-metamorphoses such as metaphors, pretenses, disguises, or stage images. They are distinctive in that they may be temporary or reversible and that they are often finally progressive rather than static or regressive.

Whereas in Ovid people turn into animals, a primary motif of *The Taming of the Shrew* is the elevation of animals into people—indeed, not only into people but into suitable spouses—a rather more difficult feat. Characters initially contaminated by the Wild are creatively co-opted into Culture.[4] In the Induction Sly is transformed from a monstrous swinelike beast (Ind.1.34) into a happy husband and a lord. And Kate and Petruchio move through a whole zoo of animal metaphors to the dignity of a human marriage. Each tries insistently and repeatedly to demote the other to bestial status, and though their refusal to respect the gap between animal and human in the Chain of Being (taken for granted at least by the young Shakespeare) and their efforts to shove each other over the Culture/Wild line are the stuff of low comedy, they are also violations of human interrelation. Animal analogies range from the lowly domestic ass, wasp, and hen to the wilder wildcat and devil's dam. More central is the hawk, which partakes of both Wild and Culture and links the two under Cultural control. For Kate and Petruchio a most important progressive image is that of the horse, and I shall pay particular attention to its uses throughout the play.

For the purposes of my discussion it will be helpful to abandon, at least for the moment, the received view of this play as a realistic farce controlled by the masterful Petruchio. It is true that the title invites this view and that folktales and analogs support it, but it is worthwhile to entertain the possibility of a subtext that runs counter to this traditional interpretation—a subtext resonant of romance and fairy tales in its depiction of two flawed lovers' quest for an ideal union. The quest is, of course, primarily male, but one feels in this play a mutual interplay of interests. To suppress the work's farcical qualities flies in the face of long critical practice and requires a considerable suspension of disbelief but will, I believe, prove fruitful.[5]

First consider the Induction. Why is it there? Why is it open-ended? Why does it linger repeatedly and, it seems, needlessly on details of sport and hunting? Why the persistent talk of dreams? Why the theme of deferred sexual consummation? And finally, why is Sly taken for his metamorphosis to the Lord's "fairest chamber" hung round with "wanton pictures," presumably those described later by the servants as representations of the metamorphoses of Adonis, Io, and Daphne? These scenes, like the whole play, announce the theme of blurring of boundaries.

An induction or frame is, of course, a standard device of distancing, of signaling the movement from the "real" world to a domain of instincts, romance, and supernatural possibility. The classic instances are *The Thousand and One Nights* and *The Decameron*, and there are many other examples. The frame is not, however, a favorite Shakespearean device. The closest approaches to it in others of his plays are the Theseus-Hippolyta plot in *A Midsummer Night's Dream* and the use of Gower in *Pericles*. In both cases the frame encloses a fluid romantic world within the fixed perimeters of known history, an excursus into a fantasy Wild from a Cultural perspective. The repeated references to dreams in the Induction of *The Shrew* and Sly's resolve at the end to "Let the world slip" can be seen as creating a similar effect. The chief difference is that the frame is open-ended. The real and romance worlds seem to have merged by the end of the play. Culture and Wild are, at least for the protagonists, momentarily harmonized.

Metaphors of the hunt and the use of hunting scenes serve regularly in Shakespeare as transitions between the worlds of history and romance, especially between the city and the forest, between Culture and Wild.[6] On one level this is predictable and obvious. Hunting is a sport that takes civilized people into the woods. But in myth and fairy tale the journey into the forest world is commonly an exploration of the instinctual and especially of the sexual Wild. In *The Shrew* the Lord moves from his offer to Sly of a "couch / Softer and sweeter than the lustful bed" of Semiramis (Ind.2.37–39) by natural progression to his offer of gorgeously trimmed horses, soaring hawks, and baying hounds. The fantasy of a complaisant female Wild is nicely blended with the male Wild of the hunt. The servants switch easily back to images of lust—Venus's, Jupiter's, and Apollo's. These assembled metaphors alert us to the important themes of animality and sexual pursuit in the play proper and ought to sensitize us to their mythological overtones.

The fair chamber hung round with wanton pictures prepares, of course, for sexual themes. But even more important, it is a landmark on the road to romance. Northrop Frye points out that what he calls "romances of descent" frequently begin with scenes of passing through a mirror—as in the case of Lewis Carroll's Alice—or of sleep in a room with such modulations of mirrors as tapestries, or pictures. Such sleep, says Frye, is typically followed by dreams of metamorphoses (*Secular Scripture* 108–9). In the case of Sly, as in the case of the chief protagonists in the play proper, the metamorphoses we behold represent improvement, progress from animal to human. Although Sly's transformation is superficial and externally imposed, we are not allowed to witness his regression. And we are convinced that Kate and Petruchio are permanently altered. Only the merest trace of true Ovidian metamorphosis—the revelation of stasis—remains buried in the play. I hope to demonstrate this, as well as to show that the deferral of sexual consummation—made bearable for Sly by the diversion of the players—also energizes the courtship of Kate and Petruchio (premarital and postmarital), not consummated, I believe, until the latter's final invitation, "Come, Kate, we'll to bed" (5.2.184). The fusion of Culture and Wild, previewed but not actually portrayed, permits at least the illusion of harmonious consummation to come.

As we turn from the Induction to the play itself, the most obvious romance convention is that of the paired heroines. It is never safe, of course, to ignore the influence of available actors on Shakespeare's characterization, and one remembers perforce the dark and blonde pairs of *A Midsummer Night's Dream* and the doubled female roles of most of the comedies. But although available actors may facilitate the realization, multiplication of lovers seems thematically central to Shakespeare's romantic comedy. It permits alternative male visions of female inhabitants of the Wild and facilitates the expression of conflicting forces in the male psyche when confronting those visions. Often the multiplication serves to emphasize the urgency and irrationality of sexual instincts. In *The Taming of the Shrew* it suggests rather two sides of one psyche, as imagined by the male. One cannot make too much of the fact that Bianca and Katherina are sisters—the plot demands it. But the dark, sometimes demonic, older sister and the fair, milder younger sister are recurrent figures of romance, and frequently one is killed off or sacrificed in the renewal of the other's life (Frye, *Secular Scripture* 142). The argument for linking Bianca and Katherina can be made fairly explicit: the elder complains that she is being made a "stale" (one meaning of the word is *decoy,* i.e., double) for the younger (1.1.58); Bianca's suitors hope to "set her free" by finding a husband for her sister (1.1.138), and the younger sister appears literally bound and enslaved to the elder at the start of Act 2. When Katherina is carried away from her own marriage feast, her father placidly proposes to "let Bianca take her sister's room" (3.2.250). The delightful switch pulled by Shakespeare on the folktale, however, is that the apparently Wild sister turns out to be tamable, and the seemingly Culture-adapted sister turns out to be Wild.

Early in the play Katherina has been identified by everyone as an animal. She is, of course, the shrew, but she is also assaulted with the most extraordinary thesaurus of bestial and diabolical terms. She is called devil, devil's dam, fiend, curst, foul, rough, a wildcat, a wasp, and a hawk, to offer only a selection of epithets. Bianca, by contrast, appears sweet, gentle, and compliant until two wry but telltale metaphors surface toward the end from the disappointed lovers, Tranio and Hortensio. The former remarks her "beastly" courting of Lucentio; the latter calls her a "proud disdainful haggard" (4.2.39). At the very moment that Kate is graduating to full human and marital status at the play's end, Bianca reveals her own animality with her references to heads and butts and heads and horns and her overt acceptance of her revealed status: "Am I your bird? I mean to change my bush" (5.2.46). At this point she says that though "awaken'd" she means to "sleep again" (5. 2.42–43), and she virtually vanishes, reappearing only as a shrewish echo in two final rebellious lines. She and Kate have merged into one. Kate's life in the Wilds—female and male—has enriched and deepened her possibilities for participation in Culture, whereas Bianca's acceptance of Culture has reduced her to an echo.

The relationship of the two girls to their father reveals clearly the male values of patriarchy. Baptista wants a docile and disposable daughter and seems to have one in Bianca. His favoritism toward his younger daughter is abundantly clear in the first scene: he assures her of his love; he praises her delight in the Cultured virtues of music and poetry; and he singles her out for private conversation. His neglect of Katherina is equally clear. He angrily chides her (2.1.26) as a "hilding of a devilish spirit" (*hilding* is a word applied to a horse in its earliest appearance in the OED in 1589); and when a potential suitor for her appears, the father actually tries to discourage him. Reduced in the eyes of others to a clever beast, she has retreated to a Wild world that inspires fear in father and suitors, thereby providing her a refuge from fools and fortune hunters. In fairy tales children transformed into animals by parental neglect are regularly turned back to humans by love, especially in marriage; but they must also establish harmonious relationships with the offending parents.[7]

It is significant, I think, that both Bianca and Kate are married in the presence of "false" fathers—real patriarchal Culture does not prevail until rapprochement is achieved with true fathers. Baptista never acknowledges a loving relationship with Kate until her transformation is revealed at the very end of the play when he finally offers "Another dowry to another daughter, / For she is chang'd, as she had never been" (5.2.114–15). Her concessions to Culture are duly rewarded. Bianca is married with the blessing of her own father on the wrong man and that of the Pedant, Lucentio's substitute father. The potential merging of these fathers into one true father is signaled on the road to Padua after the turning point between Kate and Petruchio (to which I will return), when Kate says to Vincentio, Lucentio's true father, "Now I perceive thou art a reverend father," and Petruchio goes even farther when he discovers the old man's identity, insisting "now by law as well as reverend age, / I may entitle thee my loving father" (2.5.48, 60–61). As daughters merge into one, so do fathers. In the last scene "jarring notes" are said finally to "agree," as Bianca and Lucentio welcome each other's true fathers (5.2.1–5). Lucentio aptly sums up the situation when he declares, "Love wrought these miracles" (5.1.124). The Wilds seem tamed, and the patriarch has been duly restored. Only later do doubts reemerge, when we see that Kate has shed the animal while Bianca reveals the dehumanizing effect of female submersion in Culture, becoming the epitome of the men's fears in marriage—an irredeemably shrewish wife.

The forces working to metamorphose humans into animals are not just parental, however. Katherina has been associated with more animal metaphors than any other female character in Shakespeare (Yoder 67). The terms come from all sides, but especially from Petruchio. A great deal of the humor of the first meeting between Kate and her suitor (2.1.181–278) depends on the determination of each to reduce the other to subhuman status. Their humorous descent to the animal Wild (though, significantly, a domestic animal Wild—they are playing) seems to lighten the tensions of male/female confrontation. Kate connects Petruchio successively with a join'd-stool, a jade, a buzzard, a cock, and a crabapple. He responds by associating her with a turtledove, a wasp, and a hen—and, of course, his resolution to tame her implies the sustained hawking analogy underlying most of his behavior. In their first encounter each wishes to "ride" the other. Kate starts with "Asses are made to bear, and so are you," and the double (or perhaps triple) entendre of Petruchio's riposte, "Women are made to bear, and so are you," helps to activate a second animalistic analogy that underlies the play—the fallacious picture of female horse and male rider as a suitable emblem for harmonious marriage. The controversy over proper marital roles is illustrated by the famous Veronese painting of a husband with riding crop controlling his wife by means of a bit and bridle and by the shocking and much copied woodcut by Hans Baldung Grien of the nude Phyllis astride the kneeling aged Aristotle (Fig. 9). English Renaissance artists quickly domesticated this portrait of the evils of female insubordination (Fig. 10).[8]

There can be no doubt that the equation of women with horses was operative in Elizabethan culture. Perhaps the most relevant example is in one of the possible sources of Shakespeare's play, the long anonymous poem called "A Merry Jeste of a shrewde and curst Wyfe, Lapped in Morrelles Skin for Her Good behavyour." The poem is of special interest because, like Shakespeare's play, it features two sisters (rather than the three of the anonymous *Taming of a Shrew* or the one of the source of the subplot, Gascoigne's *Supposes*).[9] The younger, more docile sister is cherished by the father and disappears early in the tale. In the poem the groom (the double meaning of this word invites equine elaboration) quarrels with his wife and in his anger mounts his old horse Morrell, a blind, lame nag unable to draw and given to falling in the mire, and as he rides away conceives the idea of killing the horse, flaying it, and wrapping his wife

9. *Aristotle and Phyllis*. Hans Baldung Grien, 1513. Berlin, Courtesy of Staatliche Museen, Kupferstichkabinett.

10. *Woman Riding Man. The Deceyte of Women.* London, [1561?]. Reproduced by permission of the Huntington Library, San Marino, California.

in Morrell's skin "for her good behavior." There is no need to recount the brutal details of how he carries out his plan—the point is clear: he wants his wife to be a horse and, in effect, succeeds in turning her into one.

The association of women and horses surfaces in other Shakespearean plays— sometimes in the mouths of his female creations. Cleopatra envies Antony's horse and wishes to be in his place (1.2.21), and in *The Winter's Tale* Hermione urges that women may be "ridden" further with the encouragement of kisses than with spurs (1.2.94–96). In *The Shrew* Gremio swears that he would give Kate's bridegroom "the best horse in Padua" as a reward for marrying her and declares that in Petruchio's search for money he would wed "an old trot with ne'er a tooth in her head, though she have as many diseases as two and fifty horses." This grim marital metaphor amazingly materializes in the description of Petruchio's arrival at his wedding mounted on exactly such a horse, but Petruchio himself has deteriorated to match his mount. The play does not accept the emblem of female horse and male rider as a proper model for marriage. On the contrary, the Petruchio of this scene is, like his specifically characterized lackey, "a monster, a very monster in apparel, and not like a Christian" (3.2.69–70). Biondello says that it is not Petruchio who comes but "his horse … with him on his back." Baptista's remonstrance, "That's all one," and Biondello's enigmatic and apparently gratuitous "A horse and a man / Is more than one / and yet not many" (3.2.79–86) might even be taken as a mock description of a marriage in which man and horse are one flesh. Petruchio has arrived like an invader from a male/animal Wild outside Cultural conventions, not like a proper bridegroom but like a parody of a centaur at the wedding feast. And yet he has none of the virility of the mythical centaur arrived to rape the bride. He looks readier for "The Battle of the Centaurs to be sung by an Athenian eunuch to the harp" than for sexual consummation.[10] Shakespeare's play omits any lines such as those in *A Shrew* which overtly reveal the bride's readiness for marriage ("But yet I will consent and marry him, / For I Methinkes have livde too long a maid" [fol. B3]). But most stage productions supply some sign of her awakened interest in her suitor. She has a stronger motive than concern over etiquette for her disappointment in his tardy and tawdry appearance. She is moving toward Culture; he has regressed to an animal Wild.

The aura of the centaur is not altogether lacking, however. Petruchio commits a sort of rape in carrying off his bride against her will. Nor is his comparison of Kate to Lucrece and Grissel unapt, for he proceeds to treat her like each of these women in turn. There have been overtones of the monster in Petruchio right from the start. He enters angrily; his servant calls him mad; and when he speaks of coming to Padua as thrusting himself "into this maze" (1.2.55) so as to wive, there may be some doubt as to whether he should be linked with Theseus or the minotaur. He compares himself and Kate to two raging fires that will consume "the thing that feeds their fury" (2.1.132–33). Frye suggests that the hunter in pursuit of his prey is never far from his own metamorphosis (*Secular Scripture* 105), and from the moment of his venereal triumph Petruchio is transformed into a beast. Granted that his transformation is presumably in part assumed, it nonetheless seems excessive and shocking. He is, says Baptista, "An eyesore at our solemn festival" (2.2.101), and his gross behavior in the church is carefully removed from view on stage. He is a "grumbling groom," "a devil, a very fiend" (3.2.155); and, indeed, Kate's journey with him to his country house is for her a kind of descent into hell, an entrapment in a relentlessly male Wild. The fairy tale of the two sisters is now eclipsed by shades of Pluto and Proserpina.

Frye notes that in romances of descent questers may be accompanied by dwarfs or animals (*Secular Scripture* 105), and it is both amusing and fitting to discover that Grumio, the first to speak in the new hellish setting of Petruchio's house, is a sort of dwarf, "a little pot" (4.1.5) and a "three-inch fool" (4.1.23), and that one of Petruchio's first acts is to call for his spaniel Troilus. Dogs, as Frye points out, are regularly resident in the lower world. They play a controlled part in fantasies of the male Wild. Rather more significant than dwarfs and dogs is the description of the newlyweds' journey. In addition to the association of horses with women, it is a Renaissance commonplace that horses represent the passions that must be reined in by the rational rider for a harmonious and moderate life. The animal Wild is powerful but must be tamed by Culture. The skilled equestrian or the chariot driver is a model for well-governed Cultural existence. The marital goal of Kate and Petruchio will be not to ride each other but to ride side by side, in control of their horses, back to Padua. It is a goal constantly frustrated. The curious account of their problems with their horses en route to Petruchio's country estate has no parallel in *A Shrew*. The idea might have been suggested by Morrell's tendency to fall in the mire or by a passage in Gascoigne's *Supposes* in which Paquetto speaks of the "foule waye that we had since wee came from this *Padua*" and of his fear that the mule "would have lien fast in the mire" (18). In Shakespeare the reported incidents (3.2.55–84) serve as fitting prologue to the scenes at Petruchio's house. Both Kate and her husband, it seems, have moved outside of Culture and lost control of their animalistic passions (i.e., they have been thrown from their horses) as they came down a "foul hill." Kate's horse has actually fallen on her, and she has waded through dirt, "bemoiled" and disoriented. At this point the "ritual assault" on the heroine, identified by Frye as a recurring hallmark of comedy, begins in earnest. The suggestion that her former identity has been destroyed is supported by the discussion among the servants of whether she has a face of her own (3.2.99–104) and later by the report that she "knows not which way to stand, to look, to speak, / And sits as one new risen from a dream" (4.1.185–86). Unlike Prosperpina she is eager to eat in this frigid underworld but instead is starved (literally and figuratively), denied proper apparel (Petruchio has predicted that Kate will prove a second patient Griselda [2.1.295] and now treats her like one), and assaulted with "sermons of continency" (4.1.182–83).

Petruchio continues to speak of his wife as an animal, explicitly as a falcon (4.1.190–96), and to treat her accordingly. She, however, no longer gets equal time. I have never found these scenes very funny. Rather, they reinforce Curtis's observation that by now "he is more shrew than she" (4.1.85–86). Kate complains justly that her husband wants to make a puppet of her (4.3.103). The promised journey to her father's house is aborted by their quarrel over the time, and the horses to be ridden to Padua remain unmounted at Long-lane end (4.3.185). A second abortion of travel plans is threatened in 4.5 when the two start out once again for Padua and momentarily disagree. The turning point of their relationship follows, of course, as Kate learns to play Petruchio's game, acquiescing in his apparently whimsical identification of the sun as the moon. It is at this point that there occurs the submerged evocation of Ovid to which I referred earlier. Petruchio continues his game by addressing Vincentio as "gentle mistress," at which Hortensio protests that it "will make the man mad, to make the woman of him." But now the "game" turns suddenly into a shared vision. Following Petruchio's lead, Kate greets Vincentio as "young budding virgin," continuing,

Happy the parents of so fair a child,
Happier the man whom favorable stars
Allots thee for his lively bedfellow.
                    (4.5.39–41)

Editors have noted that this speech echoes Salmacis's words in Arthur Golding's translation of the *Metamorphoses*:

... right happy is (I say)
Thy mother and thy sister too (if any be:) ...
But far above all other, far more blisse than these is she
Whom thou for thy wife and bedfellow vouchsafest for to bee.[11]

What has not been analyzed is the logic and significance of the connection. In Ovid Salmacis is addressing Hermaphroditus, the young man who subsequently fuses with her to become a hermaphrodite. The language takes on obvious relevance in *The Shrew*, where the speakers are metaphorically transforming a man into a woman. The reference to bedfellow certainly evokes the idea of sexual consummation; and the image of the hermaphrodite was a popular Elizabethan emblem for the miracle of marriage which joined male and female (Fig. 11). One emblem features above the figure of the hermaphrodite the sun and moon on male and female sides respectively, reinforcing the idea of union of these qualities in marriage and adding resonance to Shakespeare's scene in which the two heavenly bodies have become interchangeable (Fig. 12). Another emblem shows the male and female being joined under a burst of light from heaven, comparable to that which Kate says has "bedazzled" her eyes (Fig. 13).[12] At this moment the hell of estrangement is banished. Kate explains her vision as the result of "eyes, / That have been so bedazzled with the sun / That everything I look on seemeth green" (4.5.45–47). The couple has emerged from the Wild world of lost and mistaken identities into a special Culture of their own creation—a richer Culture than the one from which they retreated, now presided over by the true father. It is this moment that makes consummation possible. This same moment leads Hortensio to resolve to marry his widow and presumably coincides approximately with the nuptial ceremony of Bianca and Lucentio. And following this moment, Kate and Petruchio apparently mount their respective horses and ride together to Padua. Two miracles have occurred: the male and female have been momentarily joined into a harmonious whole, and human and horse are properly balanced. A rare moment of Culture/Wild equilibrium is briefly glimpsed.

Beryl Rowland suggests that the Latin word *equus* is related to the word for equal because horses drawing a chariot needed to be well matched (*Animals* 107). It is pleasant to suppose that some trace of this meaning inheres in

11. *Matrimonii Typus*. A woodcut from Barthelemy Aneau, *Picta Poesis ut Pictura Poesis Erit*. Lyons, 1552. By permission of the Folger Shakespeare Library.

12. *In sponsalia Johannes Ambii Angli & Albae Roleae D. Arnoldi Medici Gandavensis filiae*. A woodcut from Johannes Sambucus's *Emblemata*. Antwerp, 1564. By permission of the Folger Shakespeare Library.

13. *Humana Origo et Finis*. A woodcut from Barthelemy Aneau's *Picta Poesis ut Pictura Poesis Erit*. Lyons, 1552. By permission of the Folger Shakespeare Library.

Shakespeare's image, even though the idea obviously cannot be pushed too far. There can be no question but that the view of the dominant male and the submissive female survives to the end of the play. It would be absurd to argue otherwise. And yet the substitution of the vision of the hermaphrodite with its two human components for the earlier images of horse and rider or falcon and falconer is progress. And in independence of mind and liveliness of spirit the two riders do seem well matched. One can imagine that their new Culture may retain Wild resonances.

In the final scene of the play bestial metaphors and figures of the hunt reappear—but with a difference. They are no longer in the mouths of Kate and Petruchio except when Kate rebukes the other women as "unable worms" (5.2.169). The widow's reference to the shrew is dismissed by Kate as a "very mean meaning" (5.2.321). Bianca speaks of head and butt and head and horn and "becomes" a bird to be hunted and shot at (5.2.46–51). Petruchio denigrates Tranio's greyhound imagery as "something currish" (5.2.54) and, apparently forgetful of his earlier identification of Kate with a falcon, now insists on the distinction between his wife and his hawk and hound (5.2.72–73). The transformation of the protagonists bodes "peace ... and love, and quiet life." In this context the trial of Kate culminates in the revelation of her new identity and prepares the way for the long-deferred consummation. The end of this play is not the social celebration of festive comedy. It shows rather the individual salvation typical of romance. Kate and Petruchio have fashioned an idealized world that excludes conventional hypocrites. As Petruchio says, "We three are married, but you two are sped." The figurative transformation of Bianca into a bird is a true Ovidian metamorphosis—the revelation of terminal stasis. The lonely lovers, assimilating Wild to Culture, create a private sanctuary for themselves, but the surrounding Culture, mired in petty power plays, seems irredeemably static.[13]

The animal metaphors in this play are not only weapons in the war of attempted manipulation of others, they are also passing pictures in a fluid scene in which transformations are possible and possibly benign and borders can be breached. The very assertion of false images facilitates their confrontation and rejection. In the end we are permitted to believe that Petruchio has given up his view of Kate as goods and chattels or as his falcon, even as Kate has relinquished her headstrong humor. It is after all the "sped" Hortensio and Lucentio who persist in the assertion that Petruchio has succeeded in "taming" "a curst shrew." Petruchio himself is equally "tamed." Animal images, though used in conventional contexts with conventional connotations, have provided impetus for rejection of received patterns and for mutual growth. By articulating them, Kate and Petruchio have moved beyond them. In fact, the play might be seen as a demonstration of the perils of static Culture and the potential for change generated by incorporation of the Wild. Unfortunately, only the primary lovers are changed; everyone else seems committed to maintaining the status quo.

I am willing to concede that this is not the most obvious reading of the play, and one would like it to be spelled out more overtly. Still, if the subtext I have attempted to trace is actually operative, it should not be totally ignored. It demonstrates an oblique, probably unconscious, use of source materials which is, I believe, typical of Shakespeare. It also reveals the poet's uncanny ability to modify a standard tale of male supremacy with a humane vision which helps to account for the survival of his most sexist comedy as a play acceptable and even pleasureable to modern audiences—truly a miraculous metamorphosis.

Animals are used in *The Taming of the Shrew* in the expected denigratory mode as a way of degrading humans and exploiting comic incongruity. But part of the pleasure and surprise comes from the progressive transference of their application from obvious butts to supposedly superior beings. The animal Wild, though suppressed in one context, reemerges in another. Although the comic effects are finally somewhat muted by this reversal of animal reference from the minority to the majority, the results are still safely comic. The much more clearly Ovidian metamorphoses central to two later plays, *A Midsummer Night's Dream* and *The Merry Wives of Windsor*, will be discussed in the next section.

EVOLVING VISIONS

One of the theories of metaphor is that its roots are found in taboo. What cannot be faced directly is approached obliquely (Ortega y Gasset 30–31). As agents of revelation, then, animals operate effectively because they offer human beings a built-in duality, a haunting combination of the recognized and the strange. In Freudian terms they are "uncanny" (Freud, "The Uncanny" 17:224–25), both familiar and mysterious, and thus they often serve as links between the known and the unknown. In literature and in art, animals often function as guides to previously unexplored psychic landscapes—regions hitherto unsuspected, ignored, or avoided—helping to foster subtle modifications of the Cultural citadel. They serve as foils for recognition of comic incongruity, and even when the animal comparisons are playful, they guide the audience from one level of perception to another. What seems like an innocent world of fantasy leads to a leap of insight, wherein the Culturally familiar is transformed when the known and the mysterious meet. But the animal Wild also sometimes confronts Culture. In such cases comic devices cease to function comically, and the comic dramatist stops or seeks new directions. In other cases the metaphorical patterns seem to reveal an overt conflict that may be resolved by either suppressing the disturbing thoughts—as in the case of the progressive de-Naturing of the feminine green world—or gradually modifying received ideas—as in the case of *The Taming of the Shrew*.

The use of animal figures seems to become decreasingly a source of humor for Shakespeare and more and more a way of thinking about the definition of male Culture. We may trace in the comedies after *The Taming of the Shrew* sequences of man/animal associations that begin as spectacles enhancing comic vision and lead to revelations that, in bringing men ever closer to animals, work to dismantle the traditional hierarchy and put an end to laughter. In each case the animals are both objects of attention and agents of revelation. Real animals, animal metaphors, and a wide variety of animal figures generate excitement in themselves but at the same time seem to serve as catalysts to facilitate the progression of ideas. The female Wild, never fully recognized or accepted by male Culture, overlaps to some extent with the animal Wild. Male Culture admits elements of both but only with reservations. A perceived kinship between the two partially "human" alien forms is not uncommon, and I will consider some of the implications of this connection as well as those of the strictly animal.

Animal Markers
Animals frequently appear as markers of critical moments of Shakespearean narratives. These animals, predictably, almost always figure with strongly ambivalent signification, mediating between male and male, male and female, Culture and Wild.

The male valence of horses and their significance as tokens of power, especially in male/female struggles, are abundantly apparent in Richard III's famous cry for a horse at the turning point of the battle of Bosworth Field; in Richard II's grief at the defection of his horse Barbary to his victorious deposer, Henry IV;

in Troilus's anger at the capture of his horse by Diomed and Diomed's gift of it to Cressida; and in Lear's "Saddle my horses" (1.2.253) as he seeks to reassert his regal authority after his quarrel with Goneril and Albany. And yet, the horse, as we have seen, also has a strong female valence. The doubleness makes it useful in marking turning points in male/female relationships. Similarly, the deer may be a hunted animal in a male power struggle as reflected in Antony's lament over the fallen Caesar:

> Here wast thou bay'd, brave hart,
> Here didst thou fall, and here thy hunters stand,
> Sign'd in thy spoil, and crimson'd in thy lethe.
> O world! thou wast the forest to this hart,
> And this indeed, O world, the heart of thee.
> How like a deer, strooken by many princes,
> Dost thou here lie. (*Julius Caesar* 3.1.204–10)

The deer may also be a participant, male or female, in the hunt of love. The use of horses in these struggles has been discussed above, and the love hunt will be taken up below. But other examples of animal markers are numerous.

In *Venus and Adonis*, one of the richest sources of animal allusions, eagle, jennet, and snail, all linked directly or indirectly to Venus, could equally well qualify Adonis as hunter, horseman, and retarded lover. But here they seem to embody three aspects of male views of the feminine. The eagle reflects the frightful specter of the devouring crone, the randy, eager jennet projects the equally frightening image of the avidity of female desire, and the shrinking snail, which sits "smoth'red up in the shade of its shell fearing to creep forth" (1033–36), suggests the timorous virgin, frightening in its very vulnerability. In his retreat from all aspects of this triple threat, Adonis is destroyed by the never sheathed tusks of a quintessentially male beast. As I have suggested earlier, Launce's Crab helps to degrade Silvia from a pedestaled paragon of "true perfection" (2.4.196) to a sex object suitable for rape or barter. Other dog references are notoriously terms of derogation—usually of males.

Hawks share some of the aura of horses. Indeed, Walter J. Ong suggests that birds "rival horses and in some ways surpass them as symbols of power." Flight, he argues, implies dominance, superiority, "overness"; and falcons and pigeons are surrogate males (95–96). In Shakespeare hawks are more extensions of male power than surrogates. Petruchio specifically equates Kate with a falcon in need of domestication, a haggard or wild hawk who will, when tamed, do his hunting for him (4.1.190–96). And one might argue that in spite of his progress toward humanity and equality, he is using Kate in the final scene as a hawk, who, by the superiority of her training to that of the other wives, can outmanuever the other "birds" and win her trainer the prize. Offensive as Petruchio's designation of his wife as a haggard is, it may have some justification in her demonstrated Wildness; but when Othello thinks of the lively but loyal Desdemona as haggard and imagines whistling her off to prey at fortune, it is a clear sign of the deteriorating imagination of a man who once confidently boasted of his "perfect soul" and now envisions himself as a toad (3.3.260–73). Both Petruchio and Othello betray the extent to which affiliation with the female is subordinate to the need to assert male power.

Lions and snakes often lurk in the background of Shakespeare's scenes of sexual confrontation. Both carry traditional stereotyopical associations—the lion with strength and patriarchal authority, the serpent with evil and phallic suggestiveness. Both function as animals that punish sinful man and, like the three beasts that block Dante's progress at the edge of the dark wood in the *Inferno* (1.28–54), impede his journey toward salvation. The lioness and snake that confront Oliver at the edge of the Forest of Arden seem similarly emblematic, as the illustration in Joseph Fletcher's religious treatise suggests (Fig. 14). But like horse, deer, and hawk, both serpent and lion are also ambivalent in their signification. If snakes are phallic, they are limp phalluses. From the biblical collusion of Eve and the snake in Eden to Antony's addiction to his "serpent of old Nile," there is a powerful tradition connecting snakes with women. Early representations of the Triple Goddess regularly feature serpents, their power to shed their skins symbolizing female powers of regeneration. (See Fig. 1, showing serpents at the feet of Africa; Fig. 15, showing Isis with serpent hair; Fig. 30, showing Furies with serpents; and Fig. 23, depicting Luna with serpents.) Positively, the serpent woman may have the regal splendor of Cleopatra or the mysterious potency of the Great Goddess.[14] Negatively, she is deceitful, surreptitious, and deadly. Lear finds Goneril's betrayal sharper than a serpent's tooth, and Albany thinks of her as a "gilded serpent" (5.3.84). With the approach of erotic consummation Shakespeare's snakes seem to embody female threats to the male. Tamora, looking forward to a "golden slumber" wreathed in her lover's arms "([their] pastimes done)" finds the snake "rolled in the cheerful sun" a blessed omen, but Aaron, whose mind is on other things,

Man's life is short & full of miserie. Iob 14.1.

14. *The Greedy Man Tastes Living Death*. Joseph Fletcher, *The Historie of the Perfect-Cursed-Blessed Man*. London, 1629. By permission of the Folger Shakespeare Library.

15. *Nature and Isis*. Vincent Cartari, *Les images des Dieux des anciens*. Trans. Antoine Du Verdier. Lyons, 1581, p. 128. By permission of the Folger Shakespeare Library.

imagines it rather an adder (specifically female) unrolling "to do some fatal execution" (2.3.34–36). In *A Midsummer Night's Dream* Hermia's dream of a snake crawling on her breast and eating her heart while Lysander sits smiling by (2.2.145–49) presumably reflects Helena's supposed "treachery" in stealing Lysander from her; and later Lysander threatens to shake Hermia from him like a serpent (3.2.261). Most tellingly, Orlando, in *As You Like It*, must frighten off the (female) green and gilded snake that threatens either to strangle or poison his brother/double before he can achieve Rosalind.

Having frightened off the snake, Orlando faces a second female challenge—a "suck'd and hungry lioness" waiting for a prey that shows signs of life. Like the snake, the lioness seems to be, in this emblemlike description, an obstacle—not merely to fraternal reconciliation but also to sexual consummation. That she was overcome only after wounding the hero is attested by Orlando's bloodstained napkin, the token that causes Rosalind to faint, thereby signaling that she is, like Julia in *Two Gentlemen of Verona*, subsiding into an unthreatening love object. Whether or not Shakespeare knew that female lions are the hunters of the species, he certainly credits the lioness with particular fierceness—comparing her in *Titus Andronicus* to the "chafed boar" (4.2.138). There, as in *Venus and Adonis*, female hunger seems especially frightening. The lioness is a devouring female whose memory shadows male joy in the hunt of love. Lions are also regularly associated in early classical representations with various manifestations of the Great Goddess, especially Cybele (Fig. 16; see also Fig. 28 with the spirit of the province mounted on a lion.)

More often, however, Shakespeare associates lions with the frontier of masculine Culture, where the male confronts rival males as well as his own unruly erotic feelings. As in fables and in the British coat of arms, Shakespearean lions, especially in the histories, frequently connect with regal power. But lions' association with pride and hunger—both attributes with sexual connotations—seems to link them in Shakespeare's mind with scenes of imminent sexual consummation. Tarquin in *The Rape of Lucrece* gloats over the sleeping Lucrece "As the grim lion fawneth o'er his prey," while his veins "swell in their pride, the onset still expecting" (421–32). In a curious reversal, the lion is imagined as an inhibiting force in *Measure for Measure*, where the laws against fornication are said to be "like an o'ergrown lion in a cave, / That goes not out for prey" (1.3.23–24). Even here the image of a powerful force confined to a cave seems to speak more of repressed lust than potentially constraining law. It might

16. *Cybele.* Vincenzo Cartari. *Le imagini de i dei de gli antichi.* Venice, 1571, p. 207. By permission of the Folger Shakespeare Library.

almost be an emblem for marriage. But because Shakespeare situates this image in the Duke's explanation of his choice of Angelo ("a man of stricture and firm abstinence" [1.3.12]), leashed law merges with leashed lust; and the unleashing of the one precipitates the unleashing of the other. The figure of the lion suggests both the need for powerful deterrents to preserve male Culture when confronted with the female Wild and the danger of the male potency aroused by the female.[15]

In *A Midsummer Night's Dream* Lion hovers like an attendant spirit over the farcical version of the fateful erotic rendezvous between Pyramus and Thisbe; and Bottom/Pyramus later laments that the lion has "deflow'r'd" his dear. In the litany of doomed lovers in *The Merchant of Venice*, Jessica recalls the night when "Thisby [did] fearfully o'ertrip the dew, / And saw the lion's shadow ere himself, / And ran dismayed away" (5.1.7–9.) In *All's Well That Ends Well* Shakespeare has Helena imagine herself as a hind mated to a lion (1.1.91) and later suggest that she would rather have "met the ravin lion when he roar'd / With sharp constraint of hunger" (3.2.117–18) than have been responsible for Bertram's going into battle to avoid her. Silvia in *Two Gentlemen of Verona* says, "Had I been seized by a hungry lion, / I would have been a breakfast to the beast / Rather than have false Proteus rescue me," when Proteus is, in fact, on the point of raping her. Even Puck feels the need to exorcise the hungry lion before the blessing of the marriages at the end of *A Midsummer Night's Dream*. The jealous Posthumus of *Cymbeline* is surnamed Leonatus, "the lion's whelp," and the even more jealous Leontes of *The Winter's Tale* echoes the name. Shakespeare calls the intended murderer of Marina Leonine in *Pericles*, although one of his possible sources has ironically named him Theophilus. The boundary of male Culture that impinges on the female Wild is frequented by hungry and murderous lions—male or female—that must be appeased before mergers can be effected.

Numerous other animal markers provide transitions in action, mood, or psychic development, but the most memorable and most anomalous is the bear of *The Winter's Tale*. Other animals have lurked at the border of male and female terrains, expressing fear, or lust, or drive for dominance, but here the bear seems actually the agent of female Nature, liberating the play world from some of the tyranny of male Culture. The male bear puts an end to the last vestige of Leontes's savage anger against his wife and daughter, destroying Antigonus, the unwilling accessory to Leontes's jealous wrath, and magically preserving the female child who will become the sheep shearing "Queen" of her adopted land and the hope of the future for her father and Sicilia. The bear marks the change in mode of the play from tragedy to comedy. The intrusion of the animal Wild and the sacrifice of Antigonus break the spell of self-perpetuating paranoia in the male Culture of Sicilia and leave the landscape clear for things newborn—the prospect of progeny.

In the discussion that follows I will argue that the use of animal patterns marks stages in the evolution of Shakespeare's ideas and facilitates the imaginative leap from one stage to another. Viewed in sequence these patterns reveal a progression that moves from the secure hierarchy of the Great Chain of Being characteristic of the earlier plays to the fleeting recognition at the end of *The Tempest* that the paradigm for living forms is less like a ladder and more like the bush or tree favored as a model by modern scientists. Briefly the sequence is as follows. (1) As I have shown in the first section of this chapter, *The Taming of the Shrew*, in spite of its surprising reversals, uses animals in a conventional hierarchical way. In it the Chain remains intact. (2) The man/animal metamorphoses of Bottom and Falstaff, like Ovid's, reveal stasis. The Chain survives, but the usefulness of the boastful, self-assertive comic alazon is exhausted when he is baldly and overtly revealed as subhuman rather than superhuman.[16] We can laugh at the grotesqueries of animal-headed humans as long as they seem temporary jokes, but when they begin to seem to uncover the truth, they are no longer funny. (3) A different pattern emerges in the use of the love hunt in the pre-1600 comedies. These plays balance at first the comic and tragic potentialities of man/animal analogies. They turn toward the tragic with the revelation that sexual man may indeed be like an animal in his violence and uncertain fidelity. The Chain is threatened. (4) A kind of forced restriction of metaphorical structures dominates *Troilus and Cressida*, *Coriolanus*, and *Timon of Athens* in what seems like a desperate effort to restore a precarious and unstable order. The Chain lingers as a poignant but ineffective memory. (5) The blurring of the boundaries between men and women, and females and animals, and the growing confusion of man and animal destroys the efficacy of the Chain image. The breaking up of a paradigm never comes easily. Often the loss of the old way of thinking is paralyzing. Sometimes a period of madness provides the transition to the new, and I will show how such a period seems to operate in *King Lear* with the result that the Chain collapses. (6) In *The Tempest* the status of the man-monster Caliban, no longer comic, becomes increasingly ambiguous, whereas Ariel, the airy spirit, makes a virtue of metamorphosis. The man/animal hierarchy disintegrates as Prospero renounces Ariel, acknowledges Caliban, and declares that he depends on the audience to release him from the isolation of his island. The human/animal Chain is reformed as a network, albeit a restricted one. Gradations among humans remain, of course—between male and female, master and slave, and ruler and ruled. But whatever clear gap remains between species is between God and man.

The Comic Alazon

The pattern of human-to-animal metamorphosis is unusual in Shakespeare. *A Midsummer Night's Dream* and *The Merry Wives of Windsor* are the only plays to present such a change with an explicit visual representation. Puck gives Bottom the head of an ass to implement Oberon's revenge on his wife. Falstaff goes to the forest in a buck's head disguise for what he imagines to be an illicit assignation with the two wives of Windsor. Both Bottom and Falstaff appear then with their "rational" human heads supplanted by animal heads, Bottom involuntarily and Falstaff deliberately. Both are literally "translated" from Culture to Wild. In both cases, there is an initial shock that relaxes into comedy and then moves beyond. The nearly farcical tone with which the changes are treated allays the shock and apprehension that might accompany the appearance of the drastically transformed lovers, and the tension itself causes laughter. Only gradually does the comic delight of the audience change into fears about what the transformation can mean.

The same disjunction between tone and content is markedly present in Ovid. In both writers, the implications of human metamorphoses are profoundly important. The loss of male form is especially shocking because it indicates a decline from the distinguishing characteristics of Culture, particularly the ability to communicate as an equal. Human/animal confusion can be tragic, and in *King Lear* it signifies madness. But in the two Shakespearean comedies under consideration, its comic impact continues throughout the performance. Only in retrospect does metamorphosis appear to be an ironic metaphor for stasis. What seems to be change is revealed to be a sign of paralysis. In Ovid, transformations are terrifying because they are nearly always terminal. Despite rare cases in which the characters turn into exalted constellations or even return to their former selves, the cumulative effect of story after story of human form lost and human growth frozen becomes increasingly painful. In spite of apparent variations, real transformations fail to take place. People become animals or plants or stones, either because of random caprice of the gods or because they cannot move freely, cope with their problems creatively, or change. For them Cultural failure leads to demotion to the Wild. But in every case, the transformation marks the end—no further possibilities of development remain. (Perhaps the growing recognition of the failures of human existence drew Ovid to Pythagorean metempsychosis—a theory that permits some long-term hope for progress, even if only posthumously.)

By contrast to the climate of Ovid, the world of Shakespearean comedy favors growth and maturity. Change, even highly unlikely change, is possible; but Bottom and Falstaff, two of the characters most infatuated with role-playing, change hardly at all. In each case, the animal metamorphosis is a penultimate stage in a series of illusionary changes that culminate in a restored reality in which the characters remain the same. Bottom has been eager, in our first glimpse of him, to experience the widest possible spectrum of identities—lover, tyrant, lady, and lion. He has wanted to play all the parts in the mechanicals' play of *Pyramus and Thisbe*, promising rhapsodically to "move storms" as a lover, to play Hercules rarely, as a "part to tear a cat in," or to "speak in a monstrous little voice" as Thisbe. It is Bottom, in his next scene, who insists that Snug must avoid terrifying the ladies when he appears as a lion because "a lion among ladies is a most dreadful thing, for there is not a more fearful wild-fowl than your lion living" (3.1.19–31). (The overt encroachment of the Wild is intolerable.) Bottom's solution, that Snug must be called by his human name and "half his face must be seen through the lion's neck," can be seen as a prevision of Bottom's more complete transformation—the half-human/half-animal face is superseded by a completely animal face.

Bottom's appearance as an ass should be, I think, electrifying and disquieting as well as funny. The tension Bottom generates is prepared for by the emphasis on the bestial in Oberon's instruction that Titania "Wake when some vile thing is near," "Be it ounce, or cat or bear / Pard or boar with bristled hair" (2.2.30–34). The nearly speechless terror of the mechanicals at Bottom's appearance is glimpsed briefly at first hand (3.1.111–23) and described at some length (in bestial terms of derogation by Puck:

When they him spy,
As wild geese that the creeping fowler eye,

Or russet-pated choughs, many in sort
Rising and cawing in the gun's report,
Sever themselves and madly sweep the sky,
So, at his sight, away his fellows fly. . . .
And, at our stamp, here o'er and o'er one falls;
He murder cries, and help from Athens calls
Their sense thus weak, lost with their fears
   thus strong . . .
I led them on in this distracted fear,
And left sweet Pyramus translated there. . . .
            (3.2.19–32)

Not only Bottom but all the mechanicals have been degraded to animals in this speech, and both absurdity and pleasure come from the conditioned response of audience solidarity with the superior males in control. It is thinkable for women to join with animals and for the unwashed to be linked with both animals and women. For the moment at least the boundaries of the male forest Culture seem safe enough even in the forest. Puck himself, as the agent of patriarchal power, can even take pleasure in his own powers of metamorphosis:

Sometime a horse, I'll be, sometime a hound,
A hog, a headless bear . . .
And neigh, and bark, and roar . . .
Like horse, hound, hog, bear. . . .
            (3.1.108–11)

But he never joins with the females, and he maintains the power of changing back at will. The involuntarily translated Bottom takes a more disconcerting pleasure in nonthreatening birds as he improvises his song about woosel cock, throstle, wren, finch, sparrow, lark, and cuckoo. The cluster of assembled animals in these lines as well as Bottom's appearance seem to signal a dawning recognition for characters and audience. Bottom has quite literally passed into another mode of experience. As in Puck's account of his achievements, the balance between terror and pleasure in Bottom's transformation is tipped decisively toward laughter as Titania rouses to inquire, "What angel wakes me from my flow'ry bed?" The incongruity becomes irresistibly ludicrous, and it furnishes dependable comic situations for several scenes to come. But it is the conjunction of female and animal Wilds under masculine control that makes it safe for laughter. The ass-headed weaver is entertained most royally, but inevitably the vision fades. He becomes for Oberon and Puck, and in the end for Titania, a scapegoat whose "sacrifice" reunites the Faerie King and Faerie Queene. The mysterious power of Bottom's "most rare vision" does not change him and cannot be conveyed by words. His behavior implies that he ends as he began, still engagingly, if childishly, enjoying his "play" as he "dies" most pathetically for love. His transformation has not altered his destiny but merely made visible what even the most doting audience has known from the start—that he is an ass.

The case of Falstaff is similar but sadder. Its implications extend beyond the limits of *The Merry Wives*. Audiences have reveled earlier in Falstaff's riotous play with Prince Hal in 1 Henry IV, but we have also been warned that Hal will change as he grows into kingship. The scene in *The Merry Wives* prepares us for the inevitable severing of the relationship in 2 Henry IV. Since Falstaff is incapable of change, he is doomed to rejection by the necessarily altered Prince Hal when he becomes Henry V. In Falstaff's story, as in Bottom's, the recurring theme of transformation is present. In the tavern scene in 1 Henry IV Falstaff alternately played the roles of the King and Prince Hal. He has played at being a highwayman, and we first have a hint of his future as a deer in Hal's epitaph over his supposedly dead friend, "Death hath not strook so fat a deer today." Like Hal's jocular rejection of Falstaff in the tavern, the lines have a prophetic knell.

In *The Merry Wives* Falstaff sees himself as lover and cuckolder, but the audience sees him degraded first into a basket of dirty linen and then into an old woman. His climactic fantasy in Windsor Forest, as he approaches the final erotic triumph he expects, is shaped in images of himself as Jove. He imagines that he is in a male Wild divinely controlled, where women exist as objects for the taking:

The Windsor bell hath strook twelve; the minute draws on. Now the hot-blooded gods assist me! Remember, Jove, thou was a bull for thy Europa, love set on thy horns. O powerful love, that in some respects makes a beast a man; in some other, a man a beast. You were also, Jupiter, a swan for the love of Leda. O omnipotent love, how near the god drew to the complexion of a goose! A fault done first in the form of a beast (O Jove, a beastly fault!)

and then another fault in the semblance of a fowl—think on't, Jove, a foul
fault! When gods have hot backs, what shall poor men do? For me, I am here
a Windsor stag, and the fattest, I think, i'th' forest   (5.5.1–13)

Jove appears in this soliloquy as a supernatural power who changes his form
as easily and lustily as Puck and who enjoys the female Wild with impunity.
But Falstaff is no Jove. His fantasies of himself as a Jove-like lover fade when
he realizes that he is an ox (a castrated beast of burden) and an ass (a fool). There
has been no real change, and by the end of 2 Henry IV, he is, sadly but ineluctably,
a surfeit-swelled, profane old man (5.5.50), incurably tainted with gross
animality, whom the young king understandably rejects. His epiphany as deer
has simply confirmed that he has always been the lustful spirit ready to be
"dishorned," the hunter unwittingly prepared to become the prey. In the
experience of both Falstaff and Bottom, the audience is entertained by dalliances
with metamorphoses, but it must accept that what has actually diverted it is
two hopeless cases of arrested development, epitomized by their defection from
acceptable Culture. It is as if Shakespeare himself, in conjuring up the humorous
visions of the merged man and beast, had suddenly seen the inevitable limits
of the comic alazon, the braggart who pretends or tries to be more than he is.
Except for a few pale shadows and incidental appearances, the figure disappears
from his later comedy.

The Hunt of Love

In the pre-1600 comedies recurring figures of the hunt, especially the hunt of
love, work to move the playwright from the romantic comedy of courtship—the
male's foray into the Wild—to repeated studies of the hazards of marriage—the
male's effort to acclimatize his female to Culture. The scene of the hunt moves
males into female territory and exposes some of the ambiguities of male/female
relationships—the elements of risk and possible violence, the imperative of
pursuit to the "death," and often some lurking doubt as to who is the hunted
and who the hunter. The figure of the deer is one of the richest and most
provocative animal motifs in Shakespeare. In many contexts the deer is associated with movement and change that touch on courtship and cuckoldry.
The deer in rut is reputedly a lustful animal, but for Shakespeare the central
link with courtship seems to be the hunt. The effectiveness of the hunt as a
mirror for the pursuit of love is delicately balanced from the start between

comedy and tragedy. The comparisons are funny because of the incongruity of "godlike" man's abandoning his Cultural boundaries and behaving like a beast of prey; but the inevitable overtones of violence and victimization are disquietingly obvious.

Shakespeare uses the figure freely in both his early tragedies and his early comedies. Hunting scenes appear together in proximity with sexual encounters in *Venus and Adonis, Titus Andronicus, Love's Labor's Lost,* and *A Midsummer Night's Dream.* In *Twelfth Night* the mention of hunting makes Orsino think of his passion for Olivia but also turns his thoughts to Actaeon, the young hunter turned to a deer by Diana and torn apart by his hounds; Orsino "moralizes" the hounds as passion. Deer are referred to as sex objects—willing and unwilling—and the hunted, although usually female, may also be male. Chiron and Demetrius in *Titus* speak of Lavinia as a "dainty doe" they hope to pluck to ground, but in *Love's Labor's Lost* the Princess is the hunter and the killer of the deer. She is, of course, hunting the King of Navarre, and the hunt becomes the occasion of sustained bawdy dialogue that glances at the real subject (4.1.6–35; 108–39). The easy availability of puns such as "deer-dear," "hart-heart," and the double entendres constantly yoked with the word *die* further the identification already implied in the two meanings of the word *venery,* the art of pursuing the deer and the art of pursuing the love object.

Finally, the deer's horns, linked in the figure of Actaeon to both desire and infidelity, become the manifestation of cuckoldry. Shakespeare makes this association clear in *Titus* when Bassianus, after mockingly identifying Tamora with Diana and being threatened with Actaeon's fate, credits the unfaithful queen with "a goodly gift in horning" (2.3.67) and expresses the hope that her husband will escape the fate of a stag. The connection of deer horns and cuckoldry is suggested in *Love's Labor's Lost,* repeated in *As You Like It* and *All's Well That Ends Well,* and Actaeon is twice invoked as the type of the cuckold in *The Merry Wives.* In early Shakespeare the images of sexual pursuit as a hunt and of horns as signs of cuckoldry provide humor, in part because of the tensions associated with sexual behavior, but the outcome determines the tone. If we are confident of the happy ending, we can say, "Lovers behave like animals, isn't it funny?" But if we are seriously confronted with the actual destruction of the prey or with the casual and inconstant coupling rightly or wrongly associated with animals, chaos threatens and we can no longer laugh. That is what seems to happen in Shakespeare's comedies of the late 1590s.

The two links of the chain of deer association, the deer hunt as sexual pursuit and the deer's horns as signs of cuckoldry, join together most dramatically and most overtly, as we have seen, in *The Merry Wives of Windsor*. The horned Falstaff fancies himself as sexual aggressor but is revealed as the prey of the wives. In the male imagination of the male Wild, horns seem historically to have been associated with virility, power, and perhaps regeneration. Horns graced the heads of such heroes as Moses and Alexander (Graves 84) and of Viking warriors. But horns also suggest the quintessentially feminine moon; figures of Diana and Luna, of Nature, and of Egyptian queens frequently show horned head-dresses (see Nature, Fig. 15 and Luna, Fig. 23); and, of course, the devil is horned. The ambiguity of the image makes it enormously evocative. In the case of Falstaff, the glorious stag's headgear, which first signals for him divine virility, is finally reduced in his mind to the truncated, shameful ornament of the emasculated ox. In attempting to cuckold Ford (with the husband's collusion), he himself becomes the symbol of cuckoldry. The lustful intruder doesn't die but is condemned to a pseudo-castration as Falstaff is pinched by the fairies. At the same time the young lovers are united in preparation for the sexual "death" embodied in marriage. One male has successfully negotiated the female Wild; the other has been devastated by his venture into the animal/female terrain.[17]

How very closely intertwined the themes of courtship and cuckoldry are is spelled out even more clearly in *As You Like It*, 4.2., a very brief scene wherein foresters celebrate the killing of a deer and Jaques comments cynically on the deer's horns, demanding the song that climaxes with the thought that it is "no scorn to wear the horn" since all married men do it. The scene is a curious one. Its only obvious purpose is to provide for the passage of time between Rosalind's parting from Orlando (she says, "I'll go find a shadow, and sigh till he come") and the news of his misadventure with the lioness. The scene includes the recognition of the killer of the deer, the transformation of the killer of the deer into a deer himself (he shall have the "leather skin and horns to wear"), and the celebration of cuckoldry as a natural and inevitable phenomenon. The scene prefigures the moment at which Orlando conquers Rosalind, who has been identified earlier as a deer by Touchstone ("If a hart should lack a hind, / Let him seek out Rosalinde" [3.2.95–96]) and by herself ("He comes to kill my heart" [3.2.234]). The moment of victory arrives when she swoons, "dying" for love. In a sense Orlando has then, even though he is not present, "killed the deer." Both female and animal Wilds have been at least temporarily tamed and prepared for use in male Culture.[18]

The scene, like the climax of *The Merry Wives*, shows Shakespeare's sense of the indivisible union between sexual victory and the threat of cuckoldry—an insight soon to be pursued in *Much Ado About Nothing* and *Troilus and Cressida*. The merged man-animal vision indicates an unpleasant fact: success in love inescapably brings the risk of betrayal. The female is annexed but never certainly contained; and the boundaries of Culture are never quite safe. Man may behave like an animal in reality as well as in jest. It is perhaps not surprising that in *The Merry Wives* and *As You Like It* marital discord is no longer a subject of comedy; and the theme of jealousy, touched lightly in *The Comedy of Errors*, *A Midsummer Night's Dream*, and even in *The Merry Wives*, assumes fatal dimensions in *Othello*, *Cymbeline*, and *The Winter's Tale*. It is as if the figure of the deer has now exposed a frightening breach in the vulnerable frontier between male Culture and the female/animal Wild.

The new understanding achieved and shared with audiences through this use of animal figures reveals a dark side of a standard feature of Shakespearean comedy. The Hunt of Love, which has provided a reliable foundation of plot in the tradition of New Comedy, reappears in comic mutation for the last time in *Twelfth Night* and *All's Well That Ends Well*. Audrey Yoder's tabulations (unrefined as they are) show an extraordinary proliferation of animals in *1 Henry IV*, *The Merry Wives*, and *A Midsummer Night's Dream* and a surprising decline in *As You Like It*, a play set largely in the forest (66). My suggestion is that the language of animals has been a way of thinking, an exploration of male Cultural boundaries, and that the resultant revelations have led the playwright to draw back from dalliance with the animal Wild and to shore up his Cultural defenses.

The Erosion of Conventions

Later plays reveal these finally unsuccessful efforts at retreat to the once securely defined limits of male Culture. Often the proportion of expected to unexpected metaphors helps to account for the peculiar texture of a particular work. The conventional aspects of animal metaphor may dominate an entire play. J. C. Maxwell has pointed out that the animal figures of *Coriolanus* have the point-by-point correspondence of a beast-fable, their stock uses lulling audiences and characters into a false security (418–19). They are what William Empson calls "normative symbols," which tell the reader what to think of the classes named

(176). A huge proliferation of other thoroughly conventional metaphors—most notably the denunciation of men and mobs as animals—ties the tone of *Coriolanus* to that of *Timon of Athens*. Empson demonstrates that Timon's dog moves beyond the normative to become a double symbol, illustrating but never resolving the conflict between two alternative points of view (176). The strangely static metaphorical surface of these two classical plays, with their moments of unfulfilled creative potential, is anticipated in some ways by *Troilus and Cressida*. Anne Barton calls attention to the unusual predominance of similes over metaphors in that play. Quoting Winifred Nowottny's contention that similes are particularly suited to describing a familiar ordered world, Barton suggests that these similes serve to obscure identity and evade truth (447). But it seems to me more accurate to say that the superficially static metaphorical language represents a society engaged in shoring up its collapsing world, a male Culture in danger of disintegration through the threatening forces of females and foreigners. The patterns simultaneously convey a sense of the prison house of language and reveal a few desperate attempts to break out—attempts that are usually frustrated.

In some ways *Troilus* is a drama *about* metaphorical language. The lovers self-consciously play with it, belittling the well-worn figures Troilus refers to as truths "tir'd with iteration": the predictable vows of lovers to weep seas, live in fire, or tame tigers, to be as true as steel or as turtle to her mate, and to abjure the falsity of air, water, wind, sandy earth, fox to lamb, or stepdame to stepson. In each case the simile is an attempt to stabilize chaotic feelings through iteration of the familiar hyperboles. Troilus wants to find language that will avoid love talk's "monstrosity," which, he says, grows out of the disparity between the boundlessness of desire and the limitations of action; and yet, ironically, he and Cressida merely succeed in coining new clichés—as true as Troilus and as false as Cressida (3.2.174–96).

Conversely, in case after case language begins in set terms, safely stereotypical, and breaks out of its familiar boundaries, reflecting the rhythms of the play. Often the succession of similes creates the effect of a monstrous metaphor. A good example is Alexander's description of the ambiguities of Ajax: "He is as valiant as the lion, churlish as the bear, slow as the elephant. . . . He hath the joints of every thing, but every thing so out of joint that he is a gouty Briareus, many hands and no use, or purblind Argus, all eyes and no sight" (1.2.19).

What starts as the most conventional series of animal similes explodes into dizzying metaphoric visions of a giant with a hundred hands, each paralyzed by gout, and a hundred-eyed human prodigy, unable to see. The language conveys with accelerating intensity the paradoxical nature of Ajax which it begins merely by describing.

Thersites's language operates in a slightly different way. Violent and scurrilous as his speech is, his individual metaphors are surprisingly unoriginal. Such epithets as dog, bitch-wolf's son, bear, and whoreson cur are separately predictable and not remarkable. In one of his more memorable speeches, he seeks a metaphor for Menelaus, rejecting the obvious ass and ox and concluding, "To be a [dog], a moile, a cat, a fitchook, a toad, a lizard, an owl, a puttock, or a herring without a roe, I would not care; but to be Menelaus, I would conspire against destiny" (5.1.57–64). The effect derives from the accelerated succession of zoological species which operates like a speeded-up film sequence to annihilate the human figure of Menelaus. The animal Wild erases the Cultural leader.

Fascinating, surprising, and even delightful as these variations on male/animal themes are, however, all of them contain the overt or hidden common denominator of assumed hierarchy and the assumption of male definition of humanity, safely established or imperiled by erosion. But there are some notable exceptions. One of the shortcomings of Yoder's tabulations of animal comparisons is that she makes no effort to examine the relation of speakers to language. In *As You Like It* this relationship is especially striking and causes the effect to be significantly different from the expected denigration of animal/human metaphors. The animal language is overwhelmingly Rosalind's. Her speech is permeated with startling animal references applied to herself freely, with a resulting enhancement rather than tarnishing of her image. She embraces metempsychosis lightheartedly, attesting to her own earlier incarnation as an Irish rat. In rapid succession she links herself with a swan, a hind, a cat, a rat, a cony, a barbary cock-pigeon, a parrot, an ape, a monkey, a hyena, and a bird. She is paired with gods as well as beasts, appearing as "Dian in the fountain" and "a god turned shepherd." (Like the Jove of Falstaff's soliloquy, pagan gods and goddesses frequently combined human and animal forms or moved from one to the other. Such voluntary changes seem to be a sign of power. See, for example, Fig. 17, which shows Hecate Triformis with animal heads and Jove with the head of an eagle.) Although some of these woman/animal references may be antifeminine, they never seem to be anti-Rosalind. The potentially frightening female forest may have been safely

17. *Hecate Triformis*, with heads of horse, boar, and dog. Vincenzo Cartari, *Le imagini de i dei de gli antichi*. Venice, 1587, p. 90. By permission of the Folger Shakespeare Library.

colonized in this play, but Shakespeare evolves in Rosalind's androgynous presence a new human form combining species as well as sexes. Rosalind's metaphors are imaginative and freewheeling. She violates the male/female boundary with delight and impunity; she clearly enjoys her playful peregrinations through the animal kingdom; and she entertains with equanimity, indeed with elation, the idea that in an earlier existence she was not just a rat but an Irish rat—the very bastion of barbarism does not dismay her. Her creation marks the apogee of Shakespeare's vision of an imaginative and freely operating, powerfully benign female/male figure. She is a grown-up Juliet, a Prospero without need of supernatural support. Her example suggests that deviations from standard formulations of metaphor, as we would predict, mark peculiarly creative points in Shakespeare's work.

In the case of male characters—Bottom and Falstaff—the blurring of human/animal boundaries has worked primarily to degrade the human and reveal terminal stasis, but it has no such effect on Rosalind. From a male perspective the female/animal boundary is already blurred, and the transgressions, especially those generated by her own speech, are acceptable, even delightful. The determining factors here are both gender and genre. The relatively secure world of *As You Like It* and the early comedies permits and celebrates as innocuous such boundary crossing as female/male and female/animal; but male/animal and male/female mergings are much more threatening. The male entering female and animal Wilds seems always at risk. When women disguise themselves in Shakespeare, it is almost always as males and always conducive to festive endings. They are, after all, moving up in the Chain of Being and playing as unthreatening participants in Culture. The celebration of androgynous females, however, ends with marriage.[19] Older masculinized women, Lady Macbeth, the witches, Volumnia, and even Paulina, become viragoes, mankind witches, threatening and potentially destructive. When men don disguises in Shakespeare it is almost never as women (Falstaff and the boy "brides" in *The Merry Wives* are exceptions), and disguise regularly takes them down on the social scale, a descent often linked with death or near death (Kent, Cloten, the Duke in *Measure for Measure*, Edgar, Polixenes; Autolycus is an exception).[20]

If the male imagination perceives females as more subject to metamorphoses and more prone to crossing boundaries than males, it may have some basis in Cultural facts. Historically, according to Chodorow, the male has formed his identity by separating and has been more insistent on rigidly defined categories than the female. Ovid's metamorphoses are overwhelmingly transformations of women. And in other myths women copulate with animals, give birth to animals, and surround themselves with animal familiars. In prehistory the Great Goddess was Lady of the Beasts (Neumann pt. 2 ch. 14), a figure whose divinity was dissipated in later patriarchal history. The male imagination may use these images as denigratory, even disgusting, yet there may be some advantages as well as psychological accuracy in terms of female experience. Modern feminist theorists endorse the view that women's identity is more flexible and relational than men's and that their power of metamorphosis may even define their character (Gardiner 184). Shakespeare's intuitive perception of this may help to account for the pleasure his characters have accorded female as well as male audiences.

The clustering and multiplication of metaphorical animals seems in early Shakespearean comedy to signal incongruity, humor, confusion, and sometimes change. Whereas the hidden hermaphrodite of *The Taming of the Shrew* marks the beginning of harmonious male/female union, hybrid figures like those of Bottom and Falstaff, with their animal headgear, become so disturbing as to mark the end of a comic device. In later plays hidden hybrids may signal an effort to reinforce collapsing boundaries of male Culture by reiterating sharp distinctions.

Hidden Hybrids

Creatures that existed on the borderlines of male-centered Culture were at best ambiguous and unsettling figures and at worst enemies to be tamed or eliminated. In Greek myth the boundaries between man and animal were inhabited by centaurs and satyrs; on the male/female frontier were hermaphrodites and Amazons; harpies, sirens, and sphinxes shared something of the threat of both animal and female, while Amazons served with other such threatening forms as the alien Medea, Africans, and the barbarous Scythians to represent the foreign as well as the female Wild. Combining as they do the attributes of the normal and the abnormal, it is not surprising that these figures should be strikingly ambiguous.

The tradition of the satyr from Classical times to the Renaissance incorporates the same potential for *in bono* and *in malo* interpretations. Hamlet's contrast of Hyperion and satyr (1.2.140) is clear enough—a radiant, loving, and presumably orderly ruler is opposed to a demonic and lustful grotesque. But in *The Winter's Tale* the masque of satyrs comes at the culmination of the lyrical pastoral interlude. Although some critics have found the masque intrusive, the dance of three carters, three shepherds, three neatherds, and three swineherds who have made themselves "all men of hair" (4.4.324–26) operates like an anti-masque, permitting the benign intrusion of the animal Wild and at the same time accelerating the abandonment of Cultural decorum. Rough satyrs are regularly associated with Bacchanalian feasts. The Cartari drawing, with its lovely maiden and satyrs bearing food for a feast (Fig. 18), might almost be an illustration for *The Winter's Tale* except that the beautiful Perdita-like "girl" is actually Bacchus himself demonstrating, like an Elizabethan boy actor, his bisexual capability. The spirit of Shakespeare's scene begins as a festive celebration, but it moves toward Bacchanalia—with sex out of Cultural control. Immediately after the dance, the patriarchal Polixenes concludes that things are "too far gone" (4.4.344) and that it is time to part the lovers. The satyrs seem precisely to mark the boundary beyond which the parent is not willing to permit his child to pass. Culture reasserts itself over increasingly licentious Wild.

Like satyrs, harpies are ambiguous. In their *loci classici* in the tales of Aeneas and Jason, they appear as rapacious monsters, evil smelling and cruel, exacting revenge. Linked with both mermaids and sirens (Neumann 146), they have beautiful and enticing torsos but are animal from the waist down. (Dorothy Dinnerstein suggests that the mermaid is a "seductive and impenetrable female representative of the dark and magic underwater world from which our life comes and in which we cannot live," a shape, therefore, that lures voyagers to their doom [5].) Both harpies and sirens entice males and destroy them—witness the bleaching bones in Cartari's illustration (Fig. 19). Erich Neumann sees harpies as relics of the Cupid figures who served the primordial Great Goddess but were later diminished and denigrated (145–46); Beryl Rowland associates them with the devouring mother, a potentially nurturing figure turned to a predatory monster (*Birds* 75–76). Their usually voluptuous breasts and sweet faces invite, while their power of flight and rapacious talons terrify. In the Christian tradition they seem to have become symbols of remorse and repentance (Friedman 223). In their negative mode harpies are perhaps more frightening than sirens because of their activity and potency, the "overness" associated with the power of flight (Ong 95–96). Shakespeare's uses of harpies

18. *Bacchus in Female Dress with Satyrs*. Vincenzo Cartari, *Le imagini de i dei de gli antichi*. Venice, 1587, p. 342. By permission of the Folger Shakespeare Library.

19. *Harpies and Sirens*. Vincenzo Cartari, *Le imagini de i dei de gli antichi*. Venice, 1587, p. 197. By permission of the Folger Shakespeare Library.

admit of both the *in bono* and *in malo* interpretations. Antipholus of Syracuse sees Luciana as a mermaid/siren (3.2.45–52) because he thinks her seductive and unavailable but also worthy of dying for. Benedick's reference to Beatrice as a harpy in *Much Ado About Nothing* (2.1.271) conveys his experience of both her seductive and frightening qualities. The genderless Ariel, appearing "like a harpy" (3.3.s.d.) to snatch the magical banquet from the "men of sin" who have deposed Prospero, is both the minister of vengeance and the mover to repentance.

Centaurs in Shakespeare, as in Classic myth, mark boundaries, often between the male Wild and Culture. The Parthenon bas-relief of the Battle of the Centaurs celebrates this epitome of male rivalries.[21] In *The Comedy of Errors* the Centaur, the inn where the visiting Antipholus and Dromio take lodging, seems to be a neutral transitional locale. Chiron, the rapist of *Titus Andronicus*, has a name that draws one-dimensionally on the tradition of violent male sexuality, especially when it violates the marriage bond necessary to the perpetuation of Culture. But the name of the Sagittary, apparently the inn where Othello and Desdemona lodge on their wedding night, evokes both the heavenly constellation and the hybrid human-bestial archer of the legend, thus potentially betokening either blessed sensuality or forbidden lust. *Troilus and Cressida* emphasizes the warlike nature of the centaur—the "dreadful Sagittary" that appalls the Greeks (5.5.14). This fierce engine of war aids the Trojans in driving back the Greeks.[22] If Shakespeare's audience favored the Trojans in this war, the Sagittary should be a potential savior, but the text does not establish this. The fact that this legendary hybrid, like the Amazon Penthesilea, fights with the Trojans suggests, I think, the Greek origin of the tale—centaurs and Amazons embody fears of threats to the sovereignty of the Greek state and to the definition of the Greek man.

Amazons function like centaurs and other hybrid forms in Elizabethan literature. Female in appearance, they are male in behavior. They are formidable warriors and notable horsewomen, skilled like the centaurs with bow and arrow. In the Greek mythology accepted by the Renaissance they are associated with Scythia, the extreme edge of the known world and home of the barbarians. It is probably no accident that Cordelia's "rebellion" should instantly call to Lear's mind the barbarous Scythian (1.1.116). Amazons thus inhabit both the male/female and the Culture/foreign boundaries in Cultural definition. There seems to have been a fine line in the Elizabethan consciousness between the acceptable warrior woman, epitomized by Edmund Spenser's Britomart and by some representations of Queen Elizabeth, and the threatening Amazon, embodied by Radigund in Spenser's *Faerie Queene* (Bk. 5; see also Shepherd ch. 1). The distinguishing quality of the acceptable warrior is adherence to the established order—and thus Spenser makes it seem fitting that the lascivious Radigund, subjugator of men, should be destroyed by the chaste Britomart, devoted to her quest for her virtuous knight and content to be subject to him. There are other chaste Amazons, notably Penthesilea, one of the queens celebrated for heroic virtue in Ben Jonson's *Masque of Queens* in 1609. Probably the picture of Amazons most widely circulated in the Renaissance was in Mandeville's *Voyages*, first printed about 1400 and frequently reprinted (Fig. 20). Mandeville's illustration seems to domesticate the Amazons by showing them in contemporary dress, but his description incorporates the warlike legend that those of noble blood burned off their left breasts for ease in bearing a shield and that those of baser degree burned away the right breast for better shooting (fol. Lii verso). Although Jonson celebrates the heroism of Penthesilea, the costume designed by Inigo Jones for the Countess of Bedford (Fig. 21) looks exotic and erotic but hardly threatening, and its nearly bare torso leaves no doubt that both breasts are intact.[23]

The Renaissance use of the Amazon allows for the same *in bono* and *in malo* interpretations that converge around centaur and harpy. Shakespeare's references are almost equally balanced. Joan la Pucelle is Deborah-like but also an Amazon, and her illegitimate or pretended pregnancy reduces her finally to the Radigund category. Queen Margaret is a she-wolf and an "Amazonian trull," and Tamora, the woman warrior, obviously belongs to the same category. Hippolyta and Emilia in their immediate contexts in *A Midsummer Night's Dream* and *Two Noble Kinsmen* seem beyond reproach, but the hint that Hippolyta had an earlier liaison with Oberon (2.1.70–71) may cast some shadow on her character. Rosalind herself verges closely on the Amazon, with her fancy for a curtle-ax and boar spear (1.3.117–18) and her association with the super-athlete Atalanta (3.2.148), but her single-minded adherence to her chosen love keeps her comfortably closer to Britomart than to Radigund.

Timon of Athens's masque of Amazons uses their ambiguity to suggest a dramatic turning point. No doubt, the women provide a feast for the eyes, perhaps even some titillation in their presumably revealing costumes; but Apemantus calls them "madwomen," adding presciently, "I should fear that

20. *Amazons. The Voiage and Travayle of Sir John Maundeville*. Reproduction of Pyson's edition, 149_? By permission of the Folger Shakespeare Library.

21. Inigo Jones's Design for Costume of the Countess of Bedford as Penthisilea in Ben Jonson's *Masque of Queens*, 1609. Devonshire Collection, Chatsworth. Reproduced by permission of the Chatsworth Settlement Trustees. Photograph by the Folger Shakespeare Library.

those that dance before me now / Would one day stamp upon me" (1.2.133–45). After the men dance with them, and Timon thanks the Amazons, one replies, "My lord, you take us even at the best," and Apemantus adds, "Faith, for the worst is filthy, and would not hold taking" (1.2.152–54). Immediately after the masque we hear our first hint from Flavius of Timon's "empty coffers," alerting us that his fortunes are about to undergo sudden and total reversal. The masque, with its best and worst connotations, has provided the transition for Timon from Culture to the refuge of a male Wild.

Although the "bouncing" Amazonian queen of *A Midsummer Night's Dream* seems safely under the control of the rational Theseus, in the reprise of their prenuptial festivities, interrupted at the start of *Two Noble Kinsmen* by the three mourning queens, the Second Queen makes clear in her address to Hippolyta (1.1.77–85) the potential menace of the warrior woman. Hippolyta has threatened to overflow her boundaries and thus unsettle the "natural" (i.e., Cultural) pattern of creation, which posits the superiority of the male.[24]

The fact that both centaur and Amazons fought for Troy against Greece emphasizes the magnitude of the peril to traditional civilization posed in the minds of the Greeks by the Trojan war. For the Trojans these allies also suggest the extent of the erosion of their Culture.

That *Troilus and Cressida* is a play about the bewildering dissolution of boundaries is abundantly clear. The violation of the Greek/foreign border is repeatedly emphasized. The war began with the exogamous conjunction of Paris and Helen, and the play ends with the exogamous pairing of Cressida and Diomed. The Greek Achilles has been promised the Trojan Polyxena as a bride, and this prospect is one of the reasons offered for his sitting out a part of the war (5.1.37). Ajax and Hector interrupt their single combat to celebrate their kinship. Animal/human distinctions are also blurred. Ajax is the very personification of the confusion of species as well as of tribal identification. He is constantly described in animal terms. From Thersites's scurrilous but uninventive excoriations of everyone to Ulysses' pompous reiteration of what he claims as eternal verities, the characters are trying to encapsulate a dissolving world in language that can no longer contain it.

Male/female categories merge as well as others. The eponymic characters of the play are focuses for expressions both of conventional expectations and of sudden revelations. Troilus, lauded by Pandarus as the most glorious of warriors, suggests in his language a disruption of his own self-definition. He is, he acknowledges, "weaker than a woman's tear" and "less valiant than a virgin in the night." In the beginning Cressida is securely contained within conventional female/animal associations. She is identified with a "new ta'en sparrow" and a well-trained hawk; Pandarus, with clear sexual implication, confidently predicts to her that "we'll put you in the fills"—that is, use you as a cart-horse, a sexual convenience. It is an exquisitely appropriate final gesture that Diomed, after capturing Troilus's horse, should send it to Cressida, thus literally embodying her transfiguration into a nightmare for Troilus and perhaps empowering her with the possibility, in another play, of emerging as an Amazon or female centaur.

It is this ultimate humiliation rather than the loss of Cressida that arouses Troilus to rage against Diomed as a traitor—a traitor to his sex, it would seem, rather than to his nation. Troilus's words are eloquent: "O traitor Diomed! turn thy false face, thou traitor, / And pay the life thou owest me for my horse" (5.6.6–7). Only Diomed remains confident of his masculine, human, and Greek identity, and, significantly, in Caxton it is he who succeeds at last in destroying the dreadful Sagittary and bringing the Greeks one step closer to reestablishing their Cultural dominance.

The distance between the plains of Troy and the Forest of Arden is incalculable. But one index of the qualitative differences between the two universes and between the dominant genders can be found in the use of natural metaphors. Whereas those of *Troilus* are rigid and conventional, breaking out only occasionally under extreme stress, Rosalind plays with her metaphorical hybrids, as we have seen, openly and exploratively. The hidden hybrids of *Troilus* seem to hint at the emergence of insights that have been repressed or resisted. Whether Shakespeare designed his language self-consciously or intuitively, whether it reflects change in his own perception of the world or simply a rich poetic imagination adapting itself to artistic requirements, we cannot know. But a study of these two cases does lead to the conclusion, paradoxical but perhaps not surprising, that the relatively secure comedic world of Arden Forest, with its reigning female, fosters adventurous thought and language, whereas the mixed generic representation of the collapsing universe of the militantly masculine Greeks and Trojans imposes caution and constriction, impelling its characters to find refuge in conventional terms. Only in its occasional explosions and almost subliminal epiphanies of monstrous hybrids of disordered Nature does the extent of its chaos reveal itself.

THE DISRUPTED CHAIN OF BEING

Madness

Both the images of the human/bestial conflation of the centaur and the order-eroding Amazon hover behind King Lear's violent equation of women with the fitchew and the soil'd horse, and his conclusion, "Down from the waist they are Centaurs, / Though women all above" (4.6.122–25). Lear's image sequence is doubly disturbing because it evokes not only the collapsing of the categories of human and bestial but also the reversal of male and female roles. In the course of his speech the woman has moved from the position of horse to that of rider, although the final metaphor is blurred—in fact, down from the waist most centaurs are horses. Female centaurs are not unknown, but representations of such figures are rare. And horse-rider images are standard representations of male/female relationships. As we have seen above, however, the equestrian is conventionally male. To reverse the "natural" order by imagining a female centaur, a woman in control of the horse, is to call up the dreaded specter of the nightmare, the female incubus who rides a man in his worst dreams. Edgar sings in his mad song of the nightmare who alights to plight her troth:

Swithold footed thrice the 'old,
He met the night-mare and her nine-fold;
  Bid her alight,
  And her troth plight.

Surely the invocation of St. Withold is a pun on wittol, and the notion of the night-mare plighting her troth is ironic. Edgar ends by exorcising her with his refrain "aroint thee, witch" (3.4.121–24). But the exorcism is ineffective. The grotesque images remain dominant. The madness of Lear and the Fool and the feigned madness of Edgar erase Cultural boundaries and leave the scene dissolved in the confusion of female/animal Wilds with the lost Cultural center. Nature does not respond to Lear's demands. Women have betrayed him, and animals refuse to be tamed.

In the lighter vein of history/comedy, masculine Culture has the last word. Mistress Quickly orders Falstaff to repay her borrowed money, with the threat that if he does not, "I will ride thee a' nights like the mare." She imagines the possibility of being a witch, a night hag who will haunt Falstaff's dreams, in short, a nightmare. Falstaff predictably returns a bawdy and deflating reversal with a pun on the etymologically unrelated homonym for the female horse: "I am as like to ride the mare if I have any vantage of ground to get up" (2 Henry IV, 2.1.76–77).[25] Male dominance is safely reasserted. But in the later plays the hierarchy is more severely threatened.

If such plays as *Troilus and Cressida* and *Coriolanus* use metaphorical language—especially animal figures—in attempts to shore up collapsing society and at the same time reveal glimpses of cracks and dangerous weaknesses in the structure, the animals of *Timon of Athens* and *King Lear* explore the margins of sanity. When the paradigm that defines humanity—be it the Great Chain of Being or the Socratic model—depends on sharp delineation between species, violation of that system threatens the very core of received belief. Michel Foucault suggests a change in the use of animal imagery that coincides with the movement of madness to a central place in man's consciousness in the early Renaissance:

> In the thought of the Middle Ages, the legions of animals, named once and for all by Adam, symbolically bear the values of humanity. But at the beginning of the Renaissance, the relations with animality are reversed; the beast is set free; it escapes the world of legend and moral illustration to acquire a fantastic nature of its own. And by an astonishing reversal, it is now the animal that will stalk man, capture him, and reveal him to his own truth. Impossible animals, issuing from a demented imagination, become the secret nature of man; and when on the Last Day sinful man appears in his hideous nakedness, we see that he has the monstrous shape of a delirious animal … and it is animality that reveals the dark rage, the sterile madness that lie in men's hearts. (*Madness* 21)

The accuracy of E. M. W. Tillyard's assertion that everyone in Elizabethan England believed in an orderly system with clearly distinguished classes has, of course, been severely challenged, and there are many signs that by then the paradigm of the Chain was already dissolving. But such beliefs die slowly and inconclusively, as witness the survival of creationism in the post-Darwinian United States. New patterns are introduced often by such denial as is implicit in Gratiano's virulent imagination of Shylock as a wolf or by jesting assertions, like Feste's insistence in his disguise as Sir Topas, on Pythagoreanism.

But in *King Lear* species blend in grim earnest, and the image of the human form ranges in and out of focus. This is the very definition of madness—the grotesque in one root sense of the word, the mingling of human and animal. Caroline Spurgeon notes the pervasive imagery of tortured bodies in the play (342–43). Animal images work like bodily distortions to blur and obscure the ideal shape of man. Lear begins most regally—if deludedly—but he soon suggests a fall from his godlike posture in his own use of the word *crawl*. He then begins to find *clotpole*, *slave*, and *mongrel* interchangeable terms; Edgar's language, characterized on the heath by its rapid superimposition of successive animal images, and the Fool's use of partial and mutilated animals both have the same effect—the human figure all but vanishes in the "poor, bare, fork'd animal" (3.4.107–8). The clustering of animals centers dramatically in Act 3. Earlier animals have been linked to women and the Fool, both less than Man/King, but in Act 3 Lear becomes "comrade to the wolf and owl." His status sinks below that of the "cub-drawn bear" (female) and the "lion and the belly-pinched wolf" (3.1.12–14). Serpent, rat, horse, pelican, hog, fox, dog, worm, sheep, cat, cock, frog, toad, newt, cow, and mouse (3.4.) merge with "poor naked wretches" and "unaccommodated man." The question "Is man no more than this?" is that of a madman faced with the dissolution of one world picture and struggling toward a new one. It is a turning point not only for Lear but, I believe, also for Shakespeare. His later plays show an increasing openness to a horizontalized Chain of Being.[26]

As early as the late 1870s the Rev. J. Kirkman, writing about *King Lear*, called Shakespeare a "natural Darwinian," maintaining that the pattern of the play depended on "the common nature of man and his lower progenitors in the scale of creation" (400). In the same vein Robert Heilman argues, "The play never denies that man is an animal, and that he is capable of falling back wholly into the animal; in fact man's animality is asserted again and again" (112). Neither critic, however, addresses the issue that if this is true, it is an extraordinary position for an early seventeenth-century playwright only beginning to be exposed to the shifting winds of primitivism and not yet the beneficiary of the "temporalization" of the Great Chain of Being, described by Lovejoy as the product of succeeding centuries. If the model of creation as a chain or ladder with fixed links or rungs firmly and distinctly separated survives in twentieth-century minds despite all the evidence against it, how much more axiomatic must it have seemed to Shakespeare and his contemporaries? Out of Lear's madness has come a truly remarkable sense of a possible new paradigm for

Culture's relation to the animal Wild. When Lear utters his curiously flat but devastating lines over the dead Cordelia, "Why should a dog, a horse, a rat, have life / And thou no breath at all?" (5.3.307–8), he is mourning more than the loss of his daughter, catastrophic as that is. The animal Wild has eroded his Cultural definition, and his vision of human speciality has dimmed in a dementia that has made such a juxtaposition thinkable.

The New Order

Shakespeare was certainly indebted to the universe of Ovid, but there are significant differences in the worldviews of the two poets. Implicit in Ovid's *Metamorphoses* is a Chain of Being, which he outlines in his introduction (1977:22–23). In spite of the light tone, I think it is clear that Ovid regards almost all of the transformations he describes as painful. Man is unique in his "stately looke repleate with majestie" (23). The loss of this status is a disaster. But in the end Ovid's work incorporates an acceptance of fluidity of forms and leads him, as we have seen, to an acceptance of metempsychosis and vegetarianism. The insistence on a rigid hierarchy with a crucial chasm fixed between man and animal is foreign to him. Such a vision of living things is a legacy of the Christian tradition.

The early church fathers, anxious to destroy primitive nature worship, rigidified the hierarchy suggested in Genesis and emphasized the difference between man and beast. Advancing this view, Augustine wrote: "Christ himself shows that to refrain from the killing of animals and the destroying of plants is the height of superstition, for, judging that there are no common rights between us and the beasts and trees, he sent the devils into a herd of swine and with a curse withered the tree on which he found no fruit" (quoted in Passmore 111). Beryl Rowland points out that the church, "although it identified its great figures with animals because of certain traits, refuted ideas of direct transference; its penitentials ... inveighed against the ceremonial wearing of animal heads and skins. . . . While animals shared in the Fall, they had no part in the great plan of Redemption: their purpose was to provide moral lessons that would assist in man's regeneration" (*Human Faces* xvi).

With the authority of the New Testament and the church behind it, this doctrine became axiomatic, and its emphasis on the gulf between species provides the shock of recognition which energizes Shakespeare's comic success with metamorphoses and hunt analogies and adds savage power to the animal forms in such plays as *King Lear* and *Timon of Athens*.

Probably much earlier, but certainly by the time he wrote *The Tempest*, Shakespeare had read Montaigne. I do not want to enter into the controversy about how detailed and specific his knowledge of Montaigne was or to argue that the influence was narrow and decisive, but the derivation of Gonzalo's commonwealth from the essay "Of the Caniballes," as translated by John Florio in 1603, has long been acknowledged. Eleanor Prosser has demonstrated very persuasively that Prospero's speech on forgiveness echoes "Of Cruelty," the essay immediately preceding "An Apologie of Raymond Sebond," with which links to Shakespeare have also been suggested (261–64).

If Shakespeare read "Of Cruelty," he found Montaigne debating Pythagoras's metempsychosis, first rejecting the kinship of man and animal, insisting, "As touching that alliance betweene us and beastes, I make no great accoumpt of-it, nor do I greatly admit it," but later in the same essay coming to accept a bond:

> But when amongst the most moderate opinions, I meete with some discourses, that goe about and labour to shew, the neere resemblance betweene us and beasts, and what share they have in our greatest Priviledges, and with how much likely-hood they are compared unto us, truely I abate much of our presumption, and am easily removed from that imaginary Soveraigntie, that some give and ascribe unto us above all other creatures. . . . There is a kinde of enter-changeable commerce, and mutuall bond betweene them and us. (250–51)

It is not necessary to insist that Shakespeare learned to elevate the animal from Montaigne. But I suggest that a parallel progression of thought culminates in *The Tempest*, that the progression is revealed through metaphorical animals, and that the changing view moves author and audience through comedy to a sober acceptance of a new reality, a breached barrier between male Culture and the animal Wild. The coincidental use of specific passages from Montaigne and the reluctant acknowledgment of a human/animal kinship similar to that delineated by Montaigne is striking. The struggle to redefine the relationship between the orders of being is evident at least as early as *King Lear*, but the resolution is delayed until *The Tempest*.

One feels that in this play Shakespeare is indeed imagining a new kind of world. On the strictly human level he plays with Gonzalo's fantasy of a Culture without magistrate, riches, poverty, contracts, or sovereignty; and, although his vision is scorned by Antonio and Sebastian, the human hierarchy on the island is temporarily confused. The Prince is enslaved; Stephano becomes briefly a petty god; and Ariel plays tricks on King and Duke. This is more than simply a Saturnalian world turned upside down. The "proper" hierarchy is restored by the end of the play. And yet the memory of the experience of the new world remains powerful, and the definition of Culture is subtly changed.

It is significant, I think, that Prospero's island seems to be in the Mediterranean, poised between Wild Africa and Cultured Europe, with resonances of the New World Wild. Fluidity and movement are signaled from the start by the tempest and are reinforced throughout by the emphasis on air and water and by references to birds and fish. The merging and blurring of figures is characteristic of the entire play. The opposing qualities of stasis, paralysis, and isolation are restraints and punishments. Caliban is confined by Prospero, and the enchanter uses the threat of a return to that fate to subdue Ariel. But played off against these images of stasis are figures of movement and transformation. The metaphorical shifts are activated by the yoking of surprising opposites, one of which is often animal. Miranda is both a worm and a goddess. Bones are made into coral and eyes are linked with the pearl-creating oyster. Alonzo wonders what strange fish has eaten his son. Prospero compares Ferdinand to a slightly worm-eaten blossom, and both the noble Ferdinand and the bestial Caliban are lowly carriers of wood. The song of Ariel, the airy spirit, carries a refrain of prosaic dogs and cocks. Spirits appear as strange shapes, monstrous figures, but also as dogs, as nymphs, and as domesticated reapers, dissolving orderly hierarchies. Iris is linked with sheep, Juno (appropriately enough) with peacocks, Cupid with wasps and sparrows.[27]

Ariel himself (herself? the male pronoun occurs only in the stage directions) is the essence of motion. He flies, swims, dives, rides, and is linked with winds and flying things: owls, bees, bats, chicks. Puck's casual pleasure in transforming himself is greatly elaborated in Ariel. He is given to changing his form more than the plot requires: he appears inexplicably as a water nymph and as a harpy—both hybrid forms. But far from being terminal metamorphoses like those of Bottom and Falstaff, these are signs of life and power. Although his music is often described as "solemn," with no instrument specified, the tabor and pipe that he plays for the benefit of Stephano and his company (and for the audience) certainly conjure up the image of a martial human being. Prospero himself suggests that Ariel outdoes him in "humanity" with his forgiving spirit toward Prospero's enemies. Ariel emerges, then, as a figure poised between sea and air, moving freely among the assorted forms of life with reward rather than penalty.

Against this background of fluidity and interchangeable forms, certain earlier, characteristically Shakespearean uses of animal images remain predictable and conventional. The characters he wishes to denigrate are identified with animals, as Yoder maintains they regularly are in Shakespeare. Thus Sebastian is very early linked with dog, cur, cock, fowl, bulls and lions. Antonio is connected with rats, crow, cockrel, sort (fish), chough, cat, and monster. Together they are beasts and devils, associated with roaring, shrieking, and howling. Stephano and Trinculo are similarly joined with devils, monsters, savages, geese, monkeys, ducks, fish, colts, calves, and horse piss. In an unconventional revision of the love hunt they also become the prey of the spirits who appear as hounds to harry them. These traditional man/animal fusions contribute comic incongruity and shape the audience's attitude toward the characters.

And yet, curiously, the character who draws to himself by far the largest number of animal figures in the play is much more ambiguous than those characterized by the standard analogies. Yoder (67) tabulated a total of animal comparisons for Caliban, second only to those for Falstaff (in three plays). Caliban appears from the start as a man/animal hybrid comparable in some ways to the metamorphosed Bottom and Falstaff. He is not a cause of laughter in himself, but he is the butt for other people's coarse humor. As Hallett Smith points out, he is more grotesque than comic (*Tempest* 1609). Modern critics and adapters have perceived that the mystery of the play centers on him. Caliban is not a man become monster, he is a monster born, and although his appearance must have become specifically "fish-like" and "puppy- headed" on the stage, the text renders his true nature elusive. Shakespeare loads the dice against him from the beginning, and yet Caliban insistently and progressively rises in our esteem. He is prejudicially "a savage and deformed slave," "a freckled whelp," "not honored with a human shape," and a rapacious "villain." He is "filth," "brutish," "vild," "bestial," devilish "hag seed." Ravens, toads, beetles, and bats are his allies and the wholesome bee his enemy. And yet he has learned human arts; he responds to music; and he knows the locations of fresh springs, brine-pits, barren and fertile places, crabapples and filberts, and peanuts. He has mastered the arts of survival; he knows the true value of frippery; and he learns to distinguish drunkards from gods. And he speaks some of the most beautiful and haunting lines of the play, seeming to tap into powers unavailable to mere humans. He reassures his new companions,

> Be not afeard, the isle is full of noises,
> Sounds and sweet airs, that give delight and hurt not.
> Sometimes a thousand twangling instruments
> Will hum about mine ears; and sometimes voices
> That if I then had wak'd after long sleep,
> Will make me sleep again, and then in dreaming,
> The clouds methought would open, and show riches
> Ready to drop upon me, that when I wak'd
> I cried to dream again. (3.2.135–43)

Caliban's ambiguity has been well chronicled, and there is no need to belabor it here. The whole play seems an effort to come to terms with his paradoxical nature. Like Ariel, Caliban is a hybrid and no longer funny. But Ariel has been freed from the pejorative connotation of metamorphosis from the start. Airborne animals have always had some relish of salvation (Rowland, *Birds* xiii–xv). Caliban's shape, however, begins as deformity. Our laughter when he is made the butt of Trinculo and Stephano depends initially on our sense of his inferiority. Thus our mirth at Trinculo's choosing to join the strange fishlike man under his gabardine (a cloth that interestingly links him with Shylock) arises from the incongruity of the union and reaches a crescendo at the absurdity of the drunken Stephano's inability to distinguish man from monster.

What I am suggesting, then, is that in *The Tempest* we are witnessing a dawning perception in Shakespeare of a possible kinship between Culture and the animal Wild. Prospero, Ariel, and Caliban are not so much a hierarchy as an unorthodox committee. Prospero obviously prefers Ariel and regrets giving up his "tricksy spirit" before he returns to the real world, but he has needed Caliban perhaps as much as Ariel. Whether Caliban will go or stay is never made clear. The rigid order of *A Midsummer Night's Dream* has been turned on its side, and living beings must seek new relationships. In the history of thought, as well as in *The Tempest*, the dismantling of the Chain of Being has been a slow and erratic process, one not yet fully completed in our own time. The sketching out of the process in this play should be particularly fascinating to us. We sense that the relinquishing of the old secure hierarchy must have been as painful for

Shakespeare as it was for Prospero. We witness the magician's reluctance to give up the magic control exercised through his aerial "slave" and to acknowledge the "thing of darkness" that has been his earthly slave. Natural powers are the endowment of man and animal. Supernatural control can be extended only through grace. Perhaps not surprisingly, the strictly human hierarchy represented in Culture returns to its conventional shape. Miranda trades a father for a husband; Antonio and Sebastian return to their prerebellion status. Only the border between Culture and animal Wilds remains somewhat blurred by Prospero's acknowledgment of Caliban. And Prospero's epilogue suggests that a gulf remains between man and God.

Prospero's position at the end of *The Tempest* is remarkably like Montaigne's at the end of "Raymond Sebond." After a sustained encomium of the beast and an insistence on man's possible inferiority, Montaigne sums up his argument:

> To this so religious conclusion of a heathen man, I will only adde this word, taken from a testimonie of the same condition. . . . *Oh what a vile and abject thing is man* (saith he) *unlesse he rayse himselfe above humanitie!* Observe here a notable speach, and a profitable desire; but likewise absurde . . . . [It] is impossible and monstrous . . . . that man should mount over and above himselfe or humanity; for, he cannot see but with his owne eies, nor take holde but with his own armes ... He may elevate himselfe by forsaking and renouncing his owne meanes, and suffring himselfe to be elevated and raised by meere Heavenly meanes. It is for our Christian faith, not for his Stoicke vertue to pretend or aspire to this divine Metamorphosis, or miraculous transmutation. (351)

Consciously or unconsciously, Shakespeare has moved from the world of Ovid and his more rigid Christian successors toward the "so religious conclusion of a heathen man" that characterizes Montaigne. The poetic imagination has truly given him a way of "seeing with more than his own eyes" and of "taking hold with more than his own arms." His creative unions of men and beasts have engendered mutations that have indicated directions and made possible at every difficult turning point the discovery of a new terrain. The movement of metaphor has enabled him to push beyond the limitations of the alazon and the love hunt and has finally forced him to think the unthinkable and to accept the unacceptable: humans must acknowledge their kinship with beasts. For his audience, laughter at the absurdity of metamorphosis has sobered into a poignant recogniton of a new vision of the human condition, and the Chain connecting heaven and earth has begun to reform itself into a bridge uniting earthly orders of being. A portion of the animal Wild has been absorbed and accommodated, and the boundary is being redrawn.

Shakespeare's change again parallels seventeenth-century thought; as women have been more rigidly confined, animals have gained scope. The Culture/animal worlds still overlap, but with new emphasis. The almost routine use of animals in the histories to denigrate males—to demote them two rungs on the Chain of Being—survives through the canon, projecting revulsion or ridicule against Malvolio, Ajax, Menelaus, Claudius, Macbeth, the Roman mob, Coriolanus, Cloten, and the villains of *The Tempest*. Excoriation of Tamora and Goneril is similarly clear-cut. But anomalies appear with increasing frequency. Ambiguous males like Falstaff and Bottom confuse the picture; Katherine the shrew, Helena of *A Midummer Night's Dream*, Rosalind, and Beatrice gain vitality through their easy identification with animals. Basically heroic figures begin to be associated with animals—Romeo, Hal, Orlando, Benedick, and Hamlet. And even the animalistic vituperation directed against Desdemona and Imogene is inverted by the obvious virtue of the women. The final personification of the merging of man and animal is Caliban.

But there is, of course, another dimension to Caliban. He inherits from both animal and female Wilds, laying claim to the island through his mother, the "blue-eyed hag," "foul witch Sycorax." It would be pleasant to imagine that in freeing Ariel, who has appeared in the fantastic magical forms of sea nymph, harpy, and perhaps the divine Ceres,[28] in permitting his daughter to marry, and in accepting Caliban, offspring of the female witch wedded to the devil, that Prospero had made peace with all the facets of the female conjured up by the male mind. But his prediction that on his return to Milan every third thought will be his grave does not leave us with the sense that this has been a joyful resolution. The facets of the female continue as problematic as ever, as we will see in the next chapter.

Chapter Three

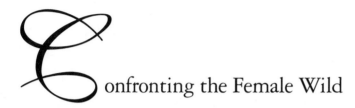 onfronting the Female Wild

RELUCTANCE AND DELAY

The Shakespearean Wild is represented by landscape, foreigners, animals, and especially women. The males' goal of incorporating women into Culture in limited and controlled ways is blocked, delayed, and perverted by factors shaping their own development and Cultural experience and by their stereotyped perceptions of females. Both problems cause deviations and delays in the accomplishment of the goal—sometimes with comic effects and sometimes in seriously damaging ways. In this chapter the Wild is women, and the focus is on the impediments that delay boundary crossing. In the forest comedies males ventured eagerly into alien territory, but in most of the plays discussed in this chapter there is an emphasis on incorporating women with the least possible risk and on restraining their dangerous impulses after incorporation. The emblematic woods have been replaced by orchards, walled gardens, cities, and pastoral settings; but the unreliable, unsettling female remains a Wild presence never wholly contained. In the following pages I will analyze first some of the crises of male self-definition that retard or abort satisfactory accommodations with women; then I will examine some of the simplistic views of women, underscored or occasionally undermined in Shakespeare's works, which frustrate satisfactory relationships and account for some of the barriers between Culture and Wild.

Shakespearean comedy and romance focus on the difficulties for the male of learning to achieve not just peaceful coexistence but harmonious union with the female. By Frye's definition the subject of these plays is sexual consummation

(*Anatomy* 44), but the body of the plays is, in fact, devoted to an elaboration of the forces blocking such consummation—forces that are usually but not always male. Indeed, one might well contend that the true "argument of comedy" is not consummation but delay, and Shakespeare illuminates brilliantly the pleasures of the skirmishes at the Culture/Wild boundary. Immoderate speed not only diminishes the pleasure of sexual consummation, it also reduces comedy to farce. Shakespeare shows impressive variety and skill in designing strategies of pleasure-enhancing delay. I am concerned here to show that these delaying strategies cast light on the behavior of the male representative of Culture when confronting the female Wild.

Problems and prejudices reflected obliquely in treatment of the Wild landscape and the animal Wild are confronted most directly in these plays in the use of the characters themselves. Male "characters" often represent fairly one-dimensionally aspects of male reluctance or resistance to the necessary process of negotiating with the female. And female "characters" endlessly recapitulate male imaginings of facets of the female which are notoriously difficult to reconcile with each other and therefore to incorporate harmoniously.

The examples of such characters that interest me especially and to which I should like to draw particular attention are in plays where romantic figures seem curiously flat and/or schematically interrelated. These cases encourage audiences to view the stage action as a sort of psychomachia, even as they appreciate its imitation of life, and to anticipate resolutions that harmonize warring psychic elements even as they resolve complications of plot.

The affinity between the dialectical nature of drama and the allegorical habit of mind is abundantly illustrated by medieval morality plays, and it is obvious that a strong taste for allegory survived into the Renaissance. To categorize Shakespeare's drama as allegory is to diminish it; but to recognize in it traces of the Renaissance proclivity for viewing human beings as composed of faculties and humours is to add resonance and historical texture to its characterizations and plots. An example of a play that invites such interpretation is *The Comedy of Errors*, where both male and female characters form stereotypical paradigms.

Although the origin of the vision of the divided male psyche represented by the twins in this play is in Plautus,[1] Shakespeare altered it in ways that point up the male/female struggle. His addition of twin servants reinforces the image of the split male, and his changing of the old man from the father-in-law of

Menaechmus I, an established part of the Culture and allied with the wife, to the alien father of two lost sons clarifies the male dilemma. On the female side Shakespeare added the wife's sister and the young men's mother and changed the male cook into the fat, amorous "Dowsabel," who pursues Dromio of Syracuse as she has, presumably, earlier pursued Dromio of Ephesus. These changes, which sharpen the picture of opposing stereotypes of male/female categories, give the play the enduring mythical resonance that helps to account for its continued popularity. Where Plautus's play is a farce, Shakespeare's partakes of comedy and romance. Because of its relative simplicity and clarity, I shall use this play to introduce the discussion of Shakespeare's diagrammatic representations of males and females.

THE MALE DILEMMAS

Reconciling Sex and Marriage
The Comedy of Errors opens with a clear and explicit depiction of the universal male dilemma. Egeon, who as father ought to be in a position of patriarchal power, is instead threatened with death because he has lost both wife and offspring. Catapulted by his shipwreck into Ephesus, a male Culture but a deranged one, which has not succeeded in assimilating the female in productive ways (there are no children), he finds that his only hope for survival, both personally and genetically, is to reclaim the progeny who can ransom him. This cannot be accomplished until his progeny, both male and both childless, can achieve a rapprochement with the females from whom they are separated or estranged.

The division of the young male into twins is a convenient device for exploring ambivalence: Antipholus of Syracuse is the eager and romantic young lover in pursuit of a virgin who thinks herself unavailable to the man she supposes to be her sister's husband and is, therefore, suitably reluctant. Antipholus of Ephesus (Shakespeare, unlike Plautus, has set the scene appropriately in the home of the fertile virgin goddess Diana of Ephesus[2]), having frozen his spouse into the role of chaste and resentful wife, seeks his pleasures with a courtesan. The obvious problem for both young men is to reconcile sex with marriage, and this is ironically and unsatisfactorily accomplished only through the miraculous importation of a *dea ex machina* in the form of the Abbess/mother, herself almost a virgin mother, after thirty-three years of separation from her spouse. Female though she is, she is here an ultimate instrument of patriarchal power, who ensures reconciliation, fertility, and the survival of the deposed and threatened patriarch by enforcing the total submission of the rebellious wife and countenancing the union of the sister, already proven suitably docile, with her eager suitor. The courtesan is tolerated but suppressed, and only the nightmarish "mountain of mad flesh" who claims marriage with Dromio of Syracuse remains a threatening remnant of the Wild, though she too is a candidate for wife at play's end.

Farcical though much of the play is, at its conclusion both male and female audiences can experience pleasure that lover, husband, and father have been successfully, if belatedly, united into a mature man. The Abbess makes the point about her sons overtly when she says,

Thirty-three years have I but gone in travail
Of you my sons, and till this present hour
My heavy burthen [ne'er] delivered.
                    (5.1.401–3)

The male dividedness, which has caused prolonged delay in consolidating Culture, has indeed seemed a heavy burden—although its elements as spelled out here have been lightened by both errors and comedy. The female Wild has seemed relatively tame. The much-feared shrewish wife has been assimilated into Culture with relative ease. The virginal "other" has been incorporated, and the threat of sexual excess (epitomized by Luce and the courtesan) has been exiled to the periphery of the Culture. Although no convincing transformation of character has been demonstrated, there is real relief that the rebirth of the male will make the birth of the future possible, and we are persuaded at least to suspend our disbelief at the miraculously imposed ending.

The Fear of Cuckoldry

A much more complex and interesting study of the divisions of the male and of delay caused by the need to integrate his parts is to be found in *Much Ado About Nothing*, a play from Shakespeare's midcareer. The parts have multiplied since *The Comedy of Errors*. Names provide some clues to the function of the parts. The name Claudio/Claudius, perhaps because of its association with such Claudian emperors as Nero and Caligula, seems to be linked in Shakespeare's mind with varieties of illicit sexuality, manifesting itself in the readiness of this

Claudio to imagine sordid sexual dalliance, in the premature embraces of the Claudio of *Measure for Measure*, and culminating in the incestuous sheets leaped to with such dexterity by Hamlet's uncle. Hero's name is mythical, androgynous, and as blankly unspecific as her character. The delightful Beatrice and Benedick, apparently Shakespeare's original inventions, are universally agreed to be the soul of the play. And yet, in spite of their vitality, their very names suggest more baldly than most Shakespearean denominations their salient qualities. Beatrice, born as she says under a dancing star, is a woman who brings blessedness. And Benedick, the receiver of blessing, also speaks well—he has more lines than anyone else in the play—and, as Beatrice remarks, he is (at least in the first two acts) always talking. In many ways he is the central character of the drama—even more than Beatrice—since we see more of him and have more insight into the stages of his conversion. And yet Beatrice, usually a reliable witness, even when she is jousting with words, calls him a "stuff'd man" (1.1.58–59) and one who has lost four of his five wits and is now "govern'd with one" (1.1.65–67). I should like to suggest that the delaying action of *Much Ado* is actually a process of restoring Benedick to his full faculties, that his psychic drama is played out by other male characters in the play, and that the union of his disparate faculties is a prerequisite to his union with Beatrice. He cannot annex her into Culture until he has collected his own wits.

Benedick arrives in Messina a successful warrior and an experienced man of the world—one whom Beatrice says she knows of old (1.1.121) and who has previously won her heart with false dice (2.1.246). He talks wittily and well, but he harps even more obsessively than other Shakespearean males on the specter of cuckoldry, which haunts his vision of the marriage bed. Beatrice says, "He hath every month a new sworn brother" (1.1.59), and asks of the messenger who announces the soldiers' imminent arrival, "Is there no young squarer now that will make a voyage with him to the devil?" Such an alter ego does indeed appear in the form of the curiously characterless Claudio, whose outstanding qualities are his youth and his vulnerability to deception. One can easily imagine him as a personification of a younger Benedick, who might have played his lover false out of his own insecurity when faced with the uncertain nature of sexual fidelity. This is the Claudio who watches with credulity the dumb show of sexual betrayal on Hero's balcony and whose rash acceptance of appearance metaphorically destroys his betrothed bride. This is the Claudio who must indeed—as Beatrice later commands—be killed or at least recognized for what he is and brought under control before Benedick can achieve a harmonious union. Benedick does successfully master this latent side of his nature, as he reveals in the final scene, when, after Claudio identifies his friend with "bull Jove" in an image that, like Falstaff's earlier, joins the divine and the animal, Benedick calmly accepts the designation, adding that such a bull was the father of the bleating, calflike Claudio. The blurring of the boundaries is necessary for offspring, even such dubious offspring as the callow Claudio.

If Claudio represents the youthful, animal-like Benedick, Don Pedro suggests a more sedate and parental aspect of his character. Don Pedro actually identifies himself with Jove when he is dancing with Hero at the masked ball. As the diviner dimension of Benedick, he twice expresses a serious desire to marry Beatrice, valuing her justly and without any sense of risk in his proposal. Beatrice declines him because she wants a complete man and sees that he is only a part to be worn on Sunday. But the noble Don Pedro is brother to Don John, the darker side of the rational psyche. He is a one-dimensional villain—the embodiment of lurking resentment and malice, which, though once forgiven, reappears to destroy the relationship. It was such a shadowy suppressed self, we feel, who could have earlier caused the young Benedick to play Beatrice false. As a manipulator of unresolved doubts and suspicions, Don John orchestrates the midnight scenario that plays out Benedick's nightmare and demonstrates the consequences of mistrust. A kinship between Benedick and Don John is first signaled by Beatrice, who, noting that Don John rarely speaks and that Benedick talks too much, suggests that an excellent man could be made "just in the midway" between him and Don John (2.1.6). Benedick himself reveals his intuitive knowledge of John's nature after Hero's betrayal when he leaps instantly to the conclusion that "The practice of it lives in John the Bastard, / Whose spirits toil in frame of villainies" (4.1.185).

The process of recognizing and dealing with Don John coincides with Benedick's realization of his ability to love Beatrice. Remarkably, this revelation changes his pattern of speech. After more than two hundred lines in the first two acts, Benedick speaks only six lines in Act 3 and gradually regains a modified and less frivolous verbal dominance in Act 5. In 3.2 Don John enters to reveal to Claudio Hero's reputed "infidelity" at precisely the moment when Benedick has retired with Leonato to request Beatrice's hand—it is almost as if the imminence of commitment has conjured up the previously suppressed malign agent. The scene on the balcony, which we see only through male planning and report, spells out the dreaded male imagination of the true nature of the female Wild. Staged on the balcony, marginal territory outside the house proper, and at night, the season of the capricious female moon, it has the quality of a nightmare which Claudio seizes on credulously and easily as truth. The enactment of the suppressed fear blocks and delays the process of incorporating the necessary females into the male future.

But this same nighttime charade calls up another figure from the murky recesses of Benedick's mind—the valiant Constable Dogberry. If Dogberry is one of Benedick's missing wits, he is the "common wit" that grounds the other four. His name suggests some affinity with both animal and Natural Wilds, with the dog and the dogwood. Bumbling, illiterate, and only dimly but stubbornly competent, he seems the obverse of the eloquent and articulate courtier, but the two men share the love of language, the experience of reverses, the hope to "comprehend all vagrom men," and the desire to have "everything handsome about" them. And it is Dogberry's stumbling progress toward the revelation of truth which condemns Don John to "everlasting redemption" and temporarily frees society of his presence. (Ominously, he is to be brought back in the end.) Dogberry is the weak but persistent voice of common sense which helps Benedick to believe Beatrice and resolve to "kill" the rejecting Claudio. Since Benedick never shares the stage with Dogberry nor Dogberry with Don John, the characters provide interesting opportunities for doubling of roles. Either Dogberry and Don John or, less plausibly, Dogberry and Benedick could be played by the same actor.

Once Benedick has, in the words of Margaret, "become a man" (3.4.75) by uniting his own quality of speaking well with the soberer aspects of Don Pedro and Dogberry and by reconciling himself to Claudio and acknowledging Don John, he can risk a commitment, reluctant as he is, to the frightening but finally receptive "other." His forays into Wild territory have been pleasurable partly because they expose so baldly the hostility between Culture and Wild and provide the satisfaction of conquering, or at least suppressing, their counterproductive effects. The amorous delay is prolonged only by the dance that Benedick insists must precede the wedding, as he says, to "lighten our own hearts and our wives' heels" (5.4.117–18). It is a way of signaling the imposition of Cultural order on its new recruits.

The future looks bright for both the loving couples. But it is not without a lingering shadow. Benedick makes one last horn joke, urging the Prince to marry and assuring him, "There is no staff more reverent than one tipp'd with horn." It is as if the word *horn* evokes the memory of Don John, and the play ends with the news that his flight has been arrested and that he will be brought back to Messina. This is not good news, and it is perhaps significant that Benedick rather than Don Pedro or Leonato promises to devise "brave punishments" for him on the morrow. We are left to wonder whether he can also live at peace with this thing of darkness, this spectral horned beast, which he has now implicitly acknowledged as his own. By incorporating the female Wild, marriage will permit progeny, which will assure a male future, but it cannot banish from the male mind the risk of female betrayal.

In *Much Ado About Nothing* the slow, painfully pleasurable process of uniting Benedick's five wits and effecting his betrothal to Beatrice reminds us of the importance of reluctance as well as delay in the argument of comedy. It would be hard to imagine two more determinedly reluctant lovers than Beatrice and Benedick. This reluctance adds greatly to our pleasure in their courtship and capitulation. It is not just that easy victories are boring, though it is partly that. And it is not just that we enjoy seeing long-vaunted independence humanized. It is also that reluctance is a genuine and powerful component of sexual encounters. One does not give up individual identity easily or relinquish it permanently. From the male perspective, Culture does not readily incorporate Nature, and Nature is both terrifying and resistant. By embracing the risks and recompenses of blurred boundaries, the opportunity for offspring, and the perils of parentage, however, Benedick becomes a suitable spouse for Beatrice. The union, reminiscent of Kate's and Petruchio's and considerably more promising than those of the Antipholuses, brings at least the hope of growth into the stagnant male Culture of Messina.

The specter of cuckoldry that shadowed the comedy of *As You Like It* and *The Merry Wives of Windsor* has been confronted in this play with deadly seriousness, and it later moves to center stage in *Othello* and *The Winter's Tale.* The fear it inspires is one of the main barriers to male acceptance of the female. It haunts courtship and marriage and, even when it is allayed, there is never a guarantee that it will not be suddenly reawakened as it is in the repulsive images that swarm so swiftly and explicitly to the surface of Leontes's mind when he suspects his wife of infidelity. He imagines a cuckoldry that by emasculating him would propel him toward engulfment in the female Wild and by horning him would drag him down into the animal Wild, which he, melding female and animal, conceives of as a pond waiting to be illicitly fished by a neighbor. And yet Leontes's rejection of the female who can so humiliate him leads inevitably to his loss of progeny. Like Egeon at the opening of *The Comedy of Errors*, he must begin again if he is to create a future. I will come back to *The Winter's Tale* in the section "*The Imagined Female*."

The Triangulation of Desire

Two Noble Kinsmen offers overt explorations of several recurrent male themes— frequently familiar ones. All center on the problems of the male in accepting the female. Delay is prolonged and no longer pleasurable. As in *The Comedy of Errors* and *Much Ado About Nothing*, the male psyche is split, and the warring parts are even more difficult to reconcile. Approaching the frightening female Wild, the male finds his attention repeatedly deflected to another male—a known quantity with which he can cope. He apparently finds it easier to make war than to make love. Thus "love" becomes a triangular affair rather than the male/female dyad we tend to imagine. In this play Diana, Venus, and Mars are featured in a triangular power struggle, which, as in the early comedies, seems primarily an affair between men. A good example of such triangulation of desire is George Wither's emblem (Fig. 22), which shows two men fighting, supposedly over Helen of Troy. Helen's torso is visible at a window on the sidelines, but the focus is clearly on the fighting men.

Females also appear in fractured forms in *Two Noble Kinsmen* in variants of the familiar stereotypes of virgin, whore, and crone—here virgin, wife, and widow. The most interesting variation on earlier Shakespearean patterns of multiplied female sex objects is that the two females available to the nobility are Amazons. (A third available woman, the Jailer's daughter, who might have provided a mate for one of the kinsmen, is never seriously considered because of her low rank.) As we have seen, the appearance of an Amazon in the scenario of a Classical or Renaissance tale is an infallible clue to an area of male anxiety, a signal of threatened erosion to a systematically constructed patriarchal worldview.[3] She is a potentially unassimilable Wild. As a virginal or only rarely sexual (and then exclusively for procreation) female, the Amazon was tradition- ally impervious to male charms; living without men, she fought them as their equal or superior; as horsewoman, archer, and hunter, she impinged on and sometimes invaded male domains, threatening even such strongholds of "civi- lized" (patriarchal) sanctity as Athens itself.[4] For the Greeks she was an

Where Hellen *is, there, will be* Warre;
For, Death *and* Luft, *Companions are.*

22. *Battle over Helen.* George Wither, *A Collection of Emblems.* London, 1635, p. 27. By permission of the Folger Shakespeare Library.

intriguing and terrifying male nightmare. For the Elizabethans the Amazonian image was revivified by the real presence of a queen whose formidable virginal power conjured up but never completely coincided with memories of the Classical myth.[5] We have seen some evidence of the domestication of the Amazon image.

The Middle Ages may have had fewer problems with these women, accepting them as mythical constructs from alien antiquity. Boccaccio in the *Teseida* (Book I) lingers with apparent pleasure over his descriptions of the Amazons and their fortress, but the certainty of the impending subjugation of the females by Theseus prevents titillation from escalating into alarm. For Chaucer in "The Knight's Tale" the Amazonian threat seems safely contained from the start. As the tale begins, Theseus, with "his wysdom and his chivalrie," has already "conquered al the regne of Femenye" and "weddede the queene Ypolita" (865–68); and although her sister Emelye loves "huntynge and venerye" and prefers "to walken in the wodes wilde, / And noght to ben a wyf and be with childe" (2308–10), she is docile and conventional in accepting her marital fate. Chaucer never elaborates on the Amazonian past of the two sisters. Similarly, in A *Midsummer Night's Dream* Hippolyta's past, glimpsed perhaps in her description of the moon as a "silver bow / [New] bent in heaven" (1.1.9–10), elicits only the momentarily troubling reference by Theseus to his wooing her with his sword and winning her love by doing her injuries (1.1.16–17). It might be argued that the quarrel between Oberon and Titania with its passing remembrance of Oberon's flirtation with the "bouncing Amazon" (2.1.20) and of Titania's having incited Theseus to "break his faith" with the Amazonian Antiopa (2.1.80)—a quarrel that has precipitated major confusions and reversals in the natural order of seasons—is in fact a covert manifestation of the convulsive effects of a union contracted in defiance of Cultural expectations; but, if so, the subtext is securely buried under the relatively smooth surface of the festive comedy.

In *The Two Noble Kinsmen*, however, the threat to male definition posed by Hippolyta before her subjugation to Theseus is clearly spelled out, as we have seen, by the second widowed Queen, who specifically refers to the danger of Hippolyta's overflowing the boundaries of her Wild and invading Culture as the Amazons are said to have invaded Athens, until Theseus, "born to uphold creation," shrank her into her proper subordinate role. The Queen addresses her as a danger narrowly averted:

> Honored Hippolyta,
> Most dreaded Amazonian, that hast slain
> The scythe-tusk'd boar; that with thy arm, as strong
> As it is white, wast near to make the male
> To thy sex captive, but that this thy lord,
> Born to uphold creation in that honor
> First Nature styl'd it in, shrunk thee into
> The bound thou wast o'erflowing, at once subduing
> Thy force and thy affection. (1.1.77–85)

Furthermore, there are repeated reminders of the barbaric background of the Scythian Queen. Proposing that Hippolyta kneel to enlist Theseus's aid in recovering their husbands' bodies, the second Queen offers, presumably as a palliative appropriate to her addressee, a grotesquely violent comparison: "But touch the ground for us no longer time / Than a dove's motion when the head's plucked off" (1.1.97–98). Even more shocking to conventional expectations of women is Hippolyta's savage account of the effect of her war experiences:

> We have been soldiers, and we cannot weep
> When our friends don their helms, or put to sea,
> Or tell of babes broach'd on the lance, or women
> That have sod their infants in (and after eat them)
> The brine they wept at killing 'em. (1.3.18–22)

In addition to Theseus's bride, her sister Emilia, absent in *A Midsummer Night's Dream*, here compounds the unsettling effect of the alien women. The delays seem rooted in fear and expressed in repeated diversions from the erotic agenda.

The early Greeks, having evolved their definition of the male Cultural center, were nonetheless constantly aware of the contrasting others who lurked dangerously around this central core. The threatening erosion of the boundaries of human definition is signaled by the ubiquity of such peripheral hybrids as satyrs and centaurs, by the human/animal metamorphic shapes of Teiresias, Callisto, and many others, by partially assimilated aliens such as Medea, and by such semidivine heroes as Hercules and Achilles. Amazons rank with hermaphrodites as forms of male-female hybrid. According to legend, they usurped such male prerogatives as horseback riding, fighting, and the rejection of orderly monogamous marriage. Usually associated with distant outposts like Scythia or Colchis, they qualified as non-"human" aliens as well as non-"human" women. In Greek legend and literature Amazons appear at moments of Cultural crisis—always on the wrong side. Hippolyta/Antiope is implicated in an invasion of Athens and subdued by Theseus in a short-lived marriage that eventuates in the catastrophic destruction of their son Hippolytus (Plutarch 14–15). Penthesilea surfaces fighting along with a centaur, the "dreadful Sagittary," for the Trojans. She is killed by Achilles, who, ironically, falls in love with her as soon as she is safely dead and no longer threatening.

Both Boccaccio and Chaucer seem to have been able to adapt the story of Theseus and Hippolyta using the two characters as received legendary figures with recognizable values and suppressing disturbing overtones. Boccaccio says he wants to celebrate the "toils endured for Mars" (Bk. 12, sections 84–86), and Chaucer seems to want to demonstrate the admirable but limited philosophy available to the highest pagan society. According to V. A. Kolve, Theseus was to the Middle Ages "a man seeking consciously to embody the highest chivalric ideals of his civilization" (101). In "The Knight's Tale" Hippolyta is so much the gracious, docile aristocratic lady as hardly to evoke any memory of her origins. Most of Chaucer's characters have relatively stable allegorical significance, and Kolve has worked out a precise and consistent Christian interpretation of the tale (156–57). Allegory, like ritual, serves to repeat and reinforce accepted Cultural norms.

But allegory, like ritual, was breaking down in the England of Shakespeare and Fletcher. The hierarchy of male/female attributes had become blurred, and the struggles between Venus and Mars and Venus and Diana are shadowed with ambiguities. Allegorical affinities certainly remain in *Two Noble Kinsmen*, but they are shifting, inconsistent, and disturbing rather than reassuring. In this climate the Amazonian presence comes to life again as a signifier of marginal territory in the exploration of the human condition. Culture is severely threatened by Wild.

The outlines of crises of male self-definition in *Two Noble Kinsmen* are delineated in two three-sided patterns: the Theseus/Pirithous/Hippolyta triangle and the Palamon/Arcite/Emilia triangle. I will argue that both triangles represent the struggle of Theseus to come to grips with a central male dilemma, namely, the conflict between his need for the female Wild represented by Venus and his preference for the male Wild of Mars. The drawn-out delay and the emphasis on male/male relationships point to a tragically shadowed resolution.

By the beginning of the play, the Amazonian Hippolyta, like the bride-to-be of *A Midsummer Night's Dream*, represents the male fantasy of the Wild female tamed. Clearly disturbed by Emilia's resolution never to "Love any that's called man," the newly acculturated Hippolyta says,

> If I were ripe for your persuasion, you
> Have said enough to shake me from the arm
> Of the all-noble Theseus, for whose fortunes
>   I will now in and kneel. (1.3.91–94)

Primacy in the affections of Theseus is to be Hipployta's compensation for her capitulation, and she finds this preeminence called into question by Emilia's reminder of the "knot of love" between Theseus and Pirithous. In a non sequitur that suggests the urgency of her need to believe in her reward, she quickly resolves to reject her earlier uncertainty about "which he loves best" and asserts, without further evidence, her "great assurance / That we, more than his Pirithous, possess / The high throne in his heart" (1.3.91–96). But the evidence actually points toward the supremacy of Pirithous, Theseus's comrade in arms. The King is torn between Venus and Mars, but his heart is with Mars. Chaucer makes his loyalty more overt than Shakespeare does, describing his white banner emblazoned with "The rede statue of Mars, with spere and targe" (975), but the play also repeatedly emphasizes the King's devotion to battle and to the service of his "master Mars" (5.3.108). To subdue Hippolyta and produce death-defying progeny, however, Theseus must marry. His extraordinary description of marriage as "This grand act of our life, this daring deed / Of fate in wedlock" (1.1.163–64) and his insistence that "This is a service, whereto I am going, / Greater than any [war]; it more imports me / Than all the actions that I have foregone, / Or futurely can cope" (1.1.171–74) show his sense of the magnitude of the act and suggest his reluctance. His willingness to be diverted from his venereal purpose by the grieving queens is rewarded by their promise that his deed will earn him a deity equal to or even greater than that of Mars (1.1.227–28).

The god of war is inevitably linked with death, and the discordant reminders of the grim reaper multiply with the appearance of the widowed queens at the marriage festival. Their black veils, their memories of the stench and "mortal loathsomeness" of the rotting corpses of their lords (1.1.45–47), their imagined vision of Theseus's own corpse lying "i' th' blood-siz'd field ... swoll'n / Showing the sun his teeth, grinning at the moon," and their rapid imagistic alternation between the marriage bed and the deathbed of "rotten kings" (1.1.139–440, 175–82) effectively cancel out the elevated ceremonial mood of the initial Hymeneal procession. Theseus leaves his nuptials, going off to fight Creon as proof of his "humanity," affirming that "As we are men / Thus should we do, being sensually subdu'd / We lose our human title" (1.1.232–34). The "human title" is validated by male bonding. Theseus leaves Hippolyta for Pirithous, chooses Mars, at least for the moment, over Venus, opts for the known pleasures of the male Wild over the unknown perils of the female Wild.

Immediately following this temporary resolution of the first triangle, we are introduced to the developing second triangle. We discover Palamon and Arcite similarly concerned that "Widows' cries / … have not / Due audience of the gods" (1.2.79–81). They describe the perils of peace—the forgotten soldier, the dissolute city "where every evil / Hath a good color, where ev'ry seeming good's / A certain evil" (1.2.38–40), and where men are monsters. Lamenting Mars's "scorn'd altar," Palamon wishes that Juno would stir up trouble enough to start a new war. Their response to their revulsion from the corruption of Creon is to plan to leave his court until they are reprieved from the threatened peace by a new war. At this point Palamon and Arcite are scarcely distinguishable. If anything, Palamon is more concerned than Arcite with Mars and his soldiers and more determined to be "forehorse in the team" or none. Sisters' children, Palamon and Arcite are essentially undifferentiated adolescents fearful of sullying their "gloss of youth" with "crimes of nature" (1.2.3–5). Content with the male bonding of war, the excitement of the male Wild, they are reluctant to incorporate themselves even into the center of male Culture. Enamored of war, they are eager to escape the unknown perils (probably venereal) of the peaceful city. They are younger versions of Theseus and Pirithous, who have "Fought out together where death's self was lodg'd" and woven a "knot of love," which, it seems, "May be outworn, never undone" (1.3.40–44).

Viewing the hearse-drawn bodies of Palamon and Arcite after he has defeated them in battle, Theseus reveals that he instantly recognized them as kindred spirits when he saw them in battle like "a pair of lions smear'd with prey." He adds, "I fix'd my note / Constantly on them; for they were a mark / Worth a god's view" (1.4.18–21), and concludes, "their lives concern us / Much more than Thebes is worth" (1.4.32–33). He fears them and would rather have them dead than free, adding, "But forty thousand fold we had rather have 'em / Prisoners to us than death" (1.4.36–37). Fearing and cherishing them, he confines them to prison, and from this point on Palamon and Arcite act out almost emblematically the Venus-Mars struggle in Theseus's mind and in the male progress toward adulthood.

Together in a narcissistic prison Palamon and Arcite think wistfully of war and women. Palamon remembers the two of them in battle, "like twins of honor" enjoying the feeling of their "fiery horses / Like proud seas under" them (2.2.18–20), and Arcite yearns self-absorbedly for "The sweet embraces of a loving wife" (2.2.30), who might furnish him with a kind of immortality by providing him with a replica of himself to memorialize him in victorious combat. The two find consolation, however, in regarding their prison as a "holy sanctuary" to keep them from the "corruption of worse men" and the menace of seductive women (2.2.71–72). They resolve, with ludicrously shortsighted assurance, to be content to be "one another's wife" and heir (2.2.80–83). Immediately there appears the figure of Emilia, plucking, appropriately enough, the narcissus flower and remarking of its namesake, "That was a fair boy certain, but a fool / To love himself " (2.2.119–21). Like Actaeon's confrontation with Diana, the vision of Emilia results in a second male crisis, a fragmentation of the identity of her viewers, which dominates the rest of the play. It is a curious but psychologically acute fact that in Renaissance mythologizing the sight of the naked virgin goddess Diana transforms the male viewer into a victim of Venus, pursued and ultimately torn apart by the hounds of desire.[6] Other-directed passion fractures the narcissistic self-absorption of Palamon and Arcite, and in transferring their affection from each other to Emilia they recapitulate Theseus's earlier progression from Pirithous to Hippolyta. But as in the case of Theseus, their new-found recognition of Venus remains weak and ineffectual. They are torn in this crisis between conflicting goals. Their rivalry and imprisonment conveniently delay the necessity of facing Venus directly.

In a patriarchy the male cherishes the female's virginity, which certifies her as his inviolate possession, but he also depends on her fecundity for the propagation of his species.[7] Divided between Diana and Venus, he resents and yet retreats to the presence of other males. Theseus has faced one side of this problem, accepting belatedly, in a bow to Venus, the responsibilities of marriage; but he imprisons his younger "rivals" who may challenge his proprietary interest in his sister-in-law. Male rivalry (the arena of Mars) is at least as powerful as heterosexual lust (the arena of Venus) in this play. The fractured friendship of

Palamon and Arcite reflects both the Mars-Venus conflict and the struggle between Venus and Diana. Their instant Venus-induced enmity propels them toward martial conflict, while their contrasting attitudes toward the lady reveal the male Diana/Venus dilemma posed by women. Palamon perceives Emilia as a goddess to be worshiped (Chaucer says as Venus, but the play's lack of specificity makes the symbolically more apt connotation of Diana available), whereas Arcite sees her "as a woman, to enjoy" (1.2.163–64). In both cases, however, their passion begins and remains a distant infatuation, and we suspect its roots are firmly fixed in the violent male rivalry suggested by Palamon's threat to nail Arcite to the window and Arcite's reciprocal vow, "I'll throw my body out, / And leap the garden, when I see her next, / And pitch between her arms *to anger thee*" (2.2.215–17, italics added).

In a neatly constructed allegory we might expect the fragmented psyches of Palamon and Arcite—reflections of Theseus's own divided mind—to define themselves as they will appear at the end—as servants, respectively, of the goddess of love and the god of war. To some extent this does indeed occur, but the distinction is never absolute or clear-cut, and the situation is complicated by the Diana/Venus polarization. Male self-definition is not simple in this play. Although the knights are hardly fully developed and rounded characters, neither can they be classified merely as emblems. Theseus, perhaps betraying his own predilection for the male Wild epitomized by Mars, frees Arcite to return to Thebes,[8] and the languishing Palamon immediately fantasizes his rival's reappearance as a victorious warrior who will conquer the female Wild, like Theseus, with his sword. Arcite, on the other hand, imagines Palamon winning Emilia through the more seductive powers of speech because "he has a tongue will tame tempests, / And make the wild rocks wanton" (2.3.16–17). Palamon is subsequently freed from prison by love, and the amorous devotion of the Jailer's daughter secures for Palamon a more central position than Arcite's in the unfolding of the drama. Of the two knights Palamon is the gentler, the sadder, the more passive. After desire has seized him, he reveals a bizarre imagination that repeatedly identifies him with the feminine. He wants to be a blooming apricock tree that will fling wanton arms into Emilia's window and bring her fruits to make her even more godlike than she already seems to him (2.2.234–39). And he fancies that if free he would do such deeds that "This blushing virgin, should take manhood to her / And seek to ravish me" (2.2.258–60). He is playing with the erasure of the male/female border but as a fantasy of role reversal rather than a vision of possessing a woman. And he seems to enjoy the delay of gratification considerably more than the final achievement of his goal, shadowed as it is by his friend's death. Whereas Arcite's tournament companion looks like a "heated lion" and has eyes that show fire within, Palamon's follower has "a face far sweeter," colored with "The livery of the warlike maid ... / ... for yet no beard has blest him" (4.2.81–82, 95, 105–7). And it has been remarked that Palamon's puzzling prayer to Venus sounds rather more as if it should be addressed to Diana (Smith, *Kinsmen* 1641). Indeed, in the polarization between Venus and Diana, Palamon seems almost as close to the latter as to the former. And like Viola's in *Twelfth Night*, this "feminine" quality proves ultimately more "winning" than Arcite's military prowess.

Arcite is on the whole more active, more aggressive, more "masculine" than Palamon. He prides himself on being "a man's son" (2.2.182) and compares his wooing to a battle charge (2.2.195). He takes the initiative in disguising himself, seizes the opportunity to win running and wrestling matches so brilliantly that Theseus says he has not seen "Since Hercules, a man of tougher sinews" (2.5.1–2). He glories in the challenge of riding a rough horse so that he won't "Freeze in [his] saddle" (2.5.47–48). Theseus is so taken with Arcite that he advises Emilia to make him her master (2.5.62–64) and proposes prophetically that the jealous gods will want him to "die a bachelor, lest his race / Should show i' th' world too godlike" (5.3.117–18). Indeed, as the feats of Mars are inextricably linked with death, Arcite's victory in the tournament proves to be sterile. Neither Culture nor the male Wild can survive without merging with the life-giving female.

It is notable that from the moment of their separation and fragmentation, the young men are constantly referred to by their *parts*. Arcite worries about Palamon's tongue; we hear of Arcite's sinews; the Jailer's daughter fancies that Palamon has been torn to pieces by wolves; Emilia thinks of Arcite's face, eye, figure, and brow (grotesquely comparing its smoothness to Pelops's shoulder) and of Palamon's eyes, face, body, and brow, concluding of her suitors, "Were they metamorphis'd / Both into one ... there were no woman / Worth so compos'd a man" (5.3.84–86).

If the first male conflict in the play, epitomized by Theseus and played out by Palamon and Arcite, is between Venus and Mars, the second conflict, projected chiefly onto the females, is between Venus and Diana. Both conflicts prolong delay. The women of the play represent the standard Renaissance stereotypes—maid, wife, and widow. The widows vanish early, and Hippolyta, as wife, gets relatively short shrift—her wedding is upstaged by the war with Thebes, and her resolution to believe herself dearer to Theseus than Pirithous is mustered with suspicious alacrity and carried out with an arbitrary decision to repress doubts. Pirithous does not help matters when he begs Theseus to show mercy, conjuring him anticlimactically, "By all our friendship, sir, all our dangers, / By all you love most—wars, and this sweet lady—" (3.6.202–3). The female having been acquired for Culture, the males are free to enjoy their own exclusive Wild.

The Amazonian Emilia comes closer to being a simple allegorical figure than any of the men. Like Hippolyta she remains curiously static, seeming more a projection of a male problem than an interesting dramatic character. Although her portrait is more complicated than that of Chaucer's Emelye, who never expresses any erotic interest in either of her suitors and prefers right up to the end of the tale to remain a maid, Emilia is throughout most of the play clearly the servant of Diana, a creature of an inaccessible female Wild. Somewhat ironically, in view of her subsequent dismissal of Narcissus as a fool for loving himself, she proclaims her own narcissistic attachment to her childhood alter ego Flavina, asserting that she will never love any man as she has loved her friend (1.3.84–86). And in gathering flowers, although she chooses the equivocal rose (which will later become for her the emblem of Diana's concession to Venus), as well as the univocal narcissus, she wishes to preserve the flowers' springlike beauty through the art of embroidery rather than to enjoy their living presence. She has no desire to bring fecundity to Culture.

Emilia repeatedly identifies with women, defining herself as "a natural sister of our sex" (1.1.125), invoking "The powers of all women" (3.6.194), and thinking of others in terms of their mothers. On seeing Arcite she supposes his handsome face was inherited from his mother, and she asks Theseus's mercy on the two knights because of "The goodly mothers that have groan'd" for them (3.6.245). She tries to choose between them for the sake of "their weeping mothers" (4.2.4) and thinks of them as their mothers' joy (4.2.63). She embodies a female solidarity that recurringly threatens Shakespearean men and inhibits their progress toward matrimony. Her concern with maternal feelings may suggest Diana's embodiment as Lucina (specifically included by Chaucer in his description of Diana's temple), but more important to Emilia is the virginal aspect of the goddess. Like Diana, patron of Amazons, she hunts, and she apparently keeps a stable because she is able to provide Arcite with a brace of horses fit for kings (2.6.19–21). She thinks of herself as a "female knight" (5.1.140). Initially, as Amazon, she embodies one facet of the female threat to male-dominated society—the unavailable woman protected by female solidarity—"foreign" and unattainable. But the image, projected through a male lens, begins to blur—the unattainable female cannot be allowed to exist. The Wild must be co-opted. Unlike Emelye, Emilia grows increasingly interested in her two suitors. Although most often she finds them interchangeable, she confesses in one speech that she is "sotted, / Utterly lost" and that her "virgin's faith hath fled" her (4.2.45–46). Her prayer to Diana is not, like Emelye's, a request to remain a maid but includes the alternative of being won by the suitor who loves her most. As Palamon moves closer to Diana, Emilia moves closer to Venus. But whatever passion she may feel, she shows no joy in Arcite's victory and speaks not at all to Palamon after she is awarded to him by default. Culture simply absorbs her, and her will to resist melts into wifely duty. The final transaction is still between Palamon and Arcite.

The more passionate face of the Wild appears in the form of the true exemplar of Venus in the play, the Jailer's daughter. It is she who sees, pities, and loves Palamon in spite of the equal charms of Arcite, who knows that she "would fain enjoy him" (2.4.30), who frees him from his prison of arrested development, pursues him into "Dian's wood" with lascivious intent, and finally, subdued by her father and the Wooer, agrees to marry Palamon's double. Her venereal freedom and boldness are welcomed happily by the rustics as part of the May Day saturnalia; but in the sober postfestive view of the Jailer and the Wooer, such excess is alarming (mad). As the Amazonian frigidity of Emilia has been warmed by desire, so the equally menacing specter of voracious feminine appetite must be curbed. At the advice of the doctor, her father confines her to a small room with a dim light so as to dupe her into a suitable marriage that will control her "extravagant vagary." For these males she embodies the fantasy of unbridled female sexuality—a sexuality which is a necessary evil but that demands the "bridaling" enacted in wedlock.

At the end of the play, then, Diana and Venus find a compromise acceptable to the males in the unions of Palamon and Emilia and of the Jailer's daughter and her surrogate Palamon. The varieties of the Wild are tamed. Fertility is both provided for and restricted. But the Mars of the male Wild is not so easily dealt with. His deadly shadow looms darkly over all. As the action has begun with mirth and funeral so it concludes. Although both Theseus and the younger generation have yielded to the power of Venus, Theseus continues to claim Mars as his master and to focus attention on Arcite's funeral rather than Palamon's wedding (5.4.106). The refrain of the widowed queens hangs hauntingly in the memory: "This world's a city full of straying streets, / And death's the market-place, where each one meets" (1.3.15–16). A measure of the distance between Chaucer and the Renaissance is suggested by the modification of this image. In Chaucer the world is a "thurghfare" from which wandering pilgrims are released by death (2847). In the drama, death is the ultimate unconquerable Wild, the heart of the mystery, and it is ominously linked with women.

As I suggested earlier, both Palamon and Arcite can be seen as spiritual offspring of Theseus. He admires both and fears both, wishing to keep them imprisoned under his control. Later the two fight each other in Theseus's armor (3.6.54). But we sense that Arcite is closer to Theseus's own self-image. Theseus releases him freely, without ransom, at the same time confining Palamon even more strictly than before. Arcite is more successful as a warrior than a lover. Even though he has been in close proximity to Emilia as her servant, whereas Palamon has never met her, Arcite has not won her unequivocal love. And his fate is oddly premonitory of that of Hippolytus, the yet unborn son of Theseus and Hippolyta, who is similarly destroyed by his own horses, which have been frightened by a monster sent by Poseidon at the behest of Aphrodite. In both cases death is the result of addiction to male Wilds and a failure to come to terms with the goddess of love. Hippolytus has preferred the hunt of animals to the Hunt of Love, and Arcite has chosen Mars as his guardian. Both have underestimated the fury of repressed female and animal Wilds.

The animal Wild, epitomized in the figure of the horse, runs like a leitmotif through the play. Palamon and Arcite remember with pleasure their fiery steeds under them in battle (2.2.18). Arcite prides himself in particular on his horsemanship, and the two of them recall the good bright bay (3.6.76–77) that Arcite rode in the war against the three kings. Arcite boasts of the brace of fine horses given him by Emilia. In the subplot horses are a source of humor, frequently coarse. The countrymen speak of tickling work out of "the jades' tails" after their day of maying. The mad Jailer's daughter sings of a lover who will give her "a white cut ... to ride" (3.4.22) and later declares that Palamon has given her an extraordinary horse, which can dance, read, and write and is beloved by the Duke's mare (5.2.45–65). A human hobby horse, along with the

Bavian, is a usual part of the Morris dance. These mergings of man and animal, like the presence of the Amazons, suggest the erosion of conventional "human" boundaries in the world of the play.

Skillful horsemanship is an image of success in war and of the individual's ability to control passion by reason, but, as we have seen, it is also frequently an image of matrimony—with "female" passion controlled by "male" reason. In each case the rider is conventionally presumed to be male, although the mounted Diana is tolerated as image of the hunt. The horse-rider figure thus links Diana, Mars (the equestrian warrior), and Venus (the promoter of amorous conjunctions). Usually a woman in the saddle, like an unbridled horse, is profoundly disturbing (see Figs. 9 and 10). It is surely no accident that, in the play, Arcite is killed by Emilia's horse. In Chaucer's tale, Arcite is fatally wounded while parading under Emilia's eye. He is thrown on his head by his horse, which has been frightened by an infernal fury sent by Pluto at Saturn's request to placate Venus. The drama, perhaps elaborating on the brief description in the *Teseida*, introduces an extraordinary modification (the merest shadow of Saturn remains in a simile). Arcite is injured because, in spite of almost superhuman efforts, he cannot control Emilia's horse. The description is grotesquely detailed and almost explicitly sexual (5.4.70–83). The horse, excited by a spark from its own hoof, reverts to Wildness,

> ... the hot horse, hot as fire,
> Took toy at this, and fell to what disorder
> His power could give his will, bounds, comes on end,
> Forgets school-doing, being therein train'd,
> And of kind manage; pig-like he whines
> At the sharp rowel, which he frets at rather
> Than any jot obeys: seeks all foul means
> Of boist'rous and rough jad'ry, to disseat
> His lord that kept it bravely. When nought serv'd,
> When neither curb would crack, girth break, nor diff'ring plunges
> Disroot his rider whence he grew, but that
> He kept him 'tween his legs, on his hind hoofs
> [....] on end he stands,
> That Arcite's legs, being higher than his head,
> Seem'd with strange art to hang. His victor's wreath

Even then fell off his head; and presently
Backward the jade comes o'er, and his full poise
Becomes the rider's load. (5.4.65–82)

The horse whines like a pig and thrashes wildly in the effort to unseat his rider. When, in spite of all, Arcite still keeps the steed between his legs, the horse upends the rider and falls backward, crushing him. The "natural" order has been overturned. Female and animal Wilds have conspired to defeat him. Arcite, the professed servant of Mars, has been confused by Venus and defeated by Diana. Proud of his equestrian skill in battle, he succumbs to his failure to subdue the unruly spirit embodied in the horse of his Amazonian mistress. Whether the instigator is Venus or Diana is not so clear as in Chaucer. In effect the two have joined against Mars. Disruptive female forces have temporarily unsettled patriarchal order.

Theseus may have succeeded in wooing Hippolyta with his sword and winning her love by doing her injuries, but the Amazonian Emilia remains beyond Mars's power. The gentler, sadder Palamon, who has eschewed horses when fighting in the forest (3.6.59) (this may have been dictated by stage convenience) and adhered, albeit somewhat reluctantly, to Venus, and who has perhaps been secretly favored by Emilia (she wore his picture near her heart, 5.3.73–76), will inherit her. This final crisis resolves, at least for the moment, the problem of Theseus and his society. The beloved rivals merge in a way that neutralizes the menace of male aggression and yet secures potency for posterity. Theseus retains the power of Mars. Patriarchy has been shored up; the threatening Amazon will be safely married off; and the new generation will have Theseus's blessing, if not an enthusiastic one. All this has been played out not by means of subtle character distinctions but emblematically. As the simpler allegorical figures of Boccaccio and Chaucer have blurred and even merged, however, the struggle to clarify male identity is heightened. Male boundaries, threatened with erosion by the inroads of both females and their surrogate horses, have been temporarily shored up. Social definitions survive, but the embattled beachhead remains insecure and unstable.

The sense of instability is reinforced by the unconventional generic form of the play. Although the Stationers' Register identifies it as a tragicomedy, it does not conform to the definition set out by Fletcher in his preface to *The Faithful Shepherdess*.[9] The play's very structure reflects the erosion of boundaries. Palamon and Arcite are repeatedly brought near death and reprieved, and yet the progress toward a festive culmination in marriage and the triumph of a new generation is continually frustrated by the realization that one of the lovers must be eliminated to effect such a conclusion. Instead of wanting, like the audience of comedy, to hurry the action toward consummation, here the audience's impulse is similar to that aroused by tragedy—the desire to retard the relentless progress of the plot. The reluctance caused by male dividedness is not pleasurable; it is a kind of desperate deferral.

The end is, then, a disturbing compromise. It allows for neither catharsis nor satisfying social reintegration. Diana and Venus have been brought to an uneasy truce: the dual female threats of virginity and lasciviousness have been tamed by matrimony. Similarly, Mars and Venus are both in some sense victorious: following Arcite's victory, death claims the center of the stage, but it is the death of the follower of the death-dealing Mars. The victory of Venus through Palamon does at least promise new generations, though Mars, as embodied in Theseus, still remains a controlling presence. The comic and the tragic have been momentarily balanced rather than resolved. The Duke's conclusion is exceedingly apt: "For what we lack / We laugh, for what we have are sorry" (5.4.132–33).

In attempting to encompass new realities, tragicomedy, like allegory, has moved beyond the bounds of received Cultural definitions into a confusing maze like the "city full of straying streets." The struggles to possess the Amazonian Emilia, to confine the female eroticism of the Jailer's daughter, and to reconcile the conflicting male impulses of Palamon and Arcite both mirror and reenact the effort of Cultural art to build an orderly vision of the universe on the shifting sands of Stuart England. The play's "order" inevitably represents a male vision, although the artist's empathy with many sorts of humanity may sometimes seem to transcend the boundaries of his gender.

The fragmentation of the males in this play is notably different from that in *The Comedy of Errors* and *Much Ado About Nothing*. In the early comedy the underlying cause seems to be the difficulty of uniting images of father, husband, and lover. In the late comedy fear of cuckoldry seems to be the fracturing force. But in *Two Noble Kinsmen* we see the profound reluctance of the male to abandon the clearly defined male Wild of Mars—the pleasures of war—for the female Wild of Venus/Diana. There is no fear of cuckoldry—patriarchy seems too firmly entrenched for that—but the polarization of sexes is real, and the confusion over the relation of Venus and Diana adds a complicating dimension. The fragmentation of the female offers fewer options, but the Venus/Diana dichotomy remains an active problem. The next section of this chapter explores the slightly broader but still severely limited spectrum of the female roles imagined by the male playwright and shows how this fragmentation of the female engenders both reluctance and delay in the male in need of a spouse and precipitates violence in the Cultural community.

Female Trinities

Shakespeare's female characters have been viewed by diverse critics, mostly male, who have seen them with visions shaped by a variety of presuppositions. Samuel Taylor Coleridge, although he professed to find all Shakespeare's women fundamentally similar, nonetheless could single out the Helena of *All's Well That Ends Well* as Shakespeare's "loveliest character," although he also sympathized with Bertram and found Helena so lacking in delicacy that it demanded all of the author's "consummate skill to interest us for her" (1:113, 134, 357). Mary Cowden Clarke in the late nineteenth century found Shakespeare's heroines so fascinating and lifelike that she imagined five volumes of detailed and elaborate childhoods for them. L. C. Knights mocked A. C. Bradley's approach to characters as real human beings with life histories in his famous *How Many Children Had Lady Macbeth?* More recently the whole idea of "character" has fallen out of fashion. As was pointed out in the Introduction, Stephen Greenblatt has gone so far as to imply that there were not only no female actors but no females, however defined, on the Elizabethan stage. For a female Shakespearean long accustomed to identification with such characters as Portia, Rosalind, and Beatrice, this is a painful conclusion. Audiences certainly think of Shakespeare's women as female and as people—at least on the stage. But for the moment I would like to argue, unlike Greenblatt, that female characters are not disguised men, but rather aspects of male imaginings of females, and that it is useful to detach oneself, at least temporarily, from thinking of them as women, although, since Shakespeare was a keen and empathetic observer, they may actually depict traits recognizable to females—both females conditioned to accept male stereotypes of women and females attempting to reimagine femininity. Further consideration of both the presence and absence of "female" characters should be illuminating to both sexes.

Not surprisingly, the inhabitants of the female Wild appear in male representations in art repeatedly and insistently cataloged and defined according to their relationship to male Culture. It is a commonplace of modern feminist criticism that depictions of women in male works of art tend to fall into three categories, defined by their relation to males. Each figure is frightening in some way. The nomenclature varies somewhat. The Greeks might have thought of the Triple Hecate, with her aspects of the virginal Diana, the maternal Juno or Lucina, and Proserpina, goddess of the underworld (Fig. 23). (The middle figure, Luna, is a variant of Juno/Lucina, patron of fertility and childbirth.) The Elizabethans probably would have referred to maid, wife, and widow. Sigmund Freud speaks of the three "inevitable relations" that a man has with a woman: the mother who bears him, the beloved who mates him, and the "woman" who destroys him ("Caskets" 301). Art historians refer to the virgin, whore, and crone. Iconographically the whore sometimes modulates into the more benign wife and the crone into mother. It is on virgin, whore/wife, and crone/mother that I intend to focus here. In the male imagination the female Wild seems to be peopled with these three main types, and the inability to reconcile them causes paralysis, reluctance, and delay. Clearly each of the categories is defined in terms of sexual relationship to males. The virgin is young, innocent of sex, but with sexual potential; the whore/wife is sexually active and therefore dangerous; the Crone, although allied with possible motherhood, has become an infertile reminder of death. (It is instructive to discover the impossibility of finding equivalent terms for men; the suggestions that come to mind—youth/stud/codger or virgin/tomcat/geezer—seem laughably inadequate.) There are, no doubt, exceptions to this threefold pattern, but it is widespread enough to be taken seriously.

The commonplace triangulation—one might even say triage—of women is reductionist, but it is also enlightening. It is immediately obvious that the great majority of Shakespeare's female characters are virgins. I have counted thirty-five examples. A few are dubious, and there may be more. They are often striking and memorable characters such as Portia, Rosalind, and Beatrice. They often appear in multiples, and Shakespeare rings some telling changes on usual expectations. But different as these young female figures may be, they all share the primary characteristic of virginity and marriageability. All are comparatively innocent and virtuous. Indeed, virtue and virginity are inseparable. The young

23. *Triple Goddess in the forms of Diana, Luna, and Perserpina.* Vincenzo Cartari, *Le imagini de i dei de gli antichi.* Venice, 1587, p. 90. By permission of the Folger Shakespeare Library.

virgins are the candidates for the necessary incorporation into male Culture. In Shakespeare some are instruments of patriarchal power, some are rebels against that power, and some already show signs of their unsettling effect on the Culture. But it is part of the definition of comedy that all are eventually assimilated, if only for the moment.

Shakespeare's virgins are not the sole guardians of female virtue. Such qualities may also be associated with wives and mothers as well as other mature, potentially sexually active women. We might expect to find multiplied portraits of chaste wives, and a few do come to mind (Brutus's Portia, Calphurnia, Mistress Ford, Mistress Page, Hermione, Virgilia). I have counted twenty-six. But curiously, half of these women are either barren or childless (nine are mothers only of daughters, widely viewed as a form of barrenness), and sexuality is an important aspect only of those whose virtue is doubted. Almost as numerous as chaste wives among the mature women are the twenty-one who may be characterized in male eyes as whores (Gertrude, Goneril, Cleopatra, Doll Tearsheet, Mistress Overdone). Many are or have been married, but all are proven or suspected "bed-swervers." The women on this list range from faithless wives to outright bawds. Almost without exception the mothers in this group produce only sons. It seems, then, that chaste wife figures are either sexless or suspect and that they are less capable of producing male offspring than women of overt sexuality. For all practical purposes, mature, potentially sexual women on Shakespeare's stage are either virgins or whores. Wild women who have been domesticated are also frequently rendered barren.

The most underrepresented woman is, of course, the mother, and, although there are some mothers in Shakespeare (Lady Capulet, Gertrude, the Countess of Rossillion, Hermione), critics have frequently remarked that such figures are rare and that they often fade out of their plays for long periods even when they exist. The major exception is Volumnia, mother of Coriolanus, and she is so thoroughly the product of Shakespeare's imagination of patriarchal Roman society that she has almost none of the expected maternal characteristics. A widowed mother and the agent of her son's death, Volumnia seems in fact a type of crone.

Patriarchy obviously had the most trouble with the middle term of the female trinity, and it is she who is most likely to cause both delay in courtship and explosion within Culture. The confusion of names bestowed on her suggests the ambivalence about her. She was both Diana, the chaste huntress who turned Actaeon into a stag when he viewed her naked beauty in the forest, and Venus, the lascivious goddess of love and beauty whom Prospero excluded from his nuptial masque for Ferdinand and Miranda (4.1.87–101). Female sexuality, obviously essential for human preservation, was sought after but also feared and repressed. Other confusions abound. Minerva, goddess of wisdom and knowledge, was confused with Bellona, Roman goddess of war (whose bridegroom Macbeth was said to be), who was in turn merged with an Asian moon goddess linked with fertility (Linche fol. Sii verso).

One of the clearest examples of patriarchal confusion about the sexually active female is the Renaissance attitude toward Helens. The archetypal Helen was, of course, Helen of Troy, the most beautiful of women, wife—but also deceitful whore, a Cultural captive who has escaped Cultural constraints. She comes, in fact, to represent all three stages of the female trinity: a virgin to be fought over, a wife who betrays, and a bringer of death. But the middle stage is most illuminating. There is a fascinating Renaissance poem by John Trussell called "The first Rape of faire Hellen"; it is in the form of a lament by Helen that since her rape at the age of thirteen by Theseus she lacks that which makes beauty a blossom that will never fade—true chastity.[10] But coached by her nurse and her mother, she conceals her loss, adding that when she later married Menelaus, he never knew that she was marred. She concludes, "But what I knew, he did not once suspect, / What he suspected not, I did not showe: / And what I show'd not, nothing could detect, / So much I knew: my mother told me so" (Shaaber 444). She thus becomes the very epitome of the male nightmare—the woman irresistibly attractive to men who nonetheless harbors the secret power to deceive and betray them. She is a Wild spy in the Cultural sanctuary.

Another famous Helen, St. Helena, mother of the Emperor Constantine, also has a curiously ambiguous history. Geoffrey of Monmouth called her a queen and identified her as the daughter of King Coel of Britain and wife of Constantius, father of Constantine. Other historians claimed, however, that she was a public courtesan and that Constantine was born of a union consummated without benefit of clergy. Whatever the truth, she was, like the other Helen, a powerful and controversial figure, an alien and marginal woman, who co-opted a space at the very heart of the new patriarchal Christian Culture (E. G. Davis 232–33).

Because of a possibly fortuitous etymological coincidence, for speakers of English, Helens share an association with Hel, the Norse goddess of the underworld who provided early English theologians with a convenient translation of the Greek "Hades." Helens are associated with death (see Fig. 22 and Fig. 24, where the caption under the picture of death as a woman mentions Helen by name). The place of the dead was transformed by the Christians into a place of terrible torments. The goddess Hel, then, gave her name to the fearful Inferno, and the association with the female remained implicit and available (Walker 85). It is a short step from Hell to Helen. Shakespeare plays on the similarity of the words in A Midsummer Night's Dream, where Helena herself vows to follow Demetrius and "make a heaven of hell" (2.1.243), and in Troilus and Cressida, where Diomed says of Helen, "He merits well to have her that doth seek her, / With such a hell of pain and world of charge" (4.1.56–58). In 1 Henry 6 Hell is specifically connected with enforced wedlock (5.5.62).

Even in Greek it was possible to make a pun on Helen and death. Aeschylus's chorus in the Agamemnon links the name Helen with helenas, death of ships, helandros, death of men, and heleptolis, death of cities. Richard Lattimore translates the lines rhetorically directed at Helen:

Who is he that named you so
fatally in every way? . . .
Helen, which is death? Appropriately
death of ships, death of men and cities.[11]

In his middle creative years Shakespeare dealt three times with Helens; and in each case he specifically linked the Helen with threatening and aggressive sexuality. In A Midsummer Night's Dream Helena determinedly follows Lysander into the forest even though he repeatedly rejects her in no uncertain terms. Helen of Troy is identified in Troilus and Cressida as the wanton and frivolous cause of the Trojan War. And in All's Well That Ends Well Helena succeeds in capturing the reluctant Bertram even though he has resisted her throughout the play. The Helena of A Midsummer Night's Dream is both irrationally rejected and irrationally pursued. It seems that in male eyes, Helens, however innocent, are tainted with suspicion. They are manifestly protégés of that Venus who rewarded Paris for declaring her the most beautiful of goddesses by presenting him with another man's wife. They are the Wild—both feared and lusted after.

Helens, then, personify the male ambivalence toward female sexuality revealed in the wife/whore dichotomy. Women are beautiful, enticing, frightening, foreign, necessary, and potentially destructive—think of Dr. Faustus's

24. *Death as a Woman*. Gerhardt Altzenbach, engraver. Art
Collection, Harry Ransom Humanities Research Center, University
of Texas at Austin.

vision of the face that launched a thousand ships, of the Helen he calls heavenly and asks to make him immortal with a kiss, a vision that comes to him from Hell, courtesy of Mephistophilis. Beautiful women are Heaven; they are also Hell. For males to fit them into Cultural contexts is a necessary but nearly impossible task. In each Shakespearean incarnation Helen is associated with the marginal; each represents in some sense a victory of Wild over Culture. Helena effectively lures Demetrius into the forest in *A Midsummer Night's Dream*. In *All's Well That Ends Well*, Helen achieves her goal of being bedded by the reluctant Bertram in alien Italy, and in *Troilus and Cressida* Helen actually defects to the enemy Trojans.

If the wife/whore archetype arouses intense ambivalence, the mother/crone figure is so problematic that she tends to be ignored, dismissed, or detested. The crone is of particular interest because of her anomalous position in male Culture. No longer functional as a vital component of the sexual negotiation that enables the production of male progeny, she nonetheless elicits, as Freud suggests, both the memory of the powerful mother and the specter of the shadow of death. She cannot be altogether banished, but she lingers disturbingly at the margins of Culture, usually more out than in. In many of Shakespeare's plays she is notable for her absence. When crones are present, they are usually messengers of death or figures of fun. Old Queen Margaret and the widowed Duchess of York in *Richard III* are prophets of doom and destruction. The witches in *Macbeth* are either fomentors or symbols of ultimately fatal evil. The nurse in *Romeo and Juliet* and Mistress Quickly in *The Merry Wives of Windsor* act as comic erotic go-betweens. There are a few exceptions, but both statistically and aesthetically the odds against the power and appeal of women in Shakespeare's plays escalate geometrically as the women age from virgin to crone.

And yet in three instances, *The Comedy of Errors*, *All's Well That Ends Well*, and *The Winter's Tale*, Shakespeare invents an older woman not present in his sources. I should like to examine the purposes and effects of these additions.

The "Mothers" of Shakespeare's Invention

Before moving to an examination of Shakespeare's three invented maternal figures, it is enlightening to look at one such figure inherited from the source but greatly expanded—Volumnia of *Coriolanus*. It is supremely ironic that

Volumnia, the most fully developed mother in Shakespeare, should be portrayed as so thoroughly the product of patriarchal Roman society that she has almost none of the expected maternal characteristics of pity, compassion, and tenderness. Plutarch blames Coriolanus's wildness and lack of social discipline on the absence of a father, but Shakespeare never develops this hint. He makes Volumnia a towering figure. Reminiscent of Queen Margaret and Lady Macbeth, she verges on the Amazonian; but instead of becoming a warrior woman like Margaret, she has devoted all her energies, like Lady Macbeth, to promoting the career of a man—in this case, her son. But she has also internalized the ideals of the Roman republic to the point that she must put loyalty to Rome before all else. For the most part this causes her no problem—her son has been trained from early youth in military arts, and she boasts that she "was pleas'd to let him seek danger where he was like to find fame" (1.3.12–13). She clearly places his honor above his connubial happiness, "consoling" her daughter-in-law for his absence by insisting, "If my son were my husband, I should freelier rejoice in that absence wherein he won honor than in the embracements of his bed where he would show most love." Like Lady Macbeth, she seems to have unsexed herself in her single-minded devotion to the pursuit of military glory. In the most shocking lines in the play she praises her son's bloody brow with an ecstatic and grotesque comparison, proclaiming, "The breasts of Hecuba, / When she did suckle Hector, look'd not lovelier / Than Hector's forehead when it spit forth blood." (1.3.40–43). Volumnia shows only proud amusement at the tale of how her grandson has torn apart a butterfly with his teeth, and she thanks the gods for the news that her son has been wounded in achieving victory, thus adding two more to the twenty-five gashes he has earlier withstood.

Volumnia emerges, then, as a facet of the female, but a severely limited one, a mother figure divorced from sexuality and stripped of most of the qualities usually associated with the maternal nature. Ambitious for her son, she is so devoted to Rome and honor that she would rather see him dead than inactive. She tells Virgilia, "had I a dozen sons . . . . I had rather had eleven die nobly for their country than one voluptuously surfeit out of action" (1.2.22–25). Although Volumnia is in some ways admirable, surely most audiences share Sicinius's wonder when he asks her, "Are you mankind?" exposing the suspicion that she is a man/woman or perhaps not a woman at all. Her son's poignant words as he capitulates to her prayer to save Rome surely reverberate in our memory of the play:

                    O mother, mother!
What have you done? Behold the heavens do ope,
The gods look down, and this unnatural scene
They laugh at. O my mother, mother! O!
You have won a happy victory to Rome;
But, for your son, believe it—O believe it—
Most dangerously have you with him prevail'd.
                    (5.3.182–88)

He is right, of course; and soon after, he is dead. She assumes something of the stature of tragic hero when she, whose definition has been to be a Roman mother, discovers the barrenness of that role. Having abandoned her son to the violence of the Volscians whom he has betrayed, she is now celebrated by senators and people as their patroness. Having been the death of her son, she becomes, in their words, "the life of Rome" (5.5.1). The play has no whore, and indeed her spirit is sorely missed. There is, in effect, only a vestige of the female Wild and the vision of a female landscape peopled only by virginal wife and androgynous crone is very bleak indeed. The victory of Thanatos over Eros, of Mars over Venus, has rarely seemed grimmer.

Divorced from the imagined terrible, voracious, and fertile mother of the female Wild, Volumnia finally forms with the other domesticated female characters and the patriarchal Roman Culture a solid front so formidable that Coriolanus deliberately chooses to defect to the male Wild of Corioli and certain death, rather than return disgraced to his family. In her final apotheosis Volumnia becomes disturbingly reminiscent of the awful and all-powerful crone who presides inexorably over the death of the male hero.

As we have seen, the women of *The Comedy of Errors*, one of Shakespeare's earliest plays, conform precisely to the expected archetypal patterns. Adriana is the chaste, somewhat rebellious wife of Antipholus of Ephesus. She resents her husband's freedom, which includes a friendship with a local courtesan whom he describes in typical fantasy terms, de-Naturing her Wildness. He says she is "a wench of excellent discourse, / Pretty and witty; wild, and yet, too, gentle," and he promises her a gold chain intended originally for his wife. From her he receives a diamond ring. Adriana complains of her problems with her husband to Luciana, her dutiful, virginal sister, only to be reproved with the reminder of the rightness of male hierarchy. In all nature, she asserts, man rules as "Lord of the wide world and wat'ry seas." Men are properly "masters to their females, and their lords," and women's will, she says, should "attend on their accords" (2.1.21–24). Adriana, the wife, neglected and ignored, turns, by her own admission, into a nag and is in the end rebuked for that and accused of driving her husband mad. In the course of the play she also becomes tainted with the guilt of locking out her husband and unintentionally entertaining his twin brother at dinner. Chaste wife thus merges on one hand with the asexual, nagging crone and on the other with the whore. Luciana, her sister, the model of patience and decorum, is presumably to be rewarded by marriage to Antipholus of Syracuse after the various confusions have been resolved.

One might read this early play as an overt spelling out of the effort of the male—in this case the split Antipholuses, bachelor and husband—to reconcile and combine images of virgin, whore, and crone into wife. The real exemplar of the crone, or asexual older woman, is strikingly absent until the final scene, when she miraculously appears as a sort of *dea ex machina* in the form of the Lady Abbess. She now "gains a husband" in her reunion with Egeon, the twins' father, after thirty-three years of celibacy or—as she puts it—after thirty-three years of labor, she has finally delivered her sons. Virgin, wife, courtesan, and mother share the stage in this final scene, and there is some sense that they have been harmonized in relation to the men, that social needs have been served, that husbands and wives will be reunited and bachelor brother married. The delay caused by fragmentation of both sexes is ended at least for the moment, and the future seems assured. Hostility, or at least coolness, remains between the women, however. The Lady Abbess blames Adriana for her husband's defection, saying,

> The venom clamors of a jealous woman
> Poisons more deadly than a mad dog's tooth.
> It seems his sleeps were hind'red by thy railing,
> And thereof comes it that his head is light.
> Thou say'st his meat was sauc'd with thy upbraidings:
> Unquiet meals make ill digestions,
> Thereof the raging fire of fever bred,
> And what's a fever but a fit of madness? . . .
> The consequence is then, thy jealous fits
> Hath scar'd thy husband from the use of wits.
>
> (5.1.69–86)

Luciana tries feebly to defend her sister:

She never reprehended him but mildly,
When he demean'd himself rough, rude, and wildly.
Why bear you these rebukes and answer not?

(5.1.87–89)

But her words have no impact on the Abbess or the group. Even Adriana subsides, saying that she has been justly chastised. Adriana's husband thanks the courtesan for her "good cheer" and seems to remain on the friendliest of terms with her. We wonder whether nag and whore can ever really merge into wife. The male/female unions seem rather perfunctory, and we sense at best an uneasy truce. The whore remains as alternative to wife, and the memory of the overblown, voracious, and subhuman "Dowsabel" is invoked at the play's end as a reminder of the dangers of uncontrolled women.

The intriguing question is, Why has Shakespeare chosen to invent the Abbess as his *dea ex machina*? Aegeon, confronted by the two Antipholuses, could surely have figured out that they were his twin sons—as he does in Plautus. By adding a mother, Shakespeare has given the scene mythical resonance. Like Volumnia, the Abbess presides almost goddesslike over the final scene; but unlike Volumnia, she has the power to give birth to the promise of the future with her two finally mature sons. By giving the mother such power, however, Shakespeare has risked jeopardizing the patriarchal vision. He has carefully hedged the issue by making the mother an abbess—almost a virgin mother—and he has ensured that there is no united front among the women. The voice of the Abbess, like Volumnia's, is, finally, the voice of patriarchy, incorporating but confining the female. Wild and Culture are at best in uneasy equilibrium. Shakespeare will return to this scene near the end of his career, in *The Winter's Tale*, and rewrite it with far deeper understanding and much more profound emotional resonance.

All's Well That Ends Well represents an intermediate stage between *The Comedy of Errors* and *The Winter's Tale*. Unlike *The Comedy of Errors* and *Two Noble Kinsmen*, in which the multiplication of males constantly reminds us of aspects of the male dilemmas in confronting the female Wild and trying to accommodate the facets of virgin, whore, and crone, *All's Well That Ends Well* is unique among Shakespeare's sixteen comedies (if one allows for the two generations of *The Winter's Tale* and counts both Ferdinand and Caliban as "lovers" in *The*

Tempest) in focusing attention on one solitary male as the potential lover. Bertram appears from the start as enmeshed in an apparently domesticated female world that threatens to engulf him. He is obviously unprepared to deal with it; retreat to safe male military service is his only recourse. In this play the sole male hope for the future is the reluctant Bertram. (The clown Lavatch may be a minor contender, but he seems to lose interest in his Isbel after he has been at court.) Bertram's reluctance is so extreme as to seem insuperable, short of a miracle. Bertram, caught between Venus, Mars, and Diana, provides a preview of the two triangles of *Two Noble Kinsmen*, and if we remember Theseus's heroic characterization of his approaching marriage as a "daring deed / Of fate in wedlock" (1.1.163–64) and a "service ... Greater than any [war]" (1.1.171–72), we may find it harder to blame the younger, callower Bertram for his reluctance.

Bertram finds himself at the beginning of his play suddenly confronted with the reality that he is the one male upon whom hopes for a fertile future rest. His world seems curiously barren. The setting is funereal. There are no living fathers (or so we think—only much later do we discover that Lafew is indeed the father of a perennially absent daughter); and the King of France is dying. There are no other young male hopefuls on the horizon of Rossillion; Parolles is clearly unhopeful from the start. Culture expects two things of Bertram—that he prove himself a man and that he marry and produce offspring. The first proves a great deal easier than the second. *All's Well* depicts with mythical resonances the progress of the young male as he negotiates the thickets of establishing male identity and integrating himself with the female world. Like Theseus, the young Bertram is torn between Venus, Diana, and Mars; but Bertram's case is more complex. Mars is dealt with relatively simply. Parolles makes a point of mentioning that he was born under the sign of Mars, and he encourages Bertram to pursue war in preference to women. Mars prevails briefly. But I believe that Bertram's hardest problem is the universal one males face of integrating the parts they perceive of the female into an acceptable woman.

To recapitulate briefly the male dilemma, the first close relationship of the male child is with his mother; if Freud is correct, she is his earliest love object. But very soon he must learn to separate himself from her, to identify with his father, and to suppress his erotic feelings for his mother in order to avoid fatal competition with his father. (This process usually involves incorporation of a belief in male superiority—a belief all too often communicated to female children as well as male—and results in the establishment of male Culture with its definition of the inferior female as marginal and Wild.) Finally, however, the male must learn to re-relate to the female if he wishes to produce progeny. This is difficult because of his earlier separation from his mother—he now fantasizes his own virgin birth—and his tendency to associate erotic feelings with inferiors, to think of sexually available women as whores. (*She Stoops to Conquer* depicts a classic comic working out of this dilemma.)

The male's progress is perilous because it plunges him into rivalry with other males, subjects him to the risk of betrayal by the previously rejected female, and finally, even when union has been effected, leaves him without the absolute certainty that he is the parent of his wife's child. Woman becomes the unknown "other," denizen of a Wild territory inhabited by seductive shadows and imagined horrors. Even the simplified stereotypes—virgin, whore, and crone— which he constructs are confusing because each of them both attracts and repels. The male's problem, then, is somehow to unify and accept the figures of virgin, erotically active woman, and asexual older woman. It is no easy task; and male fiction, when it deals with women at all, endlessly retraces the process, often emphasizing the aspect of male rivalry over involvement with the female. Recognizing these patterns in literature is illuminating for females as well as males because female worldviews have been largely conditioned by male perceptions and because both sexes must deal with the consequences of these perceptions.

It cannot be an accident that Shakespeare has changed the name of the Giletta of Boccaccio, his source, to Helen, used the name Diana for the other woman, and given the orphaned Count Beltramo a mother. He has, in effect, surrounded his Bertram with the three faces of the female, with predominantly benign aspects of the figure he refers to elsewhere as the powerful Triple Hecate. We have seen how Helens are specifically linked in Shakespeare with threatening and aggressive sexuality and with Hell and death. In *All's Well* Shakespeare carefully sets up Helena's attractive qualities—her obvious beauty, combined, as the Countess tells us, with wisdom, simplicity, honesty, and goodness. But he also establishes her strong erotic fantasy fixed on Bertram as a "bright particular star," unattainable but unforgettable. And then, in a scene that some critics find distasteful, he shows her in a bawdy conversation with Parolles, where, although she says she is not quite ready to part with her virginity, she shows great interest in the subject of how best to lose it. What audiences remember from this scene is Parolles's persuasive argument, "It is not politic in the commonwealth of nature to preserve virginity" (1.1.126–27), and his advice to dispose of it "while 'tis vendible" (1.1.154–55). In scene 3 (66–73) Lavatch overtly associates Helena with Helen of Troy in his bawdy conversation with the Countess about marriage. Earlier Shakespeare gives Helena a surprising speech of a sort usually put in the mouths of such villains as Cassius, Iago, and Edmund, in which she announces her belief in her control over her destiny, saying, "Our remedies oft in ourselves do lie / . . . . The fated sky / Gives us free scope" (1.1.216–18). Helena is clearly established as a formidable heroine. She herself visualizes a love in which "Dian [is] both herself and Love" (i.e., Venus, 1.3.212–13). Helena seems to be an integrated woman; but as such she is unacceptable to the young Bertram. She is attractive, sensual, independent, determined, and frightening, a powerful and actively erotic woman, easily confused in the male imagination with a whore or a witch, and her miraculous healing powers encourage the latter image. Small wonder that Bertram recoils from her. He is simply not ready to brave the Wild or to merge Diana with Venus.

In the course of the play, Helena becomes the personification of the answer to a favorite Renaissance riddle—wedded but not bedded, she is a woman who seems to be neither maid, wife, nor widow. Only at the very last minute does she reveal herself as an embodiment of the vision, apparently so compelling to both sexes, of the Virgin Mother—indeed, she has experienced a miraculous, if not immaculate, conception.

As the daughter of Venus, Helena is perhaps irresistible, and Bertram makes his way gradually, and I think not altogether unwillingly, toward a rapprochement with her. At the end of the play we learn, rather surprisingly, that Bertram's eye was first taken with LaFew's daughter, whose name, Maudlin or Magdalene, like Helena's, suggests worldly eroticism. It seems to have been a distant infatuation; but he says that although he never spoke to her of it, his passion for her eclipsed his vision of all other feminine presences. His amorous fantasies of Maudlin seem to have protected him from other entanglements until he is married against his will, resisting in Helena both female virginity and female sexuality.

But Bertram's travels change him. He becomes finally disillusioned with both the male camaraderie he has enjoyed with Parolles and the indulgence of male rivalry in the war to which he has retreated in his escape from the female. The Second Lord tells us that when Bertram reads the letter from his mother telling him that his wife has left Rossillion, "he chang'd almost into another man." Once his wife is powerless, he is able to love her. Removed from his mother and the aggressive sexuality of his wife, he is able to approach a woman who is not his wife and to make a sexual assignation. Now he is ready for an encounter with a female in the flesh. Curiously, he approaches Diana, clearly named as an embodiment of virginity, under the misapprehension that her name is Fontibell—a name suggesting both fertility and beauty, perhaps even Venus herself. But even when the maiden reveals herself to be Diana, he valiantly continues his pursuit.

Much is made of Diana being "wondrous cold," and Bertram urges her to be a living woman rather than a monument, to be, indeed, as her mother was when her child was conceived. It is Bertram himself, however, who has melted; and in this context, when he says to Diana, "Here, take my ring," we see it as a moment of triumph rather than betrayal. Rings are symbolic of virginity, and the exchange of rings between Bertram and his true wife, even though he does not recognize her in the dark, symbolizes the meeting of virginal lovers and constitutes a true marital bond. For the moment Bertram has merged, unknowingly, the virgin and the whore—the coldly distant Diana and his frighteningly eager wife. His parting words to Diana as he leaves her, anticipating their coming assignation, "A heaven on earth I have won by wooing thee," have a resonance that is not wholly ironic. He has, for the moment, joined Heaven and Hell.

But even now he remains reluctant. In the final confrontation he relapses into rejection of the image of the sexual female, dismissing Diana contemptuously as "a common gamester to the camp" (5.3.188), accusing her of inciting him, even as Shakespeare's play has been inciting his audience, with sweet amorous delay. He says Diana "angled" for him, "Madding [his] eagerness with her restraint, / As all impediments in fancy's course / Are motives of more fancy" (5.3.213–15). Because she retreated, he could pursue her. Helena is surely right about the persistent ambivalence of men when she reflects after her briefly blissful interlude with Bertram,

> O strange men,
> That can such sweet use make of what they hate.
> When saucy trusting of the cozen'd thoughts
> Defiles the pitchy night; so lust doth play
> With what it loathes for that which is away—
>
> (4.4.21–25)

Only in the final moments of the play, when Helena is confirmed as mother as well as "maid" and wife does Bertram, somewhat conditionally, reiterate what he has said earlier, that he loved her after he lost her (5.3.54), and consent, if she can prove her case, to "love her dearly, ever, ever dearly." Helena, returned like Proserpina from Hell, restores fertility to Rossillion with a little help from Bertram; and we hope and believe that she will succeed in turning his Hell to Heaven.

Virgin and whore are merged, but what of the crone, the asexual older woman? Shakespeare has included her in the forms of the Countess of Rossillion and the widowed mother of Diana, both relatively benign representatives of the third member of the female trinity. The Countess is a loving mother and a witty estate manager. She says she is as sorry to lose her son as her husband, but in the first line of the play she also speaks of "delivering" him—a wonderfully ambiguous term that could mean giving him new birth, or releasing him from prison, or its opposite, consigning him to his enemies. Her parting advice to him seems somewhat perfunctory, and she has almost nothing to say to him in the rest of the play. Her letters are admonitory—she tells her steward to write "to this unworthy husband of his wife." Even in the last scene, she says almost nothing to him or he to her. Her most interesting relationship is with Helena, whom she claims as a daughter, "in the catalogue of those / That were enwombed mine" (1.3.143–44). She supports Helena's pursuit of her son, and, according to Lavatch, in Helena's absence she languishes, like Demeter mourning the lost Proserpina, wishing for death. When Bertram rejects his wife, the Countess exclaims to Helena,

> He was my son,
> But I do wash his name out of my blood,
> And thou art all my child.
>   (3.2.66–68)

And although she later says that she cannot say whether Bertram or Helena is dearer to her, her actions lead us to believe it is Helena.

Diana and her widowed mother similarly present a united front. When he finally retreats from war in search of love, Bertram is faced with two solid phalanxes of women, both of which threaten his virility. The younger ones endanger his independence and even his longevity, as we are twice reminded in references by Parolles and Lavatch to the belief that the loss of semen permanently weakens men when they "spend their manly marrow" in female arms. The older mother figures expose him to both shame and the fear of engulfment.

Having escaped the maternal bonds, he senses the danger of being sucked back into childish dependency. Diana's mother actually plants the seed that grows into Helena's plan to entrap Bertram, and the widow relishes her collusion with the abandoned wife. The strong alliance between females intensifies Bertram's anxiety. Their Wild world is a mystery that he can never fully fathom. Even after her reconciliation with Bertram, Helena's last words are to the Countess, "O my dear mother, do I see you living?" (5.3.319). Bertram seems excluded from the special bond between mother and daughter.[12] If we remember that this is a male depiction of male dilemmas when confronted with the confusing faces of the female Wild, Bertram, often dismissed (by me as well as others) as an unregenerate slob, becomes somewhat more tolerable. If the imagined females are so frightening, it becomes a little easier to sympathize with his protracted and recurring reluctance, and we understand, at least in part, why his commitment to the female is so uneasy.

The effect of adding the hero's mother to Boccaccio's tale works to soften our view of Helena. The young woman's aggression, sanctioned and encouraged by a benign and sympathetic maternal figure, helps to neutralize the "stigma" of female independence and the unease aroused in some audiences by the overt sexuality of her early scene with Parolles. But the multiplication of female figures, however benign, also seems to me to add to sympathy for Bertram. Surrounded by a male/female Cultural coalition and outnumbered, Bertram at the play's end seems almost, like Coriolanus, to be reconciling himself to a kind of death. And although I cannot applaud his lack of grace in yielding to the inevitable, unlike generations of critics I now find, in light of my new feeling for his dilemma, that I have a fresh appreciation of the odds against him as I see the Countess and Helena, Diana, and her mother, and even Lafew and the King of France lined up against him, his only ally, Parolles, having already capitulated to social demands. Such a lonely male "lover" is uncommon in Shakespeare's comedy, and the young man assumes some of the poignance of a Jaques or an Antonio as he belatedly consents to assume responsibility for wife and family.

Female readers may enjoy and admire the aggressiveness and resourcefulness of Helena, but they may also muster a bit of sympathy for Bertram if they understand that the play represents an accurate view of the world as it may look to an isolated and beleaguered man at a vulnerable point of his life. Parolles has proven a weak reed as support system, and the alternatives look overwhelming.

Henry James wrote, "In the matter of wanting the world, the deeper truth is we are divided against ourselves. We are at once both attracted and repelled. We advance on the world, we shrink from the world, we desire the world, we fear the world. It is a love affair compromised by the sick excitement of mixed feelings, and the conflict is never resolved. Most of us spend our lives poised between aggression and hesitation."[13] Substitute *Wild* for *world* and we find that Shakespeare's *All's Well*, often categorized as a "dark" or "problematic" comedy, clearly reflects this human condition. It is still a comedy, however, not only by the criteria of Frye and C. L. Barber, but also because of our own conviction that all does indeed end well. As in *Much Ado About Nothing* reluctance is an understandable stage in the discovery of marital bliss and remains a pleasurable dimension of its enjoyment.

The third older woman that Shakespeare has added to an inherited plot is Paulina of *The Winter's Tale*. This play, like *The Comedy of Errors*, once again delineates in startling detail a paradigm of male experience. The women, interesting as they are, are recognizable types of male fiction: Hermione the chaste wife, Perdita, the virginal daughter, and Paulina, the wife/widow lady-in-waiting, who assumes the role of asexual mother figure. The whore is in the mind of Leontes, the central character, and the magnified image of this nightmare blots out the true picture of his faithful wife. The Wild invades his Cultural stronghold. The importance of women as male possessions in this context triggers conflicts that often seem motivated more by male rivalry than by true concern for females. But the specter of the unrulable woman is also strong. The image of the whore is activated in the imagination of Leontes by the sight of his very pregnant wife, Hermione, in intimate conversation with Polixenes, Leontes's closest friend. We have been told in some detail that the two men have been inseparable since childhood; but nonetheless Leontes now suddenly and violently rejects both friend and wife. His stable Cultural universe simply explodes. The "twinned lambs" image that has been emblematic of his childhood now comes to indicate the most violent sibling rivalry. In his revulsion toward his manifestly sexually active, very pregnant wife, he reverts to a spouse so reluctant that he seemingly cuts himself off from all hope of a future.

After his violent rejection and imprisonment of Hermione and the escape of his "friend" Polixenes, whom he has tried to have murdered, we find Leontes much more preoccupied with the idea of revenge against his male rival than with his wife: he regrets that the "harlot king" has escaped and is therefore "beyond [his] arm" and merely consoles himself with the idea that he still can "hook" his wife. Although his thoughts return in spite of himself to Polixenes, he banishes these thoughts, reflecting rather ignominiously that Polixenes is strong enough to fight back: he says,

> Fie, fie, no thought of him;
> The very thought of my revenges that way
> Recoil upon me; in himself too mighty,
> And in his parties, his alliance. Let him be,
> Until a time may serve. For present vengeance,
> Take it on her. (2.3.18–23).

But he returns obsessively to the *males*, "Camillo and Polixenes / Laugh at me; make their pastime at my sorrow: / They should not laugh if I could reach them, nor / Shall she, within my pow'r" (2.3.23–26). In his anger and suspicion Leontes has regressed to the status of a preadolescent boy. He prefers the familiar features of male rivalry to the deeply frightening prospect of a faithless wife. He is consumed with male rivalry, but he cannot repress his revulsion from female sexuality, which could hardly be more clearly expressed than in his tortured monologue in Act 1:

> There have been
> (Or I am much deceiv'd) cuckolds ere now,
> And many a man there is (even at this present,
> Now, while I speak this) holds his wife by th' arm,
> That little thinks she has been sluic'd in 's absence,
> And his pond fish'd by his next neighbor—by
> Sir Smile, his neighbor. Nay, there's comfort in't,
> Whiles other men have gates, and those gates open'd,
> As mine, against their will. Should all despair
> That have revolted wives, the tenth of mankind
> Would hang themselves. Physic for't there's none.
> It is a bawdy planet, that will strike
> Where 'tis predominant; and 'tis pow'rful—think it—
> From east, west, north, and south. Be it concluded,
> No barricado for a belly. Know't,
> It will let in and out the enemy,

With bag and baggage. Many thousand on's
Have the disease and feel't not. (1.2.190–207)

Leontes dehumanizes his wife with the conventional association of women with fortresses to be guarded, Cultural citadels, an interesting demonstration of the desire to contain the Wild once it has been incorporated—and of the traditional linkage of sex with animality. (A medieval manuscript drawing nicely epitomizes the degradation of sexuality in the image of Venus Luxuria, with a mirror and doves, hovering over a fish pond. See Fig. 25.) In 2.3 Leontes's revulsion against the female extends to Paulina, who comes to him with the hope of winning his fatherly affection at the sight of his newborn daughter and thereby reconciling him with his wife.

Paulina deserves special consideration. She does not enter the action until 2.2 after the pregnant Hermione has been imprisoned and has prematurely given birth. Paulina is the voice of truth (audiences cheer her on in this scene and the next). She insists on the innocence of Hermione, the legitimacy of the daughter, and the falsity of Leontes's accusations. She appears to Leontes as an asexual "mother," carrying a child she has not conceived or given birth to, though she has in a sense "delivered" it from its prison. But instead of seeming to him therefore harmless, she strikes him as a threatening, ungovernable man/woman. He calls her a "mankind witch" (1.3.68), an "intelligencing bawd," a crone, a henpecking wife, a "callet" (or scold), and finally "a gross hag." His daughter is a "bastard" and a "brat." His revulsion is not simply from sexuality but from all facets of the female. His inability to reconcile them sets in motion the long-delayed reunions that seem all the more miraculous when they finally occur. The female Wild sickens him, and the "sad tale" of winter projects him with seeming inevitability toward tragedy. The male has failed to secure his necessary connection with the female. He loses not only his son but also his wife and daughter.

But in the second half of *The Winter's Tale* we are plunged into a new kind of Wild, where animals—both savage and domestic—abound, a woman reigns as queen, and a pickpocket triumphantly practices his illicit trade. Satyrs dance; shepherds lavish royal hospitality; and sexual attraction is Edenic. When the Culture of the court intrudes, it is once again, as in *A Midsummer Night's Dream*, in the form of patriarchy insisting on its control of the commodities of sexual traffic. The rest of the play is concerned with rapprochement between the Wild

25. *Venus Luxuria*. Vatican Library Ms. Pal. Lat. 1726, fol. 43r. Foto Biblioteca Vaticana.

of Bohemian shepherds and the Culture of Bohemian and Sicilian courts, with Autolycus and Paulina as unlikely catalysts.

In the sixteen-year hiatus Leontes has repented his fatal rejection of wife and daughter. Paulina, now safely removed from all threatening sexuality by the loss of her husband, has become Leontes's unquestioned mentor and has subjected him to a long process of reeducation. He has consigned to this now benignly maternal figure even the power of choice of any future wife. He is finally ready for female resurrection, reunion, and the return of the promise of the future. He is ready to embrace the Wild elements he so rigorously excluded earlier.

Shakespeare shows us Leontes's first meeting with Perdita, where he is wistfully reminded of his lost wife and children but does not yet know Perdita's true identity. Surprisingly, however, the playwright does not show us the recognition scene between father and daughter, or Leontes's reconciliation with Polixenes, or Polixenes's reconciliation with his son. All these events are merely reported. The poet's efforts are concentrated on his magnificent final scene—the miraculous playing out of a universal dream of the harmonious reunion of male and female—not just of the innocent young but also of the guilt-ridden older generation, which has seemed hopelessly alienated. Male rivalries forgotten, Polixenes is again a friend, and husband and wife embrace in poignant silence while Paulina, stage manager of the event, enjoys her triumph. She—a mature woman—has orchestrated a miracle, greatly enhanced by its long delay; and although she has earlier often seemed harsh, she now reveals herself as more of a good fairy than a mankind witch.

I am profoundly ambivalent about Leontes's sense of the necessity to procure a husband for Paulina, almost as an afterthought, in the final lines of the play. From one point of view his action seems to me eminently right. She has been in danger of isolating herself, like Jaques at the end of *As You Like It*, from the happily restored families, saying,

> I, an old turtle,
> Will wing me to some wither'd bough, and there
> My mate (that's never to be found again)
> Lament till I am lost.
> (5.3.132–35)

But Leontes will have none of that. He breaks in:

O, peace, Paulina!
Thou shouldst a husband take by my consent,
As I by thine a wife. . . .
Thou hast found mine. . . .
I'll not seek far . . . to find thee
An honorable husband.

(5.3.135–44)

This move is undeniably satisfying—a proper end to comedy and one that offers some hope of a marriage of equals. And it is amazing that Leontes now insists on recognizing and welcoming all three of the women before him, daughter, wife, and "mother," as sexual beings. It is a major triumph. But from another perspective it imposes closure on Paulina's unlimited freedom by reasserting patriarchal power. It also implies that only marriage can provide for her a happy ending. The Wild will of Paulina, though it has served Culture benignly, is tamed. And for women who have reveled in her freedom, her fate leaves a sense of loss as well as gain. Like the Abbess, she is assimilated into Culture. Only Volumnia and the Countess of Rossillion remain as unmitigated crones, and both cast some shadow of death over the ends of their plays.

If we adopt the Cultural view for the moment, however, we may find even more touching than the joining of male and female arranged by Paulina the miracle wrought by Shakespeare himself in fusing in the end of this play the fragmented facets of the female. Some productions point up this fusion by doubling the roles of Hermione and Perdita, but Paulina also belongs in the constellation. Shakespeare is careful to report on Perdita's reunion with Paulina. The Third Gentleman, entrusted with describing the poignant scene, relates that Paulina "lifted the Princess from the earth, and so locks her in her embracing, as if she would pin her to her heart, that she might no more be in danger of losing" (5.2.76–78). The restoration of daughter to father, the reunion of Perdita and Paulina, and the embrace of husband and wife are all deeply moving. For me, however, the supreme moment of the play is the tender meeting of mother and daughter, long separated and estranged by circumstances beyond their control. Surely both males and females can rejoice that the lost Perdita, earlier despised by her lover's father and by her own father as either a bastard or a socially inferior shepherdess, now recognizes herself as daughter of a queen, granddaughter of the emperor of Russia, and the legitimate heir without whom there can be no future either for Bohemia or Sicilia. For the Renaissance English audience the scene would have reverberated with memories of Queen Elizabeth and with the memory that James, their present king, had derived his crown through female right of succession. For Shakespeare himself, whose only son had died earlier, leaving him only with daughters, there must have been a particular poignancy. For modern audiences there is special pleasure in the recognition that, for a brief interval at least, the images of mother, wife, and daughter—transformed from crone, whore, and virgin—merge on Shakespeare's stage into one woman, her virtue vindicated, her sexuality acknowledged and valued, and her power celebrated. It is for me the most moving moment in all Shakespearean drama.

The addition of Paulina to this tale transforms it from tragedy to romance. The ruler of the "dead" is a figure so powerful that, like Perserpina, she can orchestrate a return to life. And the witchlike crone can be reshaped into a benign mother and finally into a wife. The stage figures at the end of *The Winter's Tale* have something in common with those at the end of *The Comedy of Errors* and *All's Well That Ends Well*. Each scene features virgin, whore/wife, and crone/"mother." But whereas the Abbess of *The Comedy of Errors* presides over an uneasy truce between men and women and seems to side with the men, and the mothers of *All's Well That Ends Well* join so firmly with Helena and Diana as to seem to overwhelm Bertram, *The Winter's Tale* culminates in a harmonizing of female elements and a joyful acceptance by the males of the reconciliation of Culture and Wild. And yet, even in this play, some vague uneasiness remains. Like the Abbess, Paulina, the crone/mother, is resexualized by the gift of a husband. Unlike the "dark" comedy of *All's Well That Ends Well*, these early and late comedies cannot tolerate the unadulterated crone. A subliminal reminder of the goddess of the underworld, she takes on also the mantle of the Great Mother as she saves the newborn child and brings Hermione, like Proserpina, back to the world of the living. But for the male her power verges on excess. Marrying her off, gratifying as it is to the coupling impulse, in the end diminishes her stature. The aura of supreme female magic evaporates in the prospect of wifely domesticity. Paulina is surely the greatest of the invented older women of Shakespeare's comedies and romances, but she has a Wildness that must be comfortably contained to accommodate the demands of patriarchal Culture. But the Great Mother is not wholly suppressed. Her memory lingers hauntingly in the background, both inviting and alarming.

Shakespeare's work is distinguished by a potential multivalency of meaning that makes it adaptable to widely varying circumstances and audiences. A good example can be found in Alden Vaughan's article "Shakespeare's Indian: The Americanization of Caliban." Vaughan shows that Caliban has been successively identified by critics, actors, and audiences with a drunken beast, a fishy monster, an apish missing link, a European wild man, an American Indian, and an African slave. Various efforts have been made to pin down Shakespeare's specific knowledge of some of these categories—contemporaneous emblems of wild men, fishy monsters, and drunken beasts have been adduced; Shakespeare's knowledge of voyages of discovery in the New World has been demonstrated; and some acquaintance with early drawings or actual encounter with American Indians has been hypothesized. But I would argue that all this evidence, interesting as it is, is almost irrelevant. It does not matter that Shakespeare knew precious little about Indians and nothing about African slaves or Darwinian theory. Perhaps because they agitate aspects of "universal" human experience or probe sensitive areas of "collective unconscious," his plays condense in some mysterious way dynamic images that continue to generate meaning even in new contexts. A play like *The Tempest* with no known primary source is often particularly provocative, but different plays have burst into sudden volatility in different periods. Individual performances explicate or exfoliate plays relevant to their time, but the text remains forever pregnant, harboring the potential for discovery of new meanings or rediscovery of old ones.

Roots of potential meanings lie in specific sources, political and social constructs, personal experience, Classical, Germanic, and Celtic mythology, and, I would argue, in prehistory and the historical patterns of patriarchy.

Consider, for example, the case of Theseus. On some level Theseus is a Western cultural hero. I wondered as I was thinking about this phenomenon why I grew up imagining Theseus as noble, brave, and true, the unsullied savior of his country; and I went back to Nathaniel Hawthorne's *Tanglewood Tales*, where, as a child, I read my first story of Theseus. Hawthorne depicts the young man in glowing and unambiguous terms as a hero. After describing his killing of the Minotaur, with the indispensable aid of Ariadne, daughter of King Minos, Hawthorne adds:

> Now, some low-minded people, who pretend to tell the story of Theseus and
> Ariadne, have the face to say that this royal and honourable maiden did really

flee away, under cover of the night, with the young stranger whose life she had preserved. They say, too, that Prince Theseus (who would have died sooner than wrong the meanest creature in the world) ungratefully deserted Ariadne, on a solitary island, where the vessel touched on its voyage to Athens. But, had the noble Theseus heard these falsehoods, he would have served their slanderous authors as he served the Minotaur! Here is what Ariadne answered, when the brave Prince of Athens besought her to accompany him:

'No, Theseus!' the maiden said, pressing his hand, and then drawing back a step or two, 'I cannot go with you. My father is old, and has nobody but myself to love him. . . . I have saved you, Theseus, as much for my father's sake as for your own. Farewell! Heaven bless you!'

All this was so true, and so maiden-like, and was spoken with so sweet a dignity, that Theseus would have blushed to urge her any longer. Nothing remained for him, therefore, but to bid Ariadne an affectionate farewell, and to go on board the vessel, and set sail. (43–44)

Perhaps because he was writing for children, or perhaps because of his own fantasy needs, Hawthorne suppressed a number of details that were certainly available to Shakespeare and his contemporaries.[14] We know, for example, that Shakespeare used Thomas North's translation of Plutarch's *Life of Theseus*, which records some of the less heroic episodes of the hero's career. Relevant stories include those that Theseus early raped Helen (later of Troy), ravished Perigenia, used and abandoned Ariadne, jilted the nymph Aegles, seduced and left the Amazon Antiope, and married the Amazon Hippolyta and later Phaedra, sister of Ariadne. He deserted Phaedra for four years while he went on a mission with his friend Pirithous to kidnap Proserpina from Hades. He was responsible for the deaths of his father, Aegeus, and of his son, Hippolytus, the offspring of the marriage bed blessed by Oberon at the end of *A Midsummer Night's Dream*. Theseus died in exile and disgrace.

Shakespeare certainly knew about Ariadne—he has Julia in *Two Gentlemen of Verona* report that she moved her audience to tears by her lively performance of "Ariadne passioning / For Theseus' perjury and unjust flight" (4.4.167–68). And Oberon in *A Midsummer Night's Dream* makes specific reference to Theseus's treatment of Perigenia, Aegles, Ariadne, and Antiopa, though he blames it all on Titania (2.1.74–80). Theseus's only really heroic acts seem to have been connected with warfare and male bonding. Even the slaying of the Minotaur has been interpreted by some modern feminists as a mythical celebration of the overthrow of matriarchal rule in Crete by the patriarchal culture of the Greeks.[15] We have seen in the discussion of *Two Noble Kinsmen* Theseus's lurking ambivalence toward women and his preference for war, which is played out in the struggle between Palamon, Arcite, and Emilia, and Venus, Mars, and Diana— the struggle that prolongs delay and ends in death as well as marriage. Even in *A Midsummer Night's Dream* some ambiguity remains. And yet males and females have been content to view Theseus as a hero. As we have seen, V. A. Kolve says that Theseus was to the Middle Ages "a man seeking consciously to embody the highest chivalric ideals of his civilization" (101), and generations of critics have seen in Shakespeare's Theseus the perfect prince and the voice of reason in *A Midsummer Night's Dream*.[16] They may be right. Readers, actors, and audiences negotiate like Hawthorne between what is somehow "in the text" and their own needs and resources. Theseus can still be seen as both hero and fragmented segment of a male psyche.

Similarly, the figure of Hecate can connote the death-dealing crone, ruler of the underworld, or present a powerful image of united female qualities combined in a goddess, usually represented as triple, but in fact more multifaceted. The benign Hecate can preside over a joyous celebration like that at the end of *The Winter's Tale*, which incorporates a recognition of death, fertility, and age. But the malign Hecate, witchlike, infects the world with death and decay, blocking forces of fertility and human feeling. She is the malevolent crone incarnate. Both Hecates inhabit a Wild, intriguing and frightening to the denizens of Culture. Two traditions lie behind Shakespeare's Hecate. The most immediate and pervasive is that of the patriarchal Judeo-Christian Western world. But behind that, rooted in prehistory, is the lingering memory of the archaic matrilinear society that predates this later tradition.

There is widespread agreement on the existence of a prehistoric society in ancient Europe, which was matrilinear and nonpatriarchal if not actually matriarchal. Remnants survive in the form of religious icons apparently celebrating female fertility and in many ancient myths and legends. The presiding deity, a goddess, seems to have been conceived of from earliest times as triform in nature. Indeed, our oldest evidence suggests that threes have always been linked with women. Neolithic figures from Thrace, Cyprus, Susa, Mesopotamia, Troy, Phoenicia, Ur, and Egypt display triangles as symbols of female genitalia;[17] and the moon, with its three phases—waxing, full, and waning or dark—is closely associated with the cyclical processes of female anatomy. Accordingly, the worship of the Triple Goddess incorporated seemingly contradictory functions. As Moon Goddess she was able to be patron of virginity, benign mother, and angel of death. Foreshadower of Diana, Venus, Cybele/Demeter, and Perserpina, she ruled over sky, earth, and underworld. In her landmark work, *The Creation of Patriarchy*, Gerda Lerner meticulously weighs the evidence for early goddess worship and concludes that, at least from the fourth millennium forward, the evidence for the primacy of the Great Goddess is abundant and convincing (148).

Critics disagree on the causes of the shift from this early culture focused on the female to the patriarchal Culture of historical record. It has been attributed to the discovery of the male role in conception, to the invention of the plow, to the development of agriculture, to the incursions of Indo-European culture into Europe, and to the influence of the Judeo-Christian tradition. Lerner attributes the change to multiple causes, concluding that "in the course of the agricultural revolution the exploitation of human labor and the sexual exploitation of women become inextricably linked" (52).

But whatever the cause of the shift, it is clear that memories of goddess worship survived, consigned to a mysterious peripheral Wild never wholly subsumed by Cultural appropriation. Its continuing power may derive from the fact that the first actual experience of most human beings is a link with a great and seemingly all-powerful mother. It has been argued that the cult of the Virgin Mary was promoted as a way of incorporating the goddess into Christianity, and it is conceivable that the very concept of the Christian Trinity was an appropriation of the memory of the Triple Goddess to patriarchal uses. We know that such appropriations were commonplace. Augustine and other church fathers countenanced the possibility that early religions foreshadowed Christianity. Edgar Wind describes a sculpture of the Triple Goddess on the tomb of Pope Sixtus IV and suggests that "as pagan goddess of the moon she foreshadows the triple glory of the Christian sun" (241–58).[18] George Wither in his emblem book of 1635 provides another interesting example. Reprinting an old emblem of three interlocking crescent moons (Fig. 26), he adds as commentary:

What in this *Emblem*, that mans meanings were,
Who made it first, I neither know nor care;

For, whatsoere, he purposed, or thought,
To serve my *purpose*, now it shall be taught;
Who many times, before this Taske is ended,
Must picke out *Moralls*, where was none intended.
   This knot of *Moones* (or *Crescents*) crowned thus,
Illustrate may a Mystery to us,
Of pious use (and, peradventure, such
As from old *Hieroglyphicks*, erres not much)
Old-times, upon the *Moone*, three *names*
                          bestow'd;
Because, three diverse wayes, her selfe she show'd
And, in the *sacred-bookes*, it may be showne,
That *holy-Church*, was figur'd by the *Moone*.
                         (III)

In keeping with his interpretation, Wither has superimposed a Christian crown over the emblem and set it in a landscape featuring a Christian church. But the emblem is strikingly similar to ancient Hecate symbols such as those preserved on early coins:

Metapontum   Croton   Megarsus

The coin designs are identified as lunar symbols showing the three phases of the moon and evoking Hecate Triformis.[19] But their Wild resonances have been tamed by Wither to Culturally acceptable emblems.

    Ernest Curtius suggests, "In messianically and apocalyptically excited periods, faded symbolic figures can be filled with new life, like shades which have drunk blood" (104). The Renaissance clearly was such a period. The widespread persecution of witches is ample evidence of the terror inspired by intuitions of an archetypical female Wild. And whether or not Shakespeare was

Shee shall increase in glory, still,
Vntill her light, the world, doth fill.

ILLVSTR. XLIX.

Hat in this *Emblem*, that mans meanings were,
Who made it first, I neither know nor care ;
For, whatsoere, he purposed, or thought,
To serve my *purpose*, now it shall be taught ;
Who, many times, before this Taske is ended,
Must picke out *Moralls*, where was none intended.

This knot of *Moones* (or *Crescents*) crowned thus,
Illustrate may a Mystery to us,
Of pious use (and, peradventure, such,
As from old *Hieroglyphicks*, erres not much)
Old-times, upon the *Moone*, three *names* bestow'd ;
Because, three diverse wayes, her selfe she show'd :
And, in the *sacred-bookes*, it may be showne,
That *holy-Church*, was figur'd by the *Moone*.

26. *Interlocking Moons.* George Wither, *A Collection of Emblems.* London, 1635.
By permission of the Folger Shakespeare Library, 99.

consciously aware of conflict between the traditions of patriarchal Christianity and memories of the goddess, remnants of the struggle can be found embedded in his works. The simplistic division of female characters into the three categories of virgin, whore, and crone might be seen as a perversion of goddess worship. Vincenzo Cartari, in his collections of lore on the ancient gods, a work certainly known to Robert Burton and possibly to Shakespeare, prints two images of the Triple Goddess—one of the virginal Diana, the maternal Luna, and a veiled Hecate/Proserpina (Fig. 23). The other is a female figure identified as Diana, with the three heads of horse, dog, and boar (Fig. 17).[20] But more specifically the figure of Hecate, repeatedly invoked by name in Shakespeare—most interestingly in *Macbeth* and *A Midsummer Night's Dream*—illustrates the force of the dual traditions extremely well.

The first known Heqit seems to have been one of the oldest goddesses of predynastic Egypt, with a name derived from the Egyptian word for *intelligence* or *tribal ruler*.[21] She first appears in Greek literature in Hesiod's *Theogony*, which describes her as a pre-Olympian Titan who later shared rule with Zeus, offering aid particularly in war, athletics, and hunting (Homeric Hymns 109–13). Very early she is referred to as triform, three-faced, the Triple Hecate, who resurfaces in *A Midsummer Night's Dream* (see Fig. 27). She appears in the work of Cesare Ripa as patron of an Italian province, seated on a lion with a headdress reminiscent of Cybele's (see Figs. 28 and 16). The goddess of the meeting place of roads, she was sometimes called Trivia—Tri-Via. The trivialization of the word is a mark of the trivialization of the goddess, and trivialization is a form of taming. (One might notice in passing how often names for women become trivialized or denigrated—belle dame becomes a name for an ugly old woman, belle mère degenerates into mother-in-law, and Gran Madre is tamed into grandmother. An element of apotropaic magic may operate here, revealing the fear of identifying unpleasant "realities" about powerful Wild figures.) As moon goddess Hecate incorporated aspects reflecting its phases: waxing, full, and waning. In archaic Greece her cyclical image was also revealed in her roles as creator/preserver/destroyer. She ruled heaven, earth, and the underworld and later acquired many names in each manifestation—Luna, Cynthia, Semele, Diana, Venus, Lucina, Ceres, Juno, Proserpina, and others.[22] Indeed, she seems to have been a manifestation of that Great Goddess who predated patriarchy. In Apuleius's *The Golden Ass*, which may have contributed something to *A Midsummer Night's Dream*, the goddess appears to Lucius in his final vision saying

27. *Hecateion.* Pausanias, *Mythology and Monuments.* London, 1980, P. 378.

28. *Marca Trivisana*—Spirit of a Province. Cesare Ripa, *Iconologia*. Padua, 1611, p. 296. By permission of the Folger Shakespeare Library.

that she is called Ceres, Mother of Gods, Minerva, Venus, Diana, Proserpine, and Hecate but that her true name is Isis (see Fig. 15).[23] As the original trinity, the goddess, whatever her name, is later linked with both the Three Fates (Fig. 29) and the Three Furies (Fig. 30), and again the degeneration of her images is clear. (The Furies were, of course, finally domesticated into Eumenides in Aeschylus). The goddess was also virgin/mother/crone. My point is that in the matriarchal tradition Hecate was an extremely powerful deity, primarily benign, even as she guided her followers from birth toward inevitable death (although her underworld was not a place of punishment but a return to the mother). Only in later history and especially in the Christian era was she demoted to the status of goddess of witchcraft, still a frightening figure but more manageable because more limited. Her decline paralleled the suppression of goddess worship, the rise of patriarchy, and the general devaluation of women.

As the aspects of the Triple Goddess shrank into commonplace clichés about women, patriarchal society easily assimilated the young virgin, who became an instrument and guardian of paternal power. We have already noted patriarchal confusion about the middle term of the female trinity, confusion revealed overtly in Renaissance attitudes toward Helens. The mother figure was effectively desexualized and incorporated in the faint echo of goddess worship, which survived in the form of veneration of the Virgin Mary. She may be glimpsed also in the figure of Elizabeth, who, according to Francis Bacon, allowed "of amorous admiration but [prohibited] desire" (6:317). The crone suffered denigration and increasingly inspired fear and revulsion as she was transformed from the holy wise woman to a "revolting hag," a witch, and bearer of the evil eye. Reginald Scot, who did not believe in witches, nonetheless described women thought to be witches as "old, lame, bleare-eied, pale, fowle ... full of wrinkles; poore, sullen, superstitious ... papists [or atheists], leane, and deformed ... [melancholy], doting, scolds, [and] mad, divelish ... [odious], miserable wretches" (7). Small wonder that the degeneration of the crone eventually reached its nadir in the witch burnings of the sixteenth and seventeenth centuries.

The spirit of Hecate is preserved in both the benign, numinous, maternal pastoral scenes celebrated by Northrop Frye and the malign, hag-ridden forest of Jan Kott. The threefold imaginations of women in the patriarchal tradition—as virgin, whore, and crone—are fascinatingly adumbrated in *Macbeth* and *A Midsummer Night's Dream*. The one has no virgins or whores; the other has only

29. *Three Fates*. Vincenzo Cartari, *Le imagini de i dei de gli antichi*. Venice, 1587, p. 242. By permission of the Folger Shakespeare Library.

30. *Three Furies*. Vincenzo Cartari, *Le imagini de i dei de gli antichi*. Venice, 1587, p. 232. By permission of the Folger Shakespeare Library.

the faint echo of the crone. *Macbeth* is the simpler of the two. There are no virgins—female, that is, for Malcolm may or may not be a virgin; and a whore would be a welcome addition. Motherhood is explicitly, even gratuitously, renounced in Lady Macbeth's unsexing of herself, in the murder of Lady Macduff, and in the denial of female participation in Macduff's birth. Lady Macbeth propels herself into the category of crone with her renunciation of fertility, and, indeed, at the moment of her death female Nature itself rebels, making it possible for Birnam wood to come to Dunsinane in defiance of Natural processes. This remnant of the fragmented female inspires neither reluctance nor delay, but rather a headlong rush toward death. There remain in the play only crones. The Weird sisters, descendants of the revered Triple Goddess Wyrd of Anglo-Saxon mythology, have diminished into "secret, black, and midnight hags" (4.1.48). The name of Hecate evokes in Macbeth not the pleasures of Natural process but a world where Nature seems dead, witchcraft celebrates "Pale Hecat's off'rings, and murder stalks ghostlike towards its innocent prey" (2.1.49–56).[24] The crones are victorious, and it is a terrible and barren victory.

Hecate certainly connotes witchcraft and fatality to Shakespeare, but her name also occasionally calls up the memory of the more positive and powerful Triple Hecate of the matrilinear tradition. King Lear parallels "the sacred radiance of the sun" with the "mysteries of Hecate and the night" (1.1.110). (There is an interesting textual crux here, the history of which reveals ambivalence: Quartos 1 and 2 read "mistresse"; F1 reads "miseries"; and F2 emends, probably correctly, to mysteries.) The lovesick Orlando in *As You Like It* invokes the aid of the "thrice-crowned queen of night" with her "chaste eye," "pale sphere," and "huntress' name" (3.2.2–5). And *A Midsummer Night's Dream* presents an extended celebration of the realm of the Queen of the Night in the moon-drenched, magical landscape where fairies run with the dragon-drawn chariot of the Triple Hecate (5.1.384). Titania's very name recalls the connection of the goddess with the pre-Olympian Titans overthrown by the patriarchal Zeus. All three phases of the moon are suggested in the play—the waning old moon which postpones the marriage of Theseus and Hippolyta, the new moon which Hippolyta imagines like a silver bow new bent in heaven, and the full moon of fertility, floods, and erotic dalliance. There are virgins and a "whore," and the play's delay derives from the efforts to join the two.

The whole play might be viewed as a contest between matriarchy and patriarchy. Hippolyta suggests both the appeal of the virgin (Mary Daly defines virgin as "wild, lusty, never captured, unsubdued" [176]) and the threat of the Amazon warrior, a woman only wooed by the sword and won by injuries. Hermia and Lysander set forth from Athens in revolt against the patriarchal decree of her father and Theseus. They intend to seek refuge with his wealthy aunt beyond the forest. But the forest, magnified and mystified, becomes the focus of the play. Titania, the Faerie Queen, is a powerful and appealing force—almost equal to Oberon—and all the faeries except Puck serve the Faerie Queene. Both the pregnant votaress of Titania, who has given birth to the changeling boy, and the chaste vestal, "imperial vot'ress of Diana," are luminous presences even though physically absent. Venus and Diana can coexist, at least in theory, in this world. Ceres, the powerful and perennially fertile mother grieving for her lost Proserpina, is recalled in the disarray of Nature caused by the quarrel of Oberon and Titania. The grimmer stepmother/witch/crone is missing from the Athenian forest. The overwhelming pressure toward the fertility and consummation appropriate to Midsummer's Eve (said to have been a day for goddess celebration in Celtic prehistory) overcomes such temporary blocking forces as the resistance of Egeus and Theseus, the confusion of sex objects, and presumably even the propriety of the city-bred Hermia herself, who insists, when lying down to sleep in the forest, that her lover "lie farther off." Oberon promotes consummation for mortals and even unleashes temporarily the extramarital lusts of his wife. Peter Brook, in his landmark production of the play, made the union of Bottom and Titania an orgiastic fertility rite; and Frank Kermode wrote in 1961 that Bottom had known the love of the Triple Goddess in a vision (219). Ambiguous as it may be, the Athenian forest displays and tolerates female eroticism. Hermia, Helena, Hippolyta, and Titania, though hardly subtly characterized, show interesting and surprising aspects of the female: Hippolyta, the vanquished but undaunted Amazon; Hermia, the confident assertive woman in pursuit of a mate; Helena, also in pursuit but a self-loather unable to believe she is loved; and Titania, strong-willed, maternal, and sensuously alive. Briefly the afterimage of the Great Goddess is allowed to survive.

But all is not sweetness and light for females. Women in this play are made the objects of a considerable amount of Old Boy humor. We laugh at the fight between Hermia and Helena because it confirms clichés about what is thought of as "feminine" behavior. Oberon gets the boy. Hermia is reconciled with her father and still gets her man, but in the farcical subplot Thisby dies as the result of her similar rebellion. The female power embodied in Titania holds out temporarily against the demands of her husband; but the frightening prospect of female insurrection and the naked revelation of female lust are safely curbed in Oberon's final victory. As I have said earlier, magic is a metaphor for male power in this play. It serves to veil unpleasant realities. Titania's display of lust, a game licensed by male magic, is at first fun, but it becomes a nightmarish memory after the restorative second application of magic juice. Oberon sees the fresh and fragrant flowers Titania has used as a coronet for Bottom's hairy temples as weeping at their own "disgrace." He taunts his wife at his pleasure, and under the magic spell she begs his patience and quickly yields up the changeling boy (4.1.51–61). The male has achieved his progeny without bothering to beget it. The threat to patriarchy is quelled even in the permissive world of the forest. Primordial memories of the Faerie Queene as Great Mother and of the mysteries of Midsummer's Eve are evoked and suppressed. The forest trope allows the idea of matriarchy to surface but ends, like *Macbeth*, by denying it. The Wild is enjoyed and then safely repressed in the return to Cultural rituals.

This is not an isolated instance of male censorship of female tradition. Prospero's masque in *The Tempest* invokes aspects of the Triple Hecate. Juno represents the powers of the sky and Ceres those of the earth; but the underworld is suppressed, a censorship perhaps understandable at an engagement celebration. More striking and more puzzling, however, is the deliberate exclusion of Venus. The same play features one of the clearest and most curious examples of male appropriation of female power in Shakespeare. The playwright has given Prospero a remarkable speech proclaiming the renunciation of his magic. But before he breaks his staff, Prospero boasts resoundingly:

> I have bedimm'd
> The noontide sun, call'd forth the mutinous winds,
> And 'twixt the green sea and the azur'd vault
> Set roaring war; to the dread rattling thunder
> Have I given fire, and rifted Jove's stout oak
> With his own bolt; the strong-bas'd promontory
> Have I made shake, and by the spurs pluck'd up
> The pine and cedar. Graves at my command
> Have wak'd their sleepers, op'd, and let 'em forth
> By my so potent art. (4.1.41–50)

It is a bit of a shock to remember that these eloquent lines are based directly on Ovid, perhaps with the benefit of Golding's Elizabethan translation, and that in Ovid the lines belong to Medea, who has been specifically identified earlier in the text as a priestess of Hecate. Prospero's words mimic her prayer, addressed in Ovid to Night, the three-formed Hecate, Earth, and the Moon. In the speech, Shakespeare has edited out all traces of the goddess (whose malign memory may survive elsewhere in the play in the African Sycorax, mother of Caliban) and has claimed the elves of hills, brooks, standing lakes, and groves as instruments of patriarchal power. Indeed, in the course of the speech Prospero seems to forget even the spirits he has begun by invoking and to take credit himself for causing eclipses, storms, earthquakes, and the resurrection of the dead. Both the feats and the hubris are awesome. But the process can be traced repeatedly in Western history. It is, in fact, so familiar that it is difficult to see it clearly. Dimly remembered Wilds are lost in the light of Cultural appropriation.

We can read *Macbeth* as a demonstration of the tragic consequences of suppressing all fertile aspects of the female; but for me it is a sterile play, hostile to the feminine. I do not mean to suggest that it is not a great play, but its brilliance lies in part in its ruthless concentration on the evils of male Culture when corrupted by the sinister female Wild. We must read and admire the play, but we must also recognize and acknowledge the extreme patriarchal language behind it. New critics, almost all male, found *Macbeth* a dense, challenging, and rewarding field for the exploration of language. But for me *A Midsummer Night's Dream*, with its tolerance of both paternal and maternal voices, its intricate interweaving of languages, and its complex modulation of Natural and Cultural forces is a far richer and more resonant play. Where *Macbeth* is dark, constricted, and repressive—reflecting in some measure the male monarch it celebrates—*A Midsummer Night's Dream* is mysterious, expansive, and luminous—partaking, it is pleasant to imagine, of the euphoria inspired even in her waning years by the female ruler glanced at obliquely as "the imperial vot'ress of Diana," immune to Cupid's dart (2.1.161–64).

To read Shakespeare's women as variations of facets of the female reflected and refracted by male eyes is disturbing and enlightening. If we could add to the two faces of Hecate explored in *Macbeth* and *A Midsummer Night's Dream* a vision of what she might mean to women educated and liberated to explore and describe their own Wild world, we might revolutionize our appreciation of the Triple Hecate and redesign Culture in ways that would restore her centrality and versatility. The pains of the male in confronting the Wild might even be softened by the pleasures of consorting with it. Shakespeare comes closest to celebrating this vision at the end of *The Winter's Tale*, but even there, as we have seen, the powerful crone is demystified into wife.

Reading Shakespeare with two ears, one attuned to archaic resonances, may not always simply alert us to the suppression of women; it may also appall us at the power of women who need so much suppressing. It is inspiring and energizing to women to invoke memories of the Triple Goddess; but I am not, I must add, proselytizing for simply calling her back. Women as well as men have been unduly constrained in creating females in her image. Her variety, though rich, is far from infinite. Women should not be defined simply in terms of their sexual status or their relation to men. Virgins may be of any age, and anatomy is not synonymous with destiny. Women do not need to be either wives or mothers, and there are many other relationships untouched by the primitive archetypical paradigm.

If female audiences could learn to recognize and creatively analyze Shakespeare's deficiencies as well as his more positive achievements, to see the limitations as well as the glories of his female characters, and to understand them as fantasy figures of a mysterious Wild generated by the exigencies of male Cultural needs and fears, we might become more adventurous and more tolerant. We need to extricate ourselves from some of the "civilizing" effects of centuries of cumulative male visions, perhaps especially from those as powerful as Shakespeare's, and to explore for ourselves the Wild realm we are seen to inhabit and the Culture that regularly co-opts us. It is a very difficult task, only recently undertaken on a serious and extensive scale by women writers. Our best clues to the possible perimeters of a reimagined world are to be found in the works of such writers. Distantly removed from Shakespeare as they are, their worlds can be illuminatingly juxtaposed to his. Wild and Culture will never merge, but boundaries do shift. If we refuse to close the frontier and choose instead to explore and enjoy collisions and interactions between the two realms, we may succeed in keeping both Culture and literature alive.

Notes

INTRODUCTION

1. The story, quoted by duBois, is told by Diogenes Laertius (1:33). He attributes it to Thales but adds that it is also told of Socrates. Note also the Orthodox Hebrew Prayer: "I thank thee, O Lord, that thou has not created me a woman" (Quoted in Daly 132).

2. Mary Daly and Jane Caputi define the Wild as "Metapatriarchal Space/Time." Their more wicked and more extensive definition of the Wild describes it as "the vast Realm of Reality outside of the pinoramic world view constructed by the bores and necrophiliacs of patriarchy; true Homeland of all Elemental be-ing, characterized by diversity, wonder, joy, beauty, Metamorphic Movement and Spirit" (273, 101).

3. Ortner does not provide a diagram, but one is implied in her discussion. See Showalter (262–63) for discussion of women's views of wilds and the problems involved. Elizabeth Gould Davis quotes from Ernest Bornemann another model of male/female relations: "Men and women stand on opposite sides of a one-way window.... On the mirror side stands the man seeing only his . . . . self reflected back at him, unaware that there is anything on the other side. On the transparent side ... stands the woman, observing clearly the man ... but unable to see or realize herself" (322). The model is suggestive, but I would add that the man does indeed have some vague apprehension of the presences on the other side of his mirror.

4. The term *immasculation* was coined by Judith Fetterley (xx) to describe the process by which "women are taught to think as men, to identify with a male point of view, and to accept as normal and legitimate a male system of values, one of whose central principles is

misogyny." She suggests that the goal of feminist critics should be "to disrupt the process of immasculation by exposing it to consciousness, by disclosing the androcentricity of what has customarily passed as universal." Patrocinio Schweickart has an incisive analysis of the difficulties of feminists reading male texts and the criteria of success; see esp. 50–51.

5. In addition to Leslie Fiedler, see Adelman's *The Common Liar*. French's analysis of the "inlaw" and "outlaw" feminine is also relevant.

6. Ripa's 1603 text mentions the abundance and fertility symbolized by the figure of Africa, but he also quotes Ovid's *Metamorphoses* 4.617–20, which reads (in the Miller translation, 1:223): "As [Perseus] was flying over the sandy wastes of Libya, bloody drops from the Gorgon's head fell down; and the earth received them as they fell and changed them into snakes of various kinds. And for this cause the land of Libya is full of deadly serpents."

7. See de Beauvoir, esp. xv–xxiii. Judith Butler has a concise discussion of Beauvoir, Wittig, and Foucault on this issue. Many other critics make similar points. See, for example, Cixous and Clement, *La jeune née*, 115–16, and "Reaching," 1.

8. Elaine Showalter, in her influential essay "Feminist Criticism in the Wilderness," first published in 1981, called for feminists to move to "gynocritics," the study of writing by women (247–50).

9. See bibliographies by Elizabeth H. Hageman and Josephine Roberts. I have made no attempt to survey feminist Shakespeare criticism in great detail because this has been admirably done by Lynda Boose in "Family" (with special emphasis on feminism, Marxism, and Cultural Materialism) and by Ann Thompson's review of the stages and problems of feminist Shakespeare criticism.

10. See, for example, Juliet Dusinberre and Irene Dash. Peter Erickson and Marianne Novy, though critical of his patriarchal structures, admire Shakespeare's depictions of gender "mutuality."

11. For example, Adelman, "'Anger's My Meat,'" and Kahn.

12. See, for example, most of the essays in *The Woman's Part*, ed. Lenz et al.

13. For example, Williamson, Bamber, and French.

14. This is the implication of McLuskie (97, 98, 106). Gerda Lerner announces more generally the need for all feminist scholarship to be woman-centered (228).

15. See, for example, Kirkman 400.

16. Lerner connects the creation of patriarchy with the Neolithic development of agriculture (ch. 11); others have offered different hypotheses.

17. The aristocratic practice of farming babies out to wet nurses does not fundamentally alter the pattern of female as primary caretaker.

18. Stone 195–206; Griffin 15–17; Keller 61, 64; Merchant 148, 173; and E. G. Davis,

286–93. Susan Amussen discusses the post-Tudor polarization of hierarchies of class and gender and the withdrawal of wealthy women from the workplace (187). Linda Woodbridge concludes that "as the Renaissance ebbed, woman after woman shrank back to the cloister of the hearth" (326). And Roger Thompson, after considering the ambiguous effects of the rise of Calvinism and capitalism, sums up: "There seems little doubt that the Stuart era was one of the bleaker ones for women, certainly a decline from that golden age of Renaissance flowering under the Tudors" (5).

19. John F. Danby was one of the first to point out the conflict of the changing concept of Nature in Shakespeare and Renaissance thought (e.g., 49). For a discussion of the changes in the role of women and in the attitude toward Nature, see Chapter 2, note 19. Montaigne is, of course, the primary source for the elevation of animals, but the evidence of the phenomenon is widespread. See, for example, William R. Elton on "theriophily" (190–97), and Boas. For a recent discussion see Keith Thomas, "The Narrowing Gap" (*Man and the Natural World* 121–36).

CHAPTER ONE

1. See Daley, "Where Are the Woods in *As You Like It?*"

2. Cassirer 83, 96.

3. René Girard and Eve Kosofsky Sedgwick are extremely helpful in analyzing the triangulation of desire which occurs so frequently in Shakespeare, the modification of what appears on the surface to be a male/female love affair by the presence of a mediator or third party, internal or external to the work, who alters the structure—in Shakespeare most often into a struggle between males. This phenomenon is discussed further in Chapter 3.

4. Alan Sommers suggests that Tamora "all but personifies riotous nature." She epitomizes the uncontrolled nature of which Marilyn French says that Shakespeare had a fear "that seems pathological to some of his twentieth-century critics" (340).

5. See Boose's fine analysis of the father's dilemma in "The Father and the Bride."

6. Susan Rubin Suleiman raises the intriguing possibility that, as women are sacrificed by men for art, women may similarly sacrifice children.

7. Dedication and ff. A1 and A2. I am indebted to Richard Marienstras's *New Perspectives on the Shakespearean World* for calling this volume to my attention. Marienstras explores in rich detail Elizabethan forest laws and the legal definition of outsiders and foreigners.

8. See Gail Paster's article for a discussion of this topos.

9. See Chapter 3 for further discussion of this play. Louis Montrose's discussion of the

ambiguity of feeling toward Queen Elizabeth in "'Shaping Fantasies'" illuminates the play's contradictory signals.

10. See Jeanne Addison Roberts, *Shakespeare's English Comedy*, esp. ch. 4.

11. Nancy Cotton (324–25) relates the horned god to the devil and the images of women to the witches of black masses.

12. Peter Erickson has a good description of the patriarchal quality of the forest (24–38).

13. Skirts were not, of course, uniquely female. Elizabethans would have been more accustomed than modern audiences to male judges, courtiers, and clergy in robes with skirts.

14. Janet Adelman's "Born of Woman" is a subtle and persuasive analysis of the male realm of the play; Marjorie Garber casts light from a different direction in "Macbeth: The Male Medusa" (87–123).

15. See Jeanne Addison Roberts, "'Wife' or 'Wise,'" for the addition of one female reference to the play. Stephen Orgel's introduction to the Oxford edition of *The Tempest* provides further discussion of women. I return to this play at greater length in Chapter 2.

16. See Susan Green's perceptive study of the role of the Jailer's daughter. For a more detailed discussion of *The Two Noble Kinsmen*, see Chapter 3 below.

17. Lawrence Stone discusses the growing subordination of women in the early seventeenth century (195–206). Carol MacCormack stresses the importance of Protestantism in encouraging the harnessing of Nature (6). Susan Griffin links the scientific revolution to the persecution of witches (esp. 15–17), as does Carolyn Merchant (esp. 148). And Evelyn Fox Keller concludes of the seventeenth century that the "nexus among ideologies of woman, nature, and science ... is essential to an understanding ... of the time." She adds that science polarized the sexes, set mind against nature, and severely curtailed the economic, political, and social options for women (61). See also my Introduction, note 18.

CHAPTER TWO

1. John Donne's poem *Progresse of the Soul* elaborates this heretical fantasy at great length.

2. Passmore III. I.H. is quoted by E. K. Chambers (4:254–55). See the final section of this chapter for further discussion.

3. For an extended analysis of Ovid's metamorphoses, see Irving Massey, *The Gaping Pig*, and for a full-scale discussion of Shakespeare's metamorphoses see Carroll.

4. Victor Turner suggests that this process may be a regular feature of Culture—a force compelling the inhabitants to rethink and thereby enabling change and growth. His conclusion, that "one dies *into* nature to be reborn *from* it," illuminates the growth of Katherina and Petruchio (252–53, 256).

5. John Bean discusses the romance qualities of the play in Lenz et al., eds., esp. 66.

6. In *Titus Andronicus*, 2.2 marks a transition from town to forest; 4.1 and 2 in *Love's Labor's Lost* precede the scenes of male capitulation; 4.1.103–39 in *A Midsummer Night's Dream* mark the end of the "dream"; and 2.1 and 4.2 in *As You Like It*, with their hunting themes, punctuate the tamer Wild of Arden Forest.

7. According to Bruno Bettelheim, children in fairy tales are turned into animals (he cites hedgehogs and porcupines; shrews seem to fit into the same category) by parental anger (70).

8. Veronese's painting is reproduced in Robertson, plate 6. Another English version of the woman riding the man can be found in "The Brideling, Sadling, and Ryding of a rich Churl in Hampshire. . . . by Judith Philips," 1595, reprinted in Rosen (215).

9. The full title of the anonymous play is *A Pleasant Conceited Historie, called The Taming of a Shrew*. Whether this play is a source, an analog, or a bad quarto of Shakespeare's play is still being debated, but opinion seems to be moving toward the idea of a bad quarto.

10. See *A Midsummer Night's Dream* 5.1.44–45 and *Titus Andronicus* 5.2.203. Shakespeare's association of centaurs with the story of how the centaurs invited to the wedding feast of Theseus's friend Pirithous tried to carry off the bride, Hippodamia (note the horse allusion in "hippo"), and thus precipitated a bloody battle is apparent in both references.

11. Quoted by Bullough (1:169–73), as a source of *Venus and Adonis*.

12. See Jeanne Addison Roberts, "Horses and Hermaphrodites," 170, for reproduction of an alchemical sign that also features sun and moon and a body with male and female heads.

13. Marianne Novy has an illuminating analysis of this unusual comic conclusion (60–61).

14. Renaissance paintings of Cleopatra also sometimes seem to evoke memories of the goddess Isis with her serpent attendants. See Garrard, ch. 4. The famous Rainbow portrait of Elizabeth features either a serpent or a serpent design on the queen's sleeve.

15. Both lion and goddess become trivialized. See, for example, the reproduction of the relief of Cybele in which the once mighty lion has become a pet lap dog, Pausanias 48.

16. Valerie Traub demonstrates that even in the Henriad Falstaff is degraded by being constructed as a female other, a degradation that could be seen as culminating in his reduction from female to animal.

17. Other representations of horned female figures are to be found in Neumann (44, 49). Mircea Eliade (164) says that the horns of oxen always denote the Great Goddess. Nancy Cotton suggests that the horned Falstaff is reminiscent of the devil at a witches' sabbath. In earlier legends the Horned God, usually equipped with deer horns, is the consort of the Great Goddess. Curiously, as the horned animal may move from an emblem of virility to an emblem of castration, so the cuckoo, whose name is thought to be reflected in the word *cuckold*, may be an invader of another bird's nest and therefore quintessentially male; but it is also peculiar in that it is indistinguishable from the female in its external anatomy (Miller E3) and therefore ostensibly lacking in virility—a kind of pseudo-eunuch.

18. Peter Erickson sees the male hunt as emblematic of male solidarity and horns as signs of potency. He also describes *As You Like It* as "primarily a defensive action against female power" (24, 37).

19. For discussion of this point see Park.

20. The boy "bride" in the Induction to *The Taming of the Shrew* is merely doing what all boy actors playing women in Shakespeare do, and so his role seems different from those of other disguised male characters; but he too feels endangered by the threatened sexual degradation of his role.

21. Some early Greek representations of centaurs have human forelegs and equine hind legs and therefore presumably two sets of male genitals. See duBois (82) for illustration.

22. Shakespeare probably got the figure of the dreadful Sagittary from William Caxton's translation of Raoul Le Fevre's *The Recuile of the Histories of Troie* 3:fol. xvii verso.

23. There is some evidence of the demystification of Amazons over time. In Greek art they were usually depicted heroically, either in battle or being carried off triumphally by victorious male heroes. Penthesilea in battle is a favorite figure. By contrast, Shakespeare has Sir Toby Belch refer ironically to the diminutive Maria as his Penthesilea (*Twelfth Night* 2.3.177).

24. For further discussion of *Two Noble Kinsmen* see Chapter 3.

25. Walker (87), argues that the mare of nightmare is related to earlier versions of Mary, the Near Eastern goddess Mari, and an old name for a clan matriarch, mara or mair, the origin of the French maire, English mayor.

26. The relationship of *King Lear* to the skeptical tradition of "theriophily" or elevation of animals is spelled out in detail in Elton (190–97). I use the term *horizontalizing* by analogy with Lovejoy's *temporalizing*.

27. Reuben Brower in *Fields of Light* speaks eloquently of the fluidity and merging of states of being and forms of life in this play (see esp. 112–17).

28. Whether or not we are to suppose that Ariel has taken the form of Ceres depends on the interpretation of his line "When I presented Ceres" (4.1.166). He may have actually impersonated the goddess or perhaps simply acted as producer of the masque.

CHAPTER THREE

1. Plautus, "The Twin Menaechmi."

2. For reproduction of a Roman second-century A.D. statue of the multibreasted Diana of Ephesus, see Neumann, Plate 35.

3. Page duBois and William Blake Tyrrell have extensive discussions of the significance of Amazons in classical Greece. For a survey and discussion of Amazons in Elizabethan literature see Wright, Shepherd, and Jackson. See also Figs. 20 and 21.

4. Many descriptions of Amazons were available to Elizabethans. The account of the Amazon attack on Athens is in North's translation of Plutarch's "Life of Theseus." A full narration of Theseus's war with the Amazons is to be found in Boccaccio Bk. I. He also furnishes a gloss (48) describing Amazons as women dedicated to war, who have killed their males and cut off their right breasts to facilitate the shooting of bows. He adds that though liberated, they are unable to remain free (21).

5. Schleiner outlines the limited identification of Elizabeth with Amazons; and Montrose traces the extreme ambiguity of Elizabethan male feelings toward their sovereign.

6. See, for example, *Twelfth Night* 1.1.17–22.

7. Tyrrell explains the significance of the classical Amazon as an expression of the patriarch's fear of what his daughter, whom he wants to preserve intact as his own possession, may become if he does not secure for her a husband, giving up his control over her for the sake of profit and progeny.

8. Theseus does this at the instigation of Pirithous, but it still reveals a greater willingness to free the spirit of Mars than that of Venus.

9. "A tragicomedy is not so called in respect of mirth and killing, but in respect it wants deaths, which is enough to make it no tragedy, yet brings some near it, which is enough to make it no comedy." The preface is omitted in the second, revised edition of 1629, which may suggest that the definition no longer seemed relevant or adequate.

10. The poem is reprinted by Shaaber.

11. Aeschylus lines 681–89, p. 56. For a discussion of the pun, see Hogan (65–66).

12. A recent production at Stratford-upon-Avon attempted to mitigate Bertram's isolation at the end by having him come and embrace the embracing women, but he was still perceived as outsider.

13. Quoted by Gornick (54).

14. For a study of Theseus's reputation in the Renaissance, see Pearson.

15. For example, Chernin (81).

16. See, for example, Brooks (cii–cv).

17. See Neumann, Plates 6, 7, 10, 11, 13, 14, 16, and 17.

18. Wind also discusses the influence of the church fathers in establishing pagan/Christian links.

19. These coins are sketched in Goblet d'Alviella (183). The Hecate image continued to be powerful at least into the romantic period, although with altered connotations. William Blake's painting of the Triple Hecate (1794?) shows her, according to Martin Bulin (5–6), as superstition—the product of woman in the fallen world. Blake's painting is reproduced in Bulin (Plate 9). Freud speaks of early Cretan worship of the great mother-goddess and the later appropriation of her powers by male gods ("Moses and Monotheism" 46n). He also connects the archaic Cretan period to the pre-Oedipal phase in female development ("Female Sexuality" 43).

20. Burton refers to images from this work and advises his readers to "see more in Carterius and Verdurius" (408). Antoine Du Verdier's translation of an earlier edition of Cartari into French appeared in 1581.

21. Budge (159) and Walker (50). Walker also suggests that the word *heq* may be related to *hag* (53), which she relates in turn to the Greek *hagia* or holy one. Most dictionaries track *hag* rather to Germanic roots with the basic meaning *wood woman* or *wild woman*.

22. See Linche esp. fols. Hiii verso and Mii verso, for descriptions of Diana and the Gran Madre.

23. The picture of Isis (Fig. 14) conforms closely to Apuleius's description (547). Both Nature and Isis feature moon symbols, one on her forehead, the other on her gown.

24. The scene in which Hecat appears in *Macbeth* (3.5) seems to have been interpolated from Middleton's *The Witch*, but the Weird sisters are clearly her ministers, and her name is invoked at 2.1.52 and 3.2.41. Presumably a play warning against witchcraft would have pleased King James, who believed that devilish practices had never been so rife and were a sign of the approach of the "consummation of the worlde" (*Demonologie* 81).

Works Cited

Adelman, Janet. "'Anger's My Meat': Feeding, Dependency, and Aggression in *Coriolanus*." In *Representing Shakespeare: New Psychoanalytic Essays*. Ed. Murray Schwartz and Coppelia Kahn. Baltimore: Johns Hopkins University Press 1980, 129–49.

———. "'Born of Woman': Fantasies of Maternal Power in *Macbeth*." In *Cannibals, Witches, and Divorce: Estranging the Renaissance*. Ed. Marjorie Garber. Baltimore: Johns Hopkins University Press, 1987, 90–121.

———. *The Common Liar: An Essay on "Antony and Cleopatra."* New Haven: Yale University Press, 1973.

Aeschylus. "Agamemnon," *Oresteia*. Trans. Richard Lattimore. Chicago: University of Chicago Press, 1953. Reprint. 1967.

Amussen, Susan Dwyer. *An Ordered Society: Gender and Class in Early Modern England*. New York: Blackwell, 1988.

Apuleius. *The Golden Ass*. Trans. W. Adlington (1566). Ed. Rev. S. Gaselee. London: Heinemann, 1925.

Ardener, Edwin. "Belief and the Problem of Women," and "The Problem Revisited." In *Perceiving Women*. Ed. Shirley Ardener. London: Malaby, 1975, 1–17, 19–28.

Bacon, Francis. "De Augmentis Scientiarum," and "In Felicem Memoriam Elizabethae." In *Works*. Ed. and trans. James Spedding et al. 7 vols. London: Longmans et al., 1868–90, 4:320, 6:31.

Bamber, Linda. *Comic Women, Tragic Men: A Study of Gender and Genre in Shakespeare*. Stanford: Stanford University Press, 1982.

Barber, C. L. *Shakespeare's Festive Comedy: A Study of Dramatic Form And Its Relation to Social Custom* 1959. Reprint. Princeton: Princeton University Press, 1972.

Barton, Anne. "Introduction to *Troilus and Cressida*." In *The Riverside Shakespeare*. Ed. G. Blakemore Evans et al. Boston: Houghton Mifflin, 1974. 443–47.

Bean, John C. "Comic Structure and the Humanizing of Kate in *The Taming of the Shrew*." In *The Woman's Part: Feminist Criticism of Shakespeare*. Ed. Carolyn Ruth Swift Lenz et al. Urbana: University of Illinois Press, 1980. 65–78.

Bettelheim, Bruno. *The Uses of Enchantment*. 1976. Reprint. New York: Vintage, 1977.

Boas, George. *The Happy Beast in French Thought of the Seventeenth Century*. Baltimore: Johns Hopkins University Press, 1933.

Boccaccio, Giovanni. *Teseida delle Nozze d'Emilia*. Trans. Bernadette Marie McCoy as *The Book of Theseus*. New York: Medieval Text Association, 1974.

Boose, Lynda E. "The Family in Shakespeare Studies; or—Studies in the Family of Shakespeareans; or—The Politics of Politics." *Renaissance Quarterly* 40 (Winter 1987): 707–42.

———. "The Father and the Bride in Shakespeare." *Papers of the Modern Language Association* 97 (1982): 325–47.

Bradbrook, Muriel C. *The Growth and Structure of Elizabethan Comedy*. 1955. Reprint. Baltimore: Penguin, 1963.

"The Brideling, Sadling and Ryding, of a rich Churle in Hampshire by ... Judith Philips. . . ." 1595. In *Witchcraft*. Ed. Barbara Rosen. London: Arnold, 1969, 214–18.

Brooks, Harold F. Introduction to *A Midsummer Night's Dream*. The Arden Shakespeare. London: Methuen, 1979, xxi–cxliii.

Brower, Reuben. *Fields of Light*. New York: Oxford University Press, 1951.

Bry, Johann Theodor de. *Proscenium vitae humanae*. Frankfurt, 1627.

Budge, E. A. Wallis. *The Dwellers on the Nile*. London: Religious Tract Society, 1926.

Bulin, Martin. *William Blake*. London: Tate Gallery, 1966.

Bullough, Geoffrey. *Narrative and Dramatic Sources of Shakespeare*. 8 vols. London: Routledge & Kegan Paul, 1957–75, 1:69–108, 111–58.

Burton, Robert. *The Anatomy of Melancholy*. Ed. A. R. Shillets. Intro. A. H. Bullen. 3 vols. London: Bell, 1893, 3:408. (From 1651 2d ed., with author's corrections.)

Butler, Judith. "Variations on Sex and Gender: Beauvoir, Wittig, and Foucault." In *Feminism as Critique: On the Politics of Gender*. Ed. Seyla Benhabib and Drucilla Cornell. Minneapolis: University of Minnesota Press, 1987. 128–42.

Carroll, William C. *The Metamorphoses of Shakespearean Comedy*. Princeton: Princeton University Press, 1985.

Cartari, Vincenzo. *Les images des Dieux des ancients*. Trans. and augmented by Antoine Du Verdier. Lyons, 1581.

———. *Le imagini de i dei de gli antichi*. . . . Venice, 1571.

———. *Le imagini de i dei de gli antichi*. Venice, 1587.

Cassirer, Ernst. *The Individual and the Cosmos in Renaissance Philosophy*. Trans. with intro. by Mario Domandi. New York: Harper & Row, 1963.

Chambers, E. K. *The Elizabethan Stage*. 4 vols. Oxford: Clarendon, 1923.

Chaucer, Geoffrey. "The Knight's Tale." In *Complete Works*. Ed. F. N. Robinson. Boston: Houghton Mifflin, 1933.

Chernin, Kim. *Reinventing Eve: Modern Woman in Search of Herself*. New York: Times Books, 1987.

Chodorow, Nancy. *The Reproduction of Mothering*. Berkeley: University of California Press, 1978.

Cixous, Hélène. "The Laugh of the Medusa." *Signs: Journal of Women in Culture* 1 (Summer 1976): 875–93.

———. "Reaching the Point of Wheat: A Portrait of the Artist as a Maturing Woman." *New Literary History* 19 (1987): 1–21.

Cixous, Hélène, and Catherine Clement. *La jeune née*. Paris: Union Generale d'Editions, 1975.

Clarke, Mary Cowden. *The Girlhood of Shakespeare's Heroines*. 5 vols. New York: Armstrong, 1891.

Clemen, Wolfgang. *The Development of Shakespeare's Imagery*. 1951. Reprint. London: Methuen, 1977.

Coleridge, Samuel Taylor. *Shakespearean Criticism*. Ed. Thomas M. Raysor. 2 vols. London: Constable, 1930.

Cotton, Nancy. "Castrating (W)itches: Impotence and Magic in *The Merry Wives of Windsor*." *Shakespeare Quarterly* 38 (1987): 320–26.

Curtius, Ernst Robert. *European Literature and the Latin Middle Ages*. Trans. Willard R. Trask. 1953. Reprint. Princeton: Princeton University Press, 1973.

Daley, A. Stuart. "Where Are the Woods in *As You Like It?*" *Shakespeare Quarterly* 34 (1983): 172–80.

Daly, Mary. *Beyond God the Father: Toward a Philosophy of Women's Liberation*. Boston: Beacon, 1973.

Daly, Mary, and Jane Caputi. *Websters' First New Intergalactic Wickedary of the English Language*. Boston: Beacon, 1987.

Danby, John F. *Shakespeare's Doctrine of Nature*. London: Faber and Faber, 1949.

Dante Alighieri. "Inferno." In *The Divine Comedy*. Trans. Charles S. Singleton. 3 vols. Princeton: Princeton University Press, 1970.

Dash, Irene G. *Wooing, Wedding, and Power: Women in Shakespeare's Plays*. New York: Columbia University Press, 1981.

Davis, Elizabeth Gould. *The First Sex*. New York: Putnam's, 1971.

Davis, Walter R. *A Map of Arcadia: Sidney's Romance in Its Tradition*. New Haven: Yale University Press, 1965.

de Beauvoir, Simone. *The Second Sex*. Ed. H. M. Parshley. 1952. Reprint. New York: Vintage, 1974.

The Deceyte of Women. London, [1561?].

Dinesen, Isak. *Out of Africa*. New York: Modern Library, 1952.

Dinnerstein, Dorothy. *The Mermaid and the Minotaur: Sexual Arrangements and Human Malaise*. New York: Harper, 1976.

duBois, Page. *Centaurs and Amazons*. Ann Arbor: University of Michigan Press, 1982.

Dusinberre, Juliet. *Shakespeare and the Nature of Women*. New York: Barnes and Noble, 1975.

Eliade, Mircea. *Patterns in Comparative Religion*. Trans. Rosemary Sheed. New York: Sheed and Ward, 1958.

Elton, William R. *King Lear and the Gods*. 1966. Reprint. Lexington: University Press of Kentucky, 1988.

Empson, William. "Timon's Dog." In *The Structure of Complex Words*. Ann Arbor: University of Michigan Press, 1967, 175–84.

Erickson, Peter. *Patriarchal Structures in Shakespeare's Drama*. Berkeley: University of California Press, 1985.

Fetterley, Judith. *The Resisting Reader: A Feminist Approach to American Fiction*. Bloomington: Indiana University Press, 1978.

Fiedler, Leslie. *The Stranger in Shakespeare*. New York: Day and Stein, 1972.

Fletcher, John. *The Faithful Shepherdess*. 1610. 2d ed. London, 1629.

Fletcher, Joseph. *The Historie of the Perfect-Cursed-Blessed Man*. London, 1623.

Fossey, Dian. *Gorillas in the Mist*. Boston: Houghton Mifflin, 1983.

Foucault, Michel. *The History of Sexuality*. Volume 1: An Introduction. Trans. Robert Hurley. New York: Vintage, 1980.

———. *Madness and Civilization: A History of Insanity in the Age of Reason*. Trans. Richard Howard. New York: New American Library, 1967.

French, Marilyn. *Shakespeare's Division of Experience*. New York: Summit, 1981.

Freud, Sigmund. "Female Sexuality" (1931). Reprinted in *Women and Analysis*. Ed. Jean Strouse. New York: Grossman, 1974, 39–56.

———. "Moses and Monotheism." In *The Standard Edition of the Complete Psychological Works*. Ed. and trans. James Strachey. 24 vols. London: Hogarth, 1953–74, 23:7–137.

———. "The Question of Lay Analysis." In *Standard Edition*, 20:183–250.

———. "The Theme of the Three Caskets." In *Standard Edition*, 12:291–301.

———. "The Uncanny." In *Standard Edition*, 17:219–52.

Friedman, Herbert. *A Bestiary for Saint Jerome: Animal Symbolism in European Religious Art*. Washington, D.C.: Smithsonian, 1980.

Frye, Northrop. *Anatomy of Criticism*. 1957. Reprint. Princeton: Princeton University Press, 1973.

———. *The Secular Scripture*. Cambridge, Mass.: Harvard University Press, 1976.

Garber, Marjorie. *Shakespeare's Ghost Writers: Literature as Uncanny Causality*. New York: Methuen, 1987.

Gardiner, Judith Kegan. "On Female Identity and Writing by Women," In *Writing and Sexual Difference*. Ed. Elizabeth Abel. Chicago: University of Chicago Press, 1982. 177–91.

Garrard, Mary D. *Artemisia Gentileschi: The Image of the Female Hero in Italian Baroque Art*. Princeton: Princeton University Press, 1988.

Gascoigne, George. "Supposes." In *The Posies of George Gascoigne*. London, 1575.

Gilligan, Carol. *In a Different Voice*. 1982. Reprint. Cambridge, Mass.: Harvard University Press, 1983.

Girard, René. *Deceit, Desire, and the Novel: Self and Other in Literary Structure*. Trans. Yvonne Freccero. Baltimore: Johns Hopkins University Press, 1965.

Goblet d'Alviella, Eugene Felicien Albert. *The Migration of Symbols*. London: Constable, 1894.

Goldberg, Jonathan. *Voice Terminal Echo*. New York: Methuen, 1986.

Gornick, Vivian. "The World and Our Mothers." *New York Times Book Review*, November 22, 1987, pp. 1, 52–54.

Graves, Robert. *The White Goddess: A Historical Grammar of Poetic Myth*. 1966. Reprint. New York: Farrar, Straus, and Giroux, 1987.

Green, Susan. "'A mad woman? We are made, boys!' The Jailer's Daughter in *The Two Noble Kinsmen*." In *Shakespeare, Fletcher, and "The Two Noble Kinsmen."* Ed. Charles H. Frey. Columbia: University of Missouri Press, 1989, 121–32.

Greenblatt, Stephen. "Fiction and Friction." In *Shakespearean Negotiations*. Berkeley: University of California Press, 1988.

Griffin, Susan. *Woman and Nature: The Roaring Inside Her.* New York: Harper, 1980.

Hageman, Elizabeth H. "Recent Studies in Women Writers of the English Seventeenth Century (1604–1674). *English Literary Renaissance* 18 (Winter 1988): 138–67.

———. "Recent Studies in Women Writers of Tudor England (1485–1603)." *English Literary Renaissance* 14 (Autumn 1984): 409–25.

Harding, Esther M. *Women's Mysteries: Ancient and Modern.* 1955. Reprint. London: Rider, 1971.

Hartman, Geoffrey. "Evening Star and Evening Land." In *The Fate of Reading and Other Essays.* Chicago: University of Chicago Press, 1975, 147–78.

Hawthorne, Nathaniel. *Tanglewood Tales.* 1853. New York: Dutton, 1950, Reprint. 1966.

Heilman, Robert B. *This Great Stage: Image and Structure in "King Lear."* Baton Rouge: Louisiana State University Press, 1948.

Hesiod. *The Homeric Hymns and Homerica.* Trans. Hugh G. Evelyn-White. London: Heinemann, 1914.

Hogan, James C. *A Commentary on the Complete Greek Tragedies: Aeschylus.* Chicago: University of Chicago Press, 1984.

Jackson, Gabriele Bernhard. "Topical Ideology: Witches, Amazons, and Shakespeare's Joan of Arc." *English Literary Renaissance* 18 (1988): 40–65.

Jardine, Lisa. *Still Harping on Daughters: Women and Drama in the Age of Shakespeare.* Brighton, Sussex: Harvester, 1983.

Kahn, Coppélia. *Man's Estate: Masculine Identity in Shakespeare.* Berkeley: University of California Press, 1980.

Keats, John. "Written before Re–Reading *King Lear.*" In *Poetical Works.* 2 vols. London: Bell, 1886, 2:482–83.

Keller, Evelyn Fox. *Reflections on Gender and Science.* New Haven: Yale University Press, 1985.

Kermode, Frank. "The Mature Comedies." In *Early Shakespeare.* Ed. John Russell Brown and Bernard Harris. London: Arnold, 1961.

King James I. *Demonologie.* Edinburgh, 1597.

Kirkman, J. "Animal Nature versus Human Nature in *King Lear.*" *New Shakespeare Society's Transactions* 7 (1877–79): 385–408.

Knights, L. C. *How Many Children Had Lady Macbeth?* Cambridge, Eng.: Minority Press, 1933.

Kolve, V. A. *Chaucer and the Imagery of Narrative.* Stanford: Stanford University Press, 1984.

Kott, Jan. *Shakespeare Our Contemporary*. Trans. Boleslaw Taborski. New York: Doubleday, 1966.

Laertius, Diogenes. *Lives of Eminent Philosophers*. Trans. R. D. Hicks. 2 vols. London: Loeb, 1925.

LeFevre, Raoul. *The Recuile of the Histories of Troie*. Trans. William Caxton. London, 1553.

Lenz, Carolyn Ruth Swift, et al., eds. *The Woman's Part: Feminist Criticism of Shakespeare*. Urbana: University of Illinois Press, 1980.

Lerner, Gerda. *The Creation of Patriarchy*. New York: Oxford University Press, 1986.

Lessing, Doris. *Children of Violence*. 5 vols., including *Martha Quest, A Proper Marriage, A Ripple from the Storm*, and *Landlocked*. 1952–58. Reprint. New York: New American Library, 1970. *The Four-Gated City*. 1969. Reprint. New York: Bantam, 1970.

Le Ver, Girard. *Vraye description de trois voyages*. Amsterdam, 1600.

Linche, Richard. *The Fountaine of Ancient Fiction*. London, 1599. (English adaptation of Cartari, without illustrations.)

Lovejoy, A. O. *The Great Chain of Being: A Study of the History of an Idea*. New York: Harper, 1936.

MacCormack, Carol P. "Nature, Culture, and Gender: A Critique." In *Nature, Culture, and Gender*. Ed. Carol P. MacCormack and Marilyn Strathern. Cambridge: Cambridge University Press, 1980, 1–24.

McLuskie, Kathleen. "The Patriarchal Bard: Feminist Criticism and Shakespeare—*King Lear* and *Measure for Measure*." In *Political Shakespeare: New Essays in Cultural Materialism*. Ed. Jonathan Dollimore and Alan Sinfield. Ithaca: Cornell University Press, 1984.

Mandeville. *See* Maundeville.

Manwood, John. *A Treatise and Discourse of the Lawes of the Forests*. London, 1598.

Marienstras, Richard. *New Perspectives on the Shakespearean World*. Trans. Janet Lloyd. Cambridge: Cambridge University Press, 1985. (French original, 1981.)

Markham, Beryl. *West with the Night*. Berkeley: North Point, 1983.

Massey, Irving. *The Gaping Pig: Literature and Metamorphosis*. Berkeley: University of California Press, 1976.

Maundeville, John. *The Voiage and Travayle*. Ed. John Ashton. London: Pickering and Chatto, 1887. (Copy of Pyson's ed. [149–] with facsimile illustrations.)

Maxwell, J. C. "Animal Imagery in *Coriolanus*." *Modern Language Review* 42 (1947): 417–21.

Merchant, Carolyn. *The Death of Nature*. San Francisco: Harper & Row, 1980.

A Merry Jeste of a shrewde and curst Wyfe, Lapped in Morrelles Skin for Her Good behavyour. London, 1580.

Miller, Frank. "The Wonderful World of Animals." *Washington Post*, February 2, 1990, p. E3.

Moers, Ellen. *Literary Women.* Garden City, N.Y.: Doubleday, 1976.

Montaigne, Michel de. *The Essayes.* Trans. John Florio. London, 1603.

Montrose, Louis Adrian. "'Shaping Fantasies': Figurations of Gender and Power in Elizabethan Culture." *Representations* 2 (1983): 61–94.

Neumann, Erich. *The Great Mother: An Analysis of the Archetype.* Trans. Ralph Manheim. 1955. Reprint. Princeton: Princeton University Press, 1974.

Novy, Marianne. *Love's Argument: Gender Relations in Shakespeare.* Chapel Hill: University of North Carolina Press, 1984.

Ong, Walter J. *Fighting for Life.* Ithaca: Cornell University Press, 1981.

Orgel, Stephen. "Nobody's Perfect: Why Did the English Stage Take Boys for Women?" *South Atlantic Quarterly* 88 (Winter 1989): 7–28.

————, ed. *The Tempest.* Oxford: Clarendon, 1987.

Ortega y Gasset, José. *The Dehumanization of Art and Other Writings on Art and Culture.* Garden City, N.Y.: Doubleday, 1956.

Ortner, Sherry. "Is Female to Male as Nature Is to Culture?" *Feminist Studies* 1 (1973): 5–32. Revised version in *Woman, Culture, and Society.* Ed. Michelle Zimbalist Rosaldo and Louise Lamphere. Stanford: Stanford University Press, 1974, 65–87.

Ovid. *Metamorphoses.* Antwerp, 1591.

————. *Metamorphoses.* Trans. Frank Justus Miller. 1916. 2 vols. Reprint. Cambridge, Mass.: Harvard University Press, 1977.

Park, Clara Claiborne. "As We Like It: How a Girl Can Be Smart and Still Popular." In *The Woman's Part: Feminist Criticism of Shakespeare.* Ed. Carolyn Ruth Swift Lenz et al. Urbana: University of Illinois Press, 1980. 100–116.

Passmore, John. *Man's Responsibility for Nature.* London: Duckworth, 1974.

Paster, Gail Kern. "Leaky Vessels: The Incontinent Women of City Comedy." *Renaissance Drama*, N.S. 18 (1987): 43–65.

Pausanias. *Mythology and Monuments of Ancient Athens, Being a Translation of a Portion of the 'Attica.'* Trans. Margaret de Gaudrion Verrall. Intro. Jane E. Harrison. London: Macmillan, 1890.

Pearson, D'Orsay W. "'Unkinde' Theseus: A Study in Renaissance Mythography." *English Literary Renaissance* 4 (1974): 276–98.

Plautus. "The Twin Menaechmi." Trans. Edward C. Weist and Richard W. Hyde. In *An Anthology of Roman Drama*, ed. Philip Whaley Harsh. New York: Holt, Rinehart and Winston, 1960, 2–48.

A Pleasant Conceited Historie, Called The Taming of a Shrew. London, 1594.

Plutarch. "The Life of Theseus." *Lives of the Noble Grecians and Romans*. Trans. Thomas North. London, 1579.

Prosser, Eleanor. "Shakespeare, Montaigne, and the Rarer Action." *Shakespeare Studies I* (1965): 261–64.

Ripa, Cesare. *Cesare Ripa: Baroque and Rococo Imagery*. Ed. and trans. Edward A. Maser. New York: Dover, 1971. Reprint of Johann Georg Hertel, *Historiae et Allegoriae. . . . Augsburg*, [1758–60].

———. *Iconologia*. Rome, 1603.

———. *Iconologia*. Padua, 1611.

Roberts, Jeanne Addison. "Horses and Hermaphrodites: Metamorphoses in *The Taming of the Shrew*." *Shakespeare Quarterly* 34 (1983): 159–71.

———. *Shakespeare's English Comedy: "The Merry Wives of Windsor" in Context*. Lincoln: University of Nebraska Press, 1979.

———. "'Wife' or 'Wise'—*The Tempest* l.1786." *Studies in Bibliography* 31 (1978): 203–8.

Roberts, Josephine A. "Mary Sidney, Countess of Pembroke." *English Literary Renaissance* 14 (Autumn 1984): 425–39.

Robertson, D. W. *A Preface to Chaucer: Studies in Medieval Perspectives*. Princeton: Princeton University Press, 1962.

Rosen, Barbara, ed. *Witchcraft*. London: Arnold, 1969.

Rowland, Beryl. *Animals with Human Faces: A Guide to Animal Symbolism*. Knoxville: University of Tennessee Press, 1973.

———. *Birds with Human Souls: A Guide to Bird Symbolism*. Knoxville: University of Tennessee Press, 1978.

Sachs, Hanne Lore. *The Renaissance Woman*. New York: McGraw-Hill, 1971.

Schleiner, Winfried. "*Divina Virago*: Queen Elizabeth as an Amazon." *Studies in Philology* 75 (1978): 163–80.

Schweickart, Patrocinio P. "Reading Ourselves: Toward a Feminist Theory of Reading." In *Gender and Reading: Essays on Readers, Texts, and Contexts*. Ed. Elizabeth A. Flynn and Patrocinio P. Schweickart. Baltimore: Johns Hopkins University Press, 1986, 31–62.

Scot, Reginald. *The Discovery of Witchcraft*. London, 1584.

Sedgwick, Eve Kosofsky. *Between Men: English Literature and Male Homosocial Desire*. New York: Columbia University Press, 1985.

Shaaber, M. A. "The First Rape of Faire Hellen by John Trussell." *Shakespeare Quarterly* 8 (1957): 407–48.

Shakespeare, William. *The Riverside Shakespeare*. Ed. G. Blakemore Evans et al. Boston: Houghton Mifflin, 1974.

Shepherd, Simon. *Amazons and Warrior Women: Varieties of Feminism in Seventeenth-Century Drama*. Brighton, Sussex: Harvester, 1981.

Showalter, Elaine. "Feminist Criticism in the Wilderness." In *The New Feminist Criticism: Essays on Women, Literature, and Theory*. Ed. Elaine Showalter. New York: Pantheon, 1985, 243–70.

Smith, Hallett. "Introduction to *The Tempest*." In *The Riverside Shakespeare*. Ed. G. Blakemore Evans et al. Boston: Houghton Mifflin, 1974.

———. "Introduction to *Two Noble Kinsmen*." In *The Riverside Shakespeare*. Ed. G. Blakemore Evans et al. Boston: Houghton Mifflin, 1974.

Sommers, Alan. "'Wilderness of Tigers': Structure and Symbolism in *Titus Andronicus*." *Essays in Criticism* 10 (1960): 275–89.

Spenser, Edmund. "The Faerie Queene." In *Poetical Works*. Ed. J. C. Smith and E. de Sélincourt. 1912. Reprint. London: Oxford University Press, 1948.

Spurgeon, Caroline. *Shakespeare's Imagery and What It Tells Us*. New York: Macmillan, 1936.

Stone, Lawrence. *The Family, Sex and Marriage in England, 1500–1800*. New York: Harper & Row, 1977.

Suleiman, Susan Rubin. "Writing and Motherhood." In *The (M)other Tongue: Essays in Feminist Psychoanalytic Interpretation*. Ed. Shirley Nelson Garner et al. Ithaca: Cornell University Press, 1985, 352–77.

Thomas, Keith. *Man and the Natural World: Changing Attitudes in England, 1500–1800*. London: Lane, 1983.

Thompson, Ann. "'The Warrant of Womanhood': Shakespeare and Feminist Criticism." In *The Shakespeare Myth*. Ed. Graham Holderness. Manchester: University of Manchester Press, 1988, 74–88.

Thompson, Roger. *Women in Stuart England and America: A Comparative Study*. London: Routledge & Kegan Paul, 1974.

Tillyard, E. M. W. *The Elizabethan World Picture*. New York: Macmillan, 1944.

Traub, Valerie. "Prince Hal's Falstaff: Positioning Psychoanalysis and the Female Reproductive Body." *Shakespeare Quarterly* 40 (Winter 1989): 456–74.

Turner, Victor. *Drama, Fields and Metaphors: Symbolic Action in Human Society*. 1974. Reprint. Ithaca: Cornell University Press, 1985.

Tyrrell, William Blake. *Amazons: A Study in Athenian Mythmaking*. Baltimore: Johns Hopkins University Press, 1984.

Vaughan, Alden T. "Shakespeare's Indian: The Americanization of Caliban," *Shakespeare Quarterly* 39 (1988): 137–53.

Walker, Barbara G. *The Crone: Woman of Age, Wisdom, and Power*. 1985. Reprint. New York: Harper & Row, 1988.

Williamson, Marilyn. *The Patriarchy of Shakespeare's Comedies*. Detroit: Wayne State University Press, 1986.

Wind, Edgar. *Pagan Mysteries in the Renaissance*. 1958. Reprint. London: Faber and Faber, 1968.

Wither, George. *A Collection of Emblems*. London, 1635.

Woodbridge, Linda. *Women and the English Renaissance: Literature and the Nature of Womankind* 1540–1620. Urbana: University of Illinois Press, 1984.

Wright, C. T. "The Amazons in Elizabethan Literature." *Studies in Philology* 37 (1940): 433–56.

Yoder, Audrey E. *Animal Analogy in Shakespeare's Character Portrayal*. 1947. Reprint. New York: AMS, 1975.

Index

Page numbers in italics indicate illustrations.